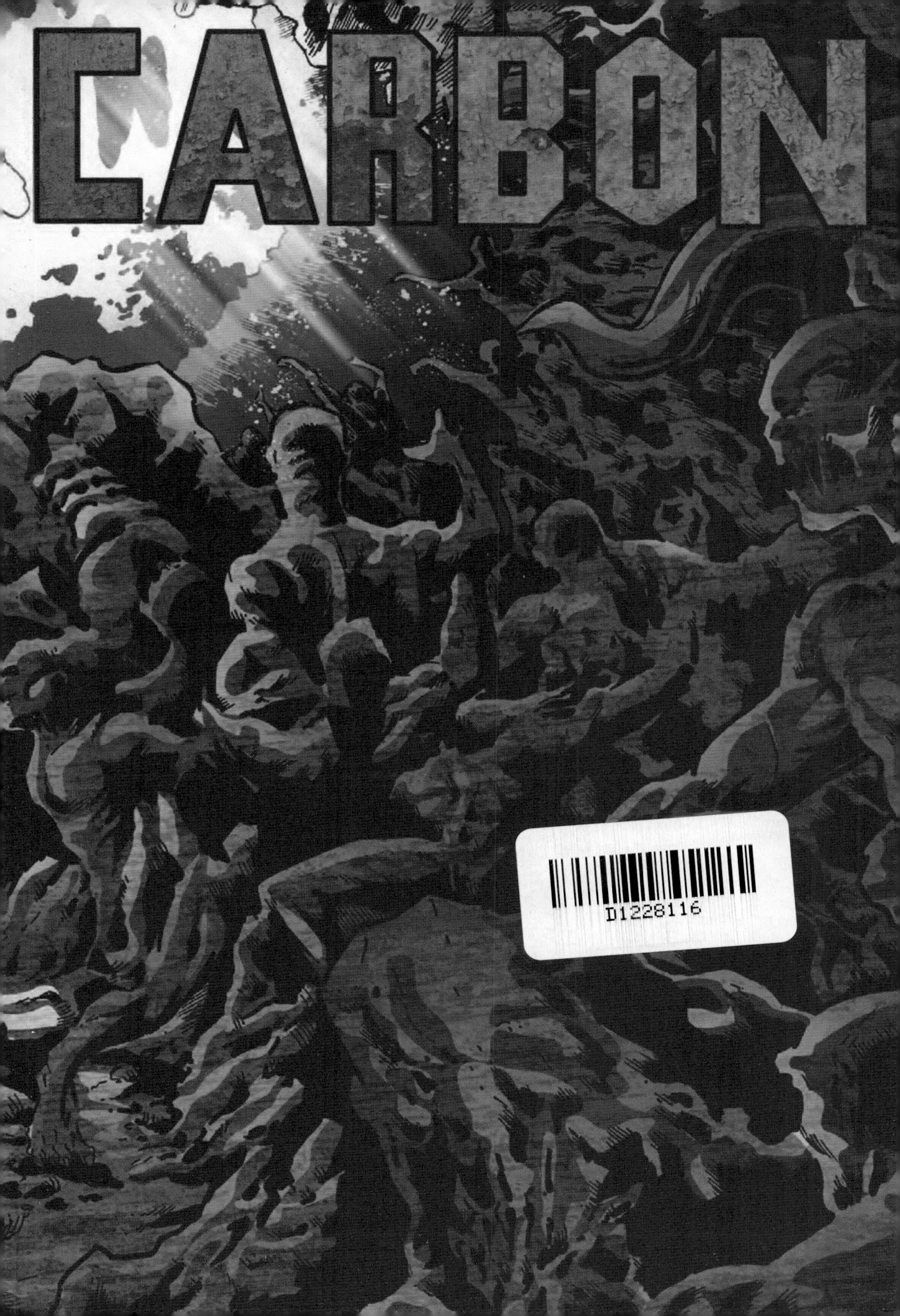
CARBON

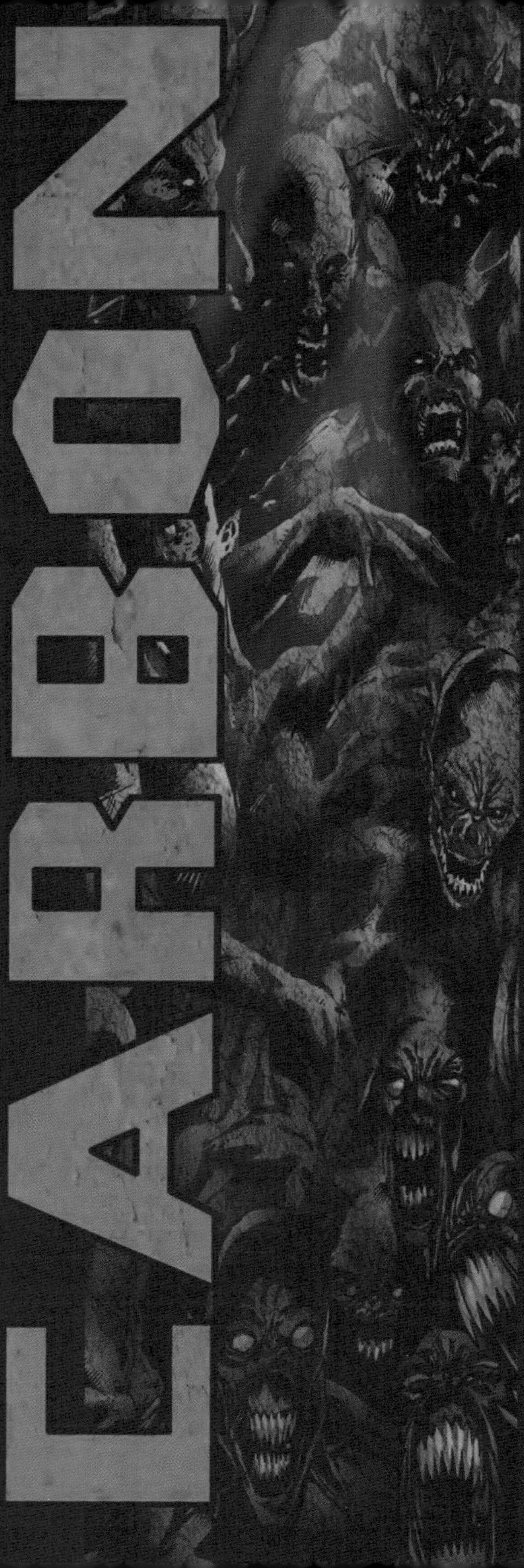
CARBON

A Big Pictures Production of
a Caliber Comics Publication

Writer
DANIEL BOYD

Artist
EDI GUEDES

Colors
ALZIR ALVES

Letters
JASON ARTHUR

Publisher
GARY REED

Editor
CHET JACQUES

Associate Editors
WILLIAM BITNER & JOSEPH NG

Logo
JOSH MARTIN

SPECIAL THANKS:
R. Charles Byers, Brunetta Dillard, Orlando McMeans, Jack Bailey, Steve Gilliland, Lisa Bragg, Charlie Cooper, Chuck Biel, Balsa Gobovich, Danielle Boyd, David Wohl, Eric Douglas, West Virginia State University, WVSU EDC, Cal Bailey, Robert L. Bandy, Ana Karla Albuquerque, L. Kevin Levine, Geoff Fuller, Nilskidoo, Morgan Spurlock.

INTRODUCTION
JOHN SAYLES

The graphic novel (or 'really long comic book' as I like to think of them) is more than a storyboard version of an unfundable movie. The medium, and it does deserve that classification, has its own unique vibe. Danny Boyd's CARBON combines three distinct genres- Lovecraftian gorefest, religious picture book and political allegory- to tell the story of our slow and conscious self-poisoning.

In an industry that combines men with picks and shovels with machines bigger than New York apartment complexes, in a state (West Virginia) carrying on a love/hate relationship with its own contentious history, Boyd sets his eco-horror Old Testament tale replete with heroes, villains, and the winged spawn of hell.

I've never seen a comic with better, more dramatic industrial illustrations, and it's a great switch to have it be the guys, not the women, who must fight for their virtue. All the iconic elements of mountain states culture are here- tight-knit families and rapacious exploiters, gonzo theology, sports fever, and the sad fact that being employed may mean helping to despoil one of the most beautiful spots on the planet.

CARBON is an ambitious addition to the long tradition, religious and secular, of that basic cautionary tale - be careful what you dig up.

John Sayles

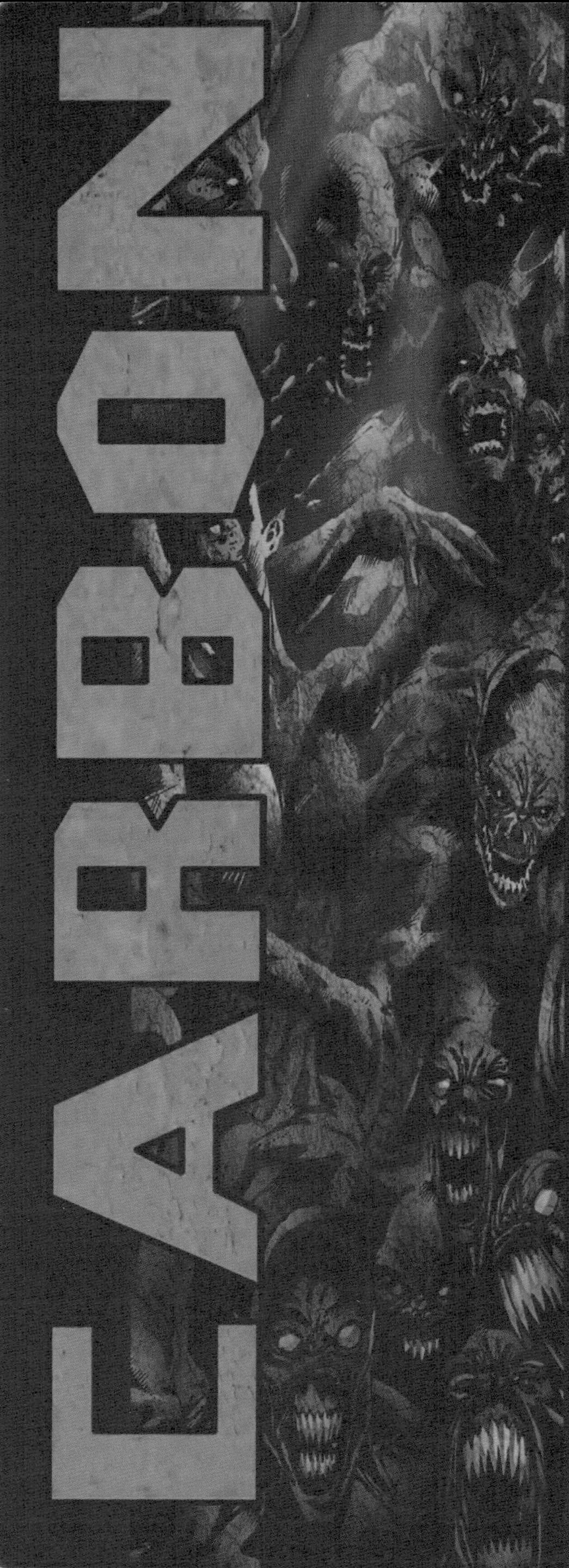
CARBON

Dedicated to
Those who toil in the darkness
- Coal Miners

BOOK I

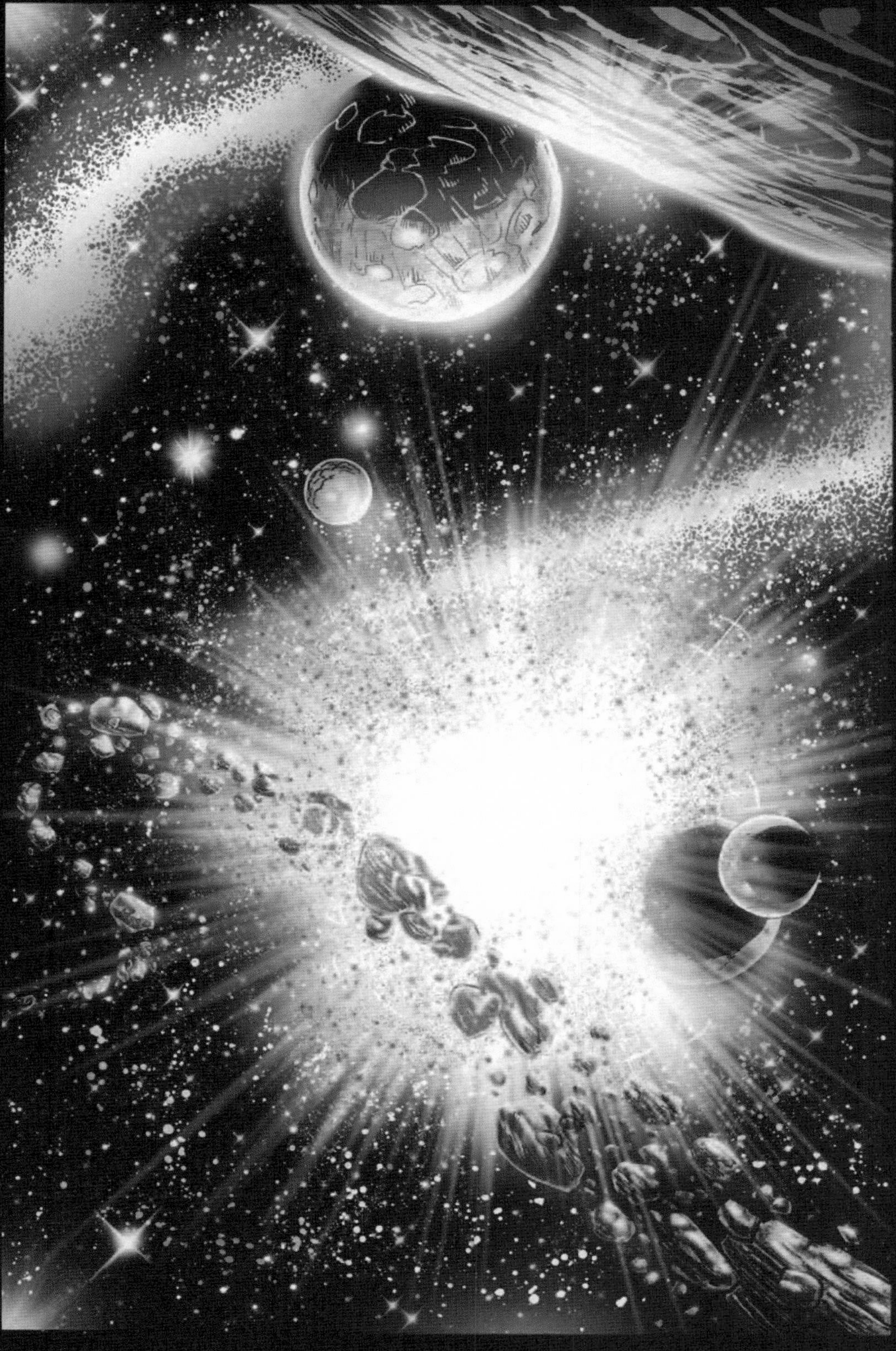

PROLOGUE -- A TIME BEFORE TIME

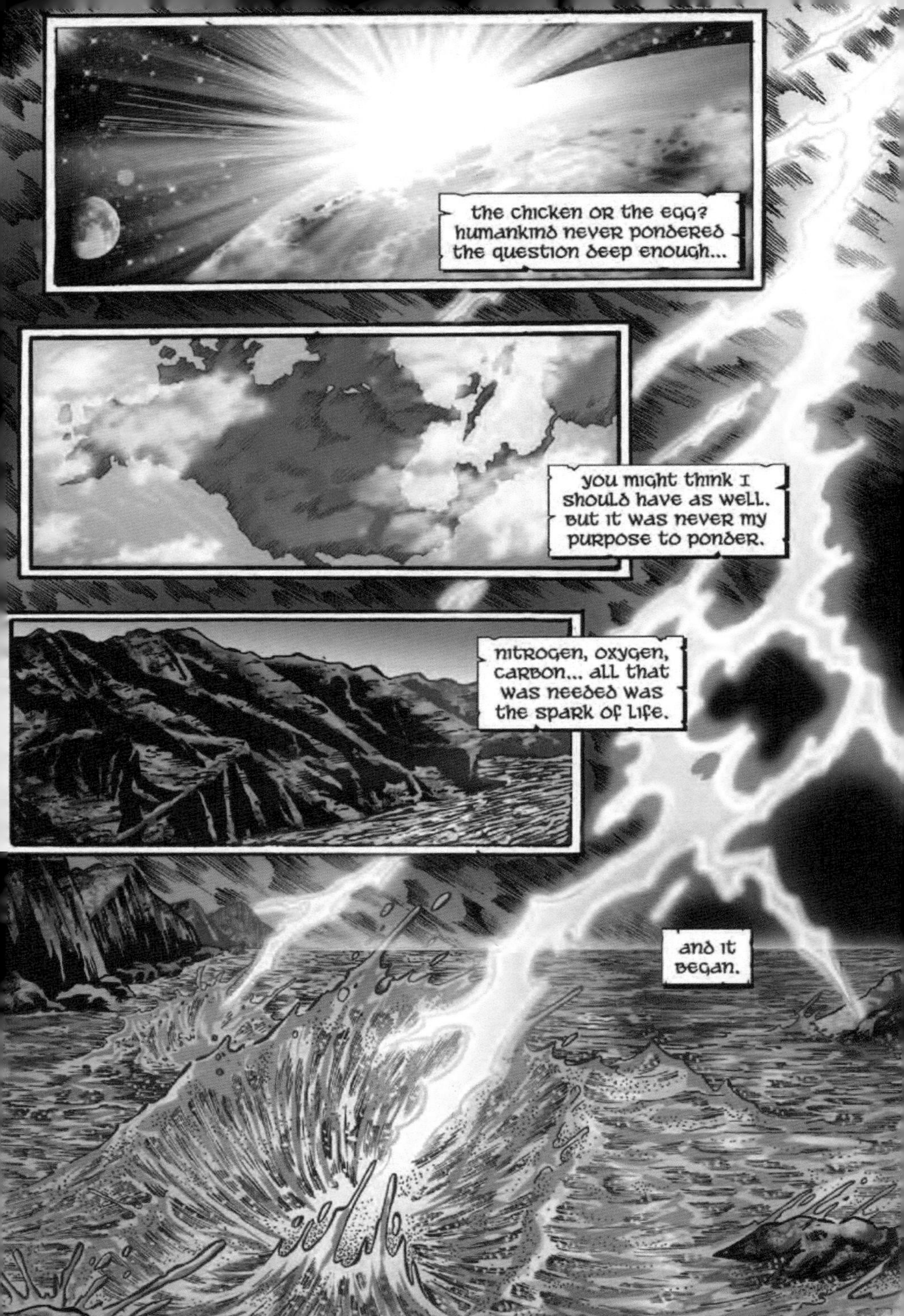

the chicken or the egg? humankind never pondered the question deep enough...
you might think I should have as well. but it was never my purpose to ponder.
nitrogen, oxygen, carbon... all that was needed was the spark of life.
and it began.

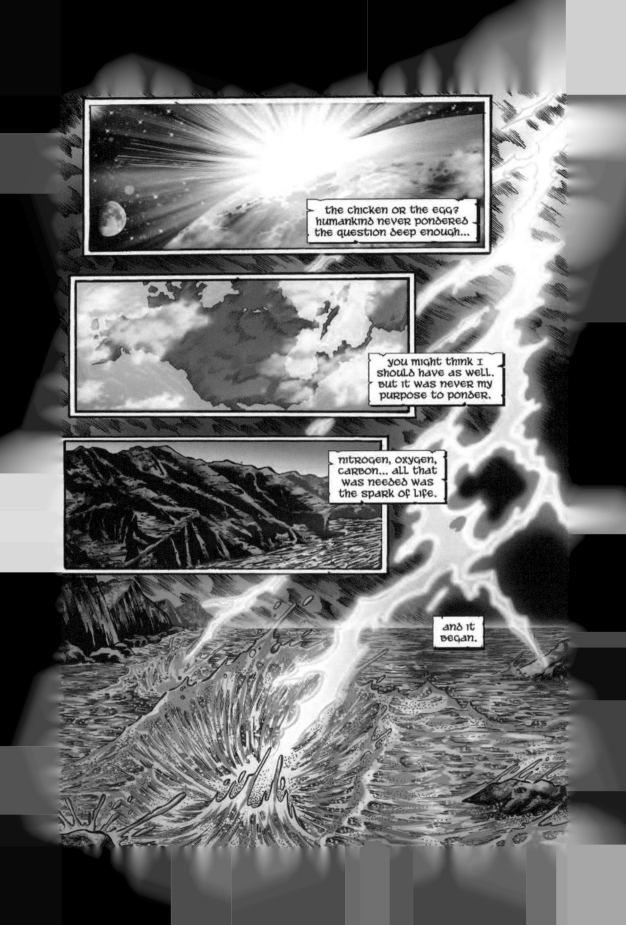

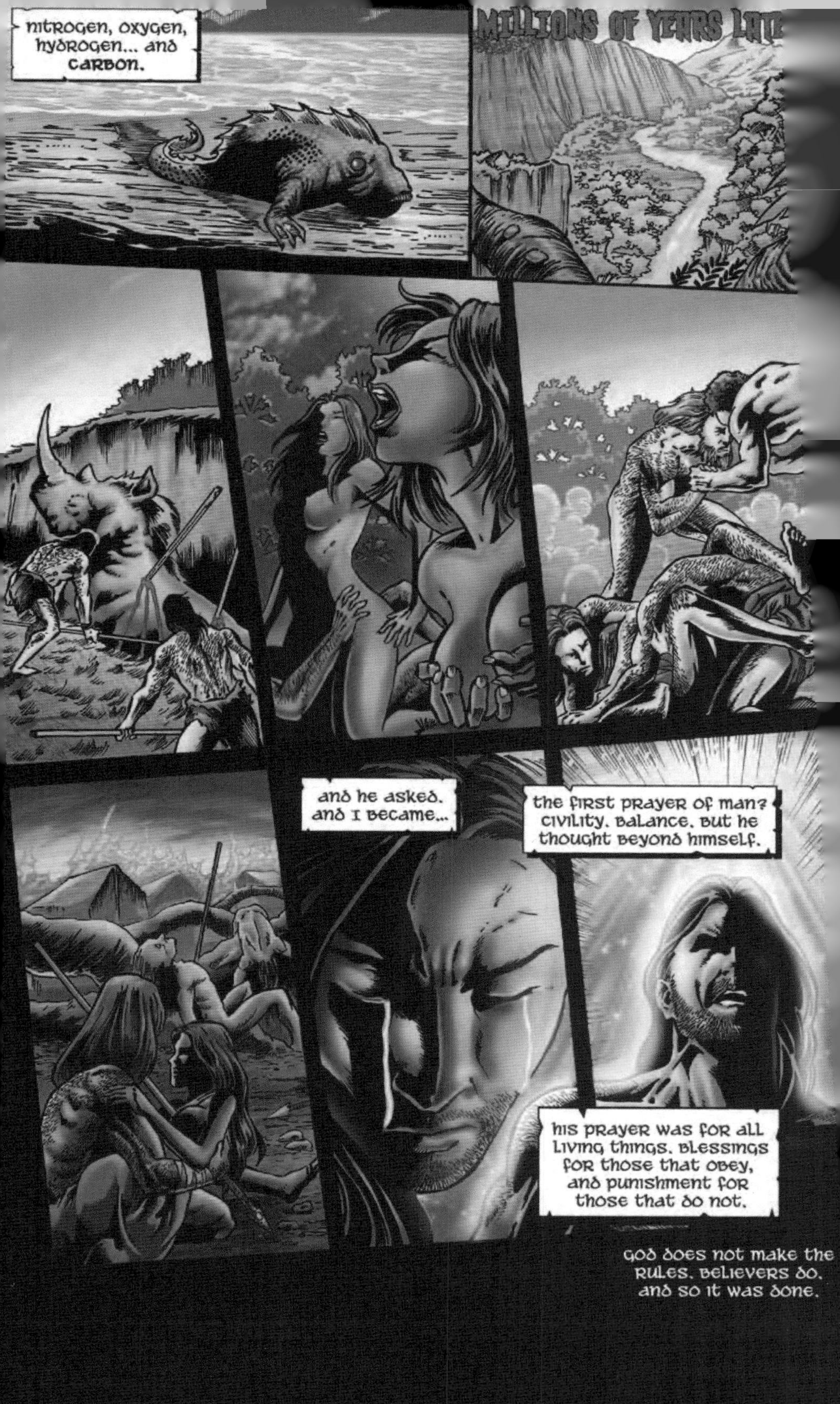
nitrogen, oxygen, hydrogen... and carbon.
MILLIONS OF YEARS LATE
and he asked. and I became...
the first prayer of man? civility. balance. but he thought beyond himself.
his prayer was for all living things. blessings for those that obey, and punishment for those that do not.
God does not make the rules. believers do. and so it was done.

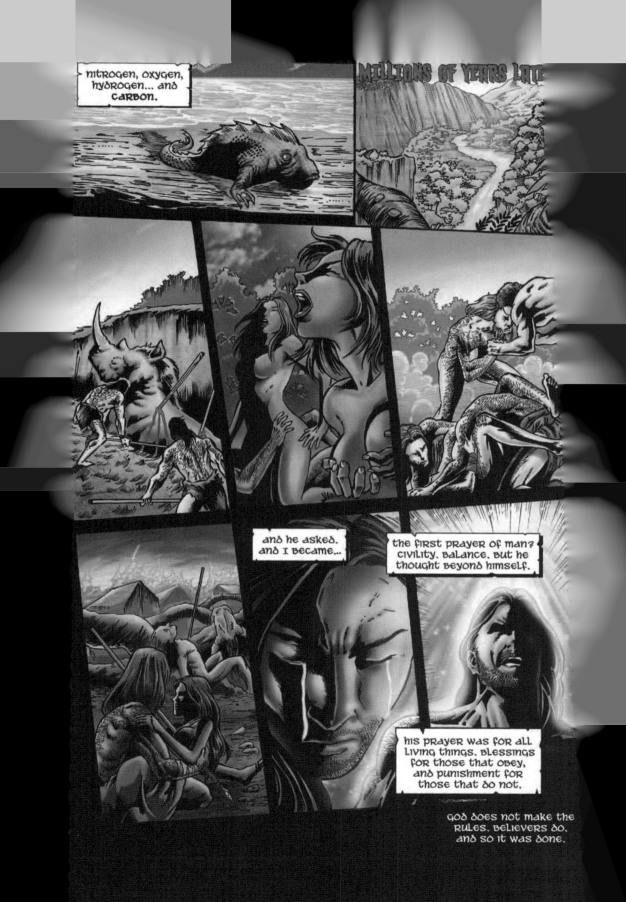

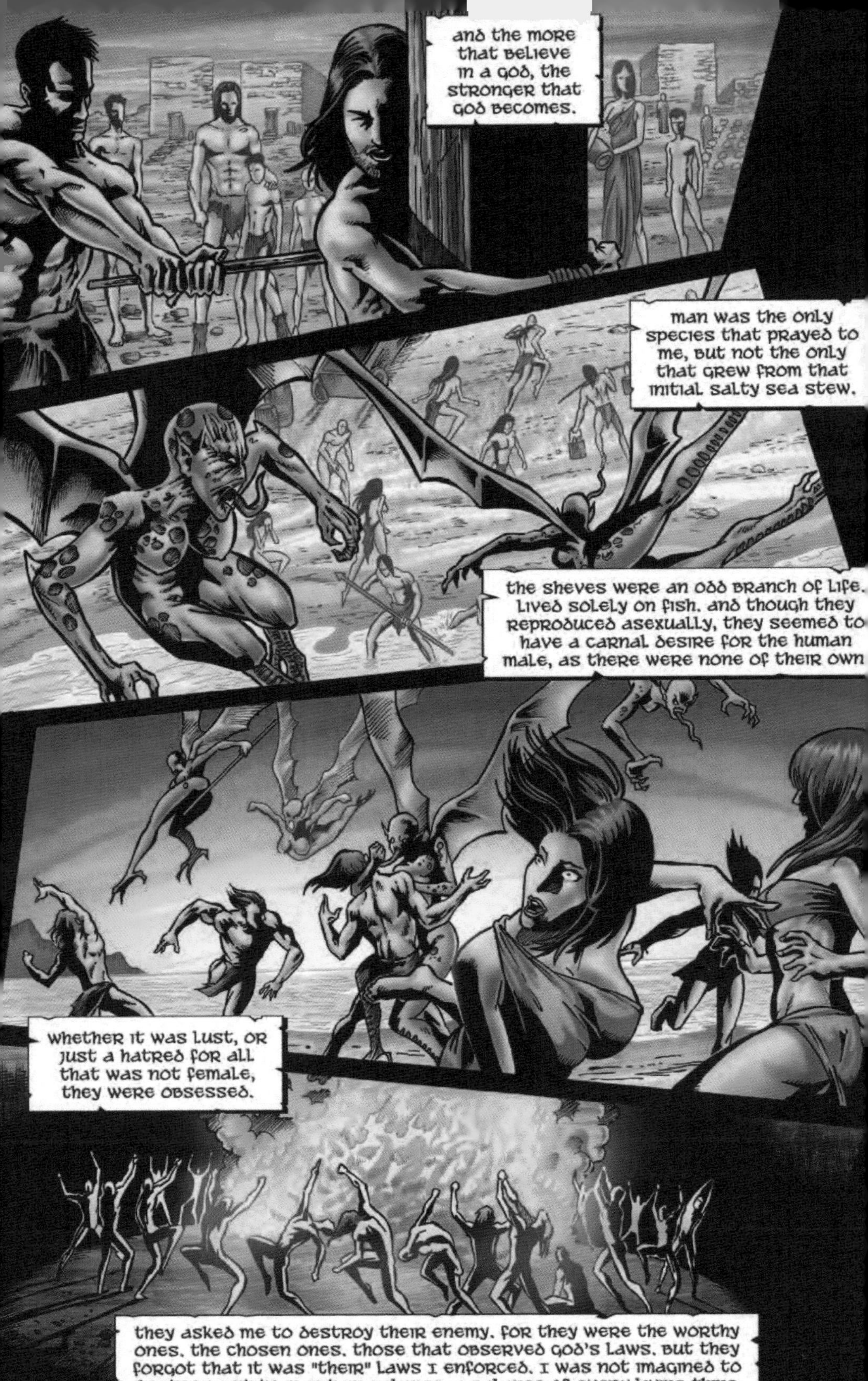
and the more that believe in a god, the stronger that god becomes.
man was the only species that prayed to me, but not the only that grew from that initial salty sea stew.
the sheves were an odd branch of life. lived solely on fish. and though they reproduced asexually, they seemed to have a carnal desire for the human male, as there were none of their own
whether it was lust, or just a hatred for all that was not female, they were obsessed.
they asked me to destroy their enemy. for they were the worthy ones. the chosen ones. those that observed god's laws. but they forgot that it was "their" laws I enforced. I was not imagined to destroy, but to maintain balance. a balance of every living thing in the natural world. man had forgotten, but I had not.

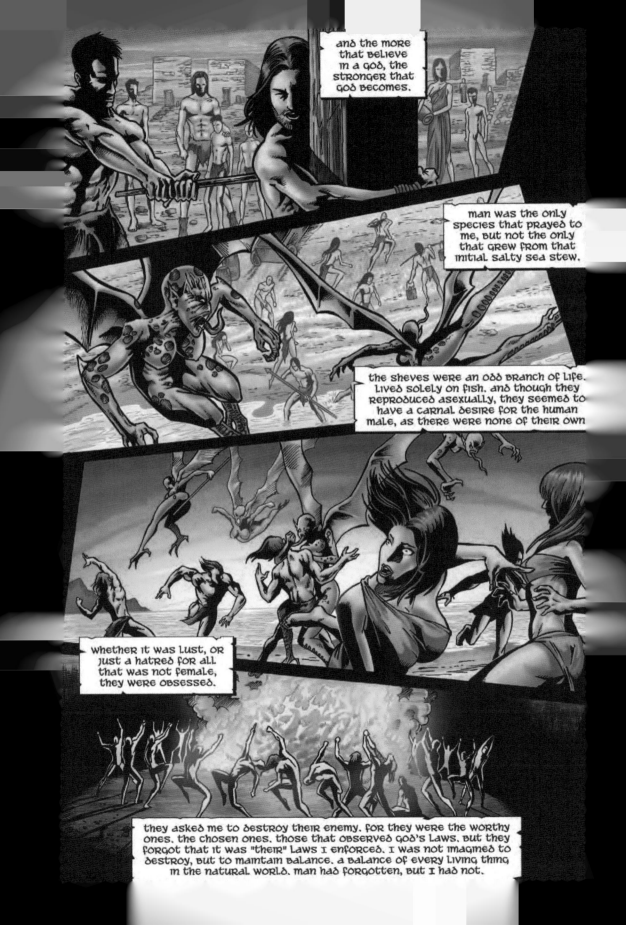

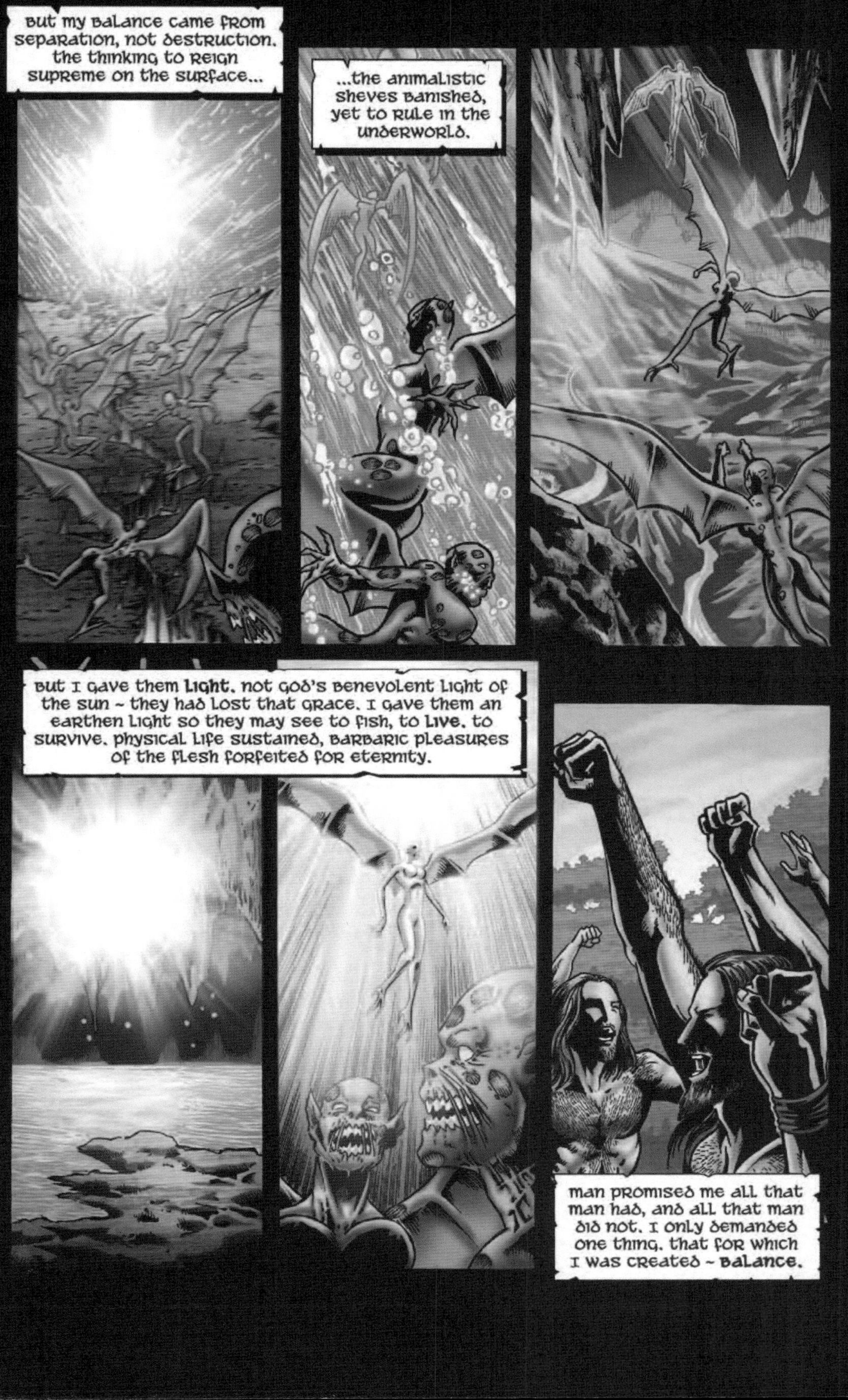
But my balance came from separation, not destruction. the thinking to reign supreme on the surface...
...the animalistic sheves banished, yet to rule in the underworld.
But I gave them light. not God's benevolent light of the sun ~ they had lost that grace. I gave them an earthen light so they may see to fish, to live. to survive. physical life sustained, barbaric pleasures of the flesh forfeited for eternity.
man promised me all that man had, and all that man did not. I only demanded one thing. that for which I was created ~ balance.

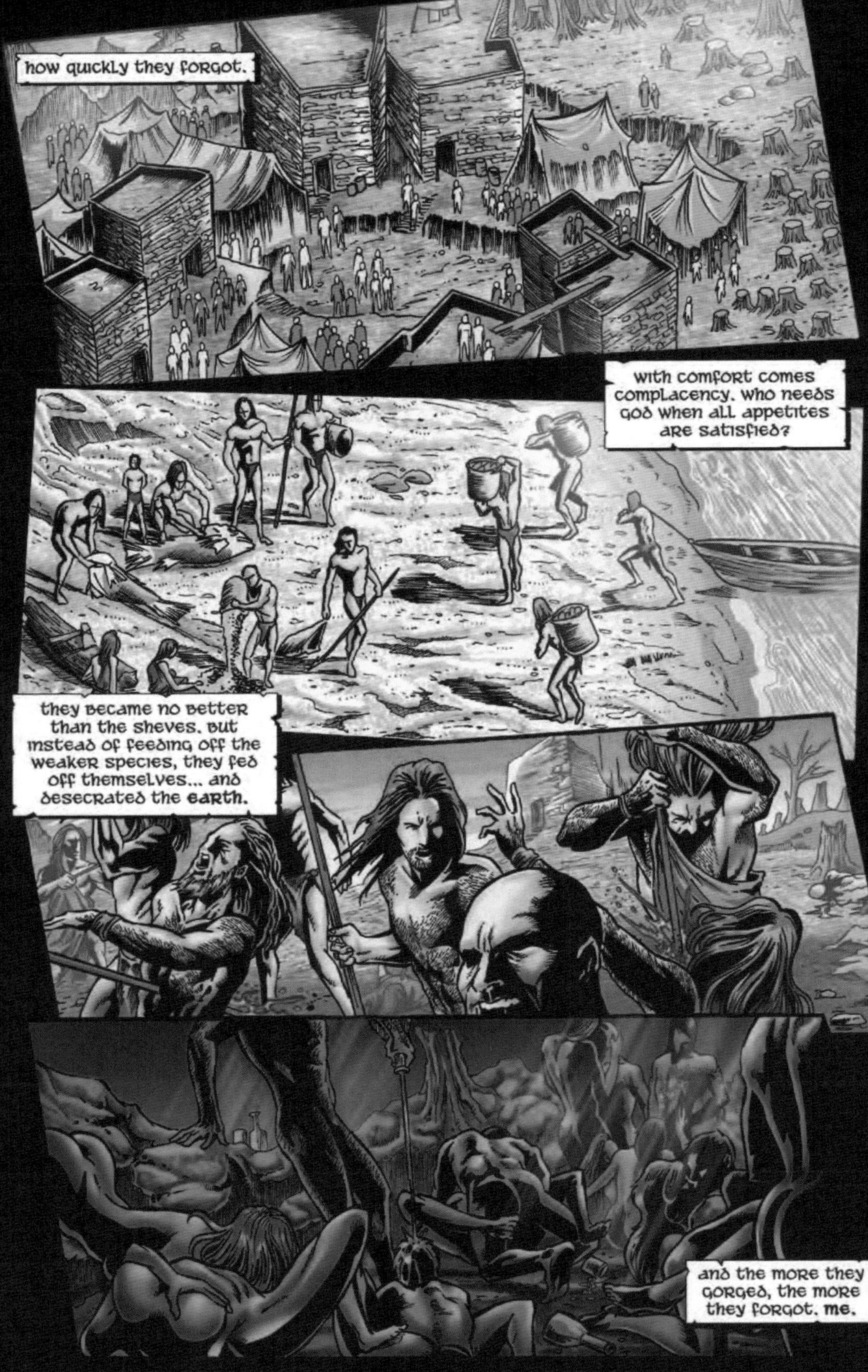
how quickly they forgot.
with comfort comes complacency. who needs god when all appetites are satisfied?
they became no better than the sheves. but instead of feeding off the weaker species, they fed off themselves... and desecrated the earth.
and the more they gorged, the more they forgot. me.

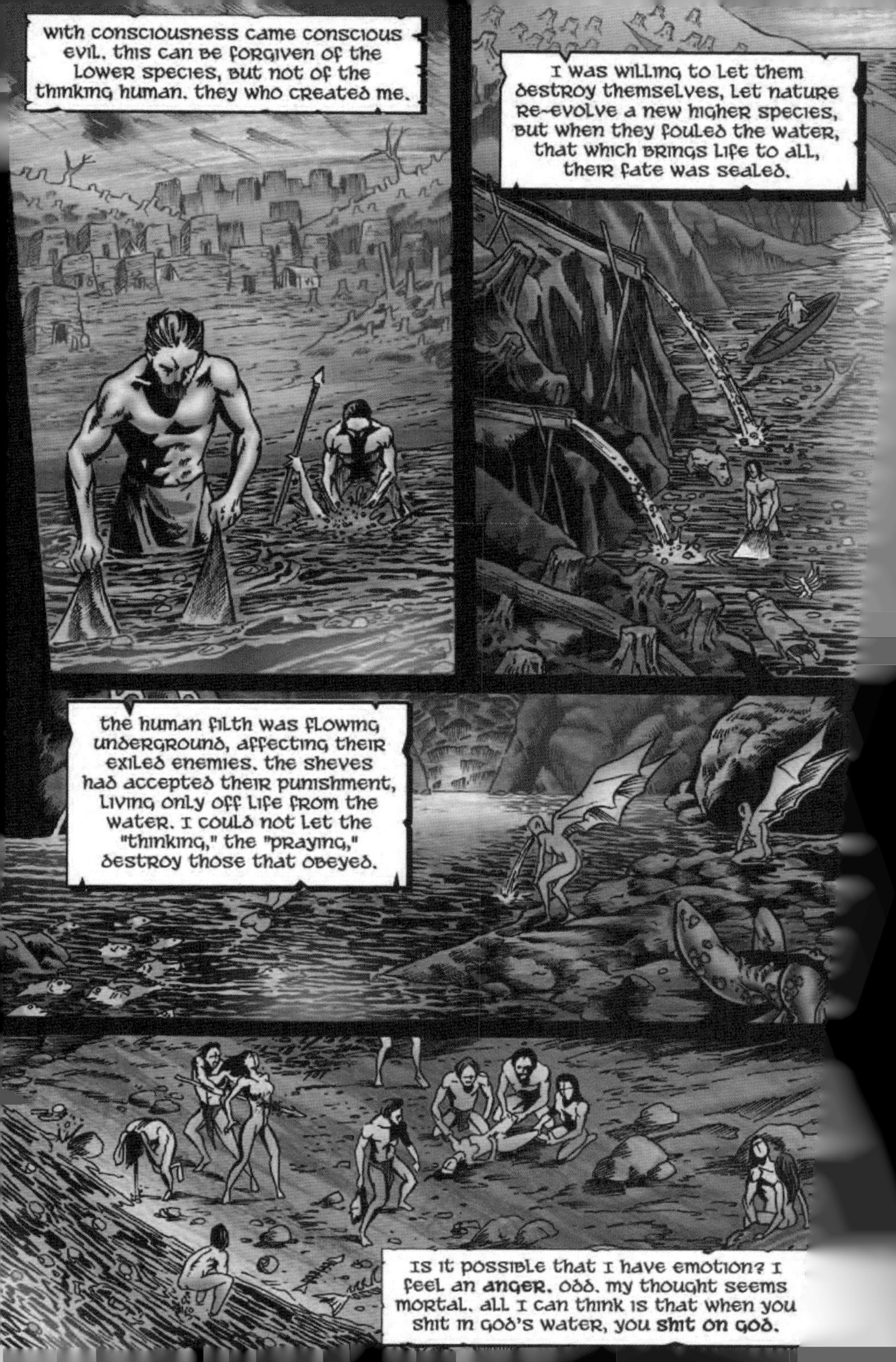
with consciousness came conscious evil. this can be forgiven of the lower species, but not of the thinking human. they who created me.
I was willing to let them destroy themselves, let nature re-evolve a new higher species, but when they fouled the water, that which brings life to all, their fate was sealed.
the human filth was flowing underground, affecting their exiled enemies. the sheves had accepted their punishment, living only off life from the water. I could not let the "thinking," the "praying," destroy those that obeyed.
Is it possible that I have emotion? I feel an **anger**. odd. my thought seems mortal. all I can think is that when you shit in god's water, you **shit on god**.

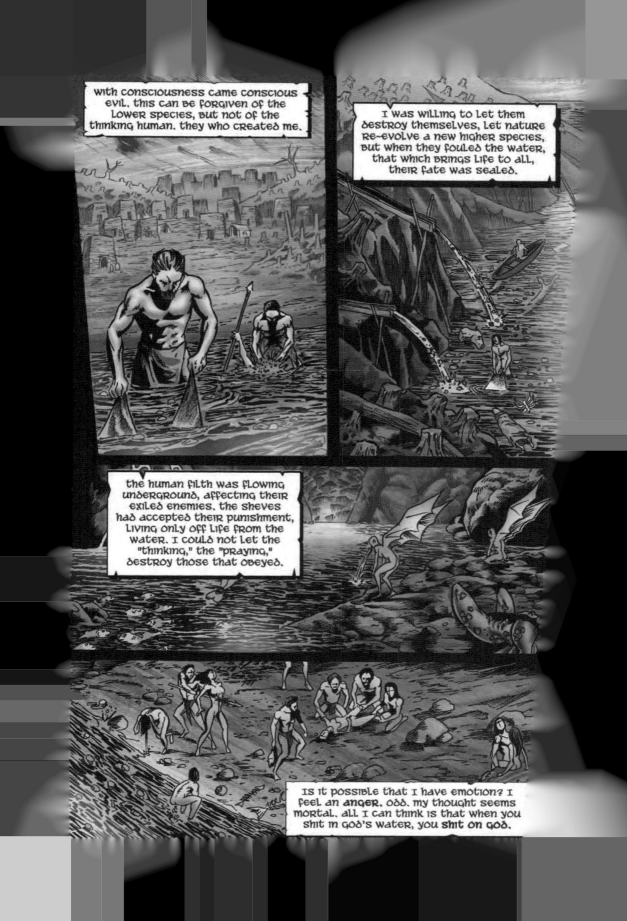

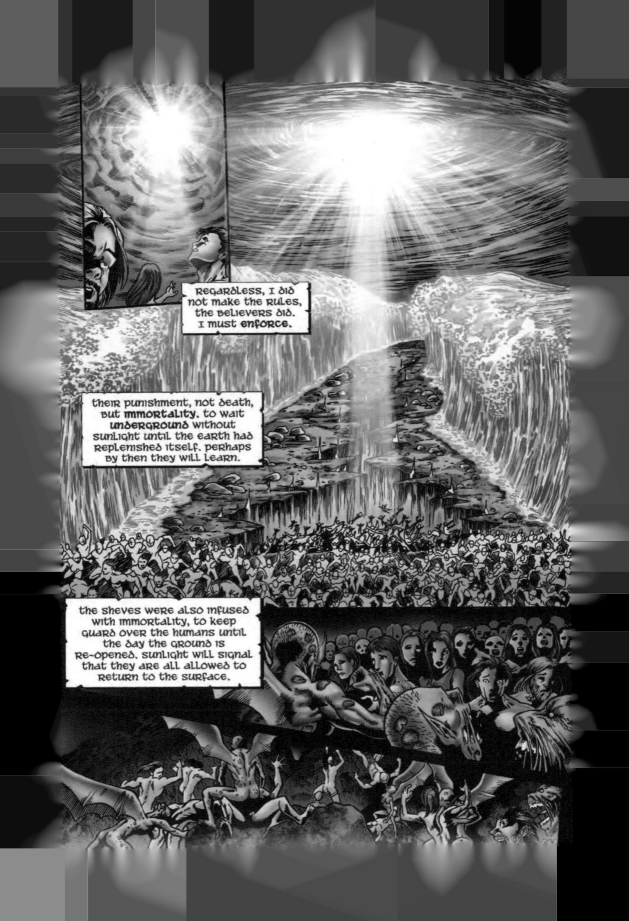

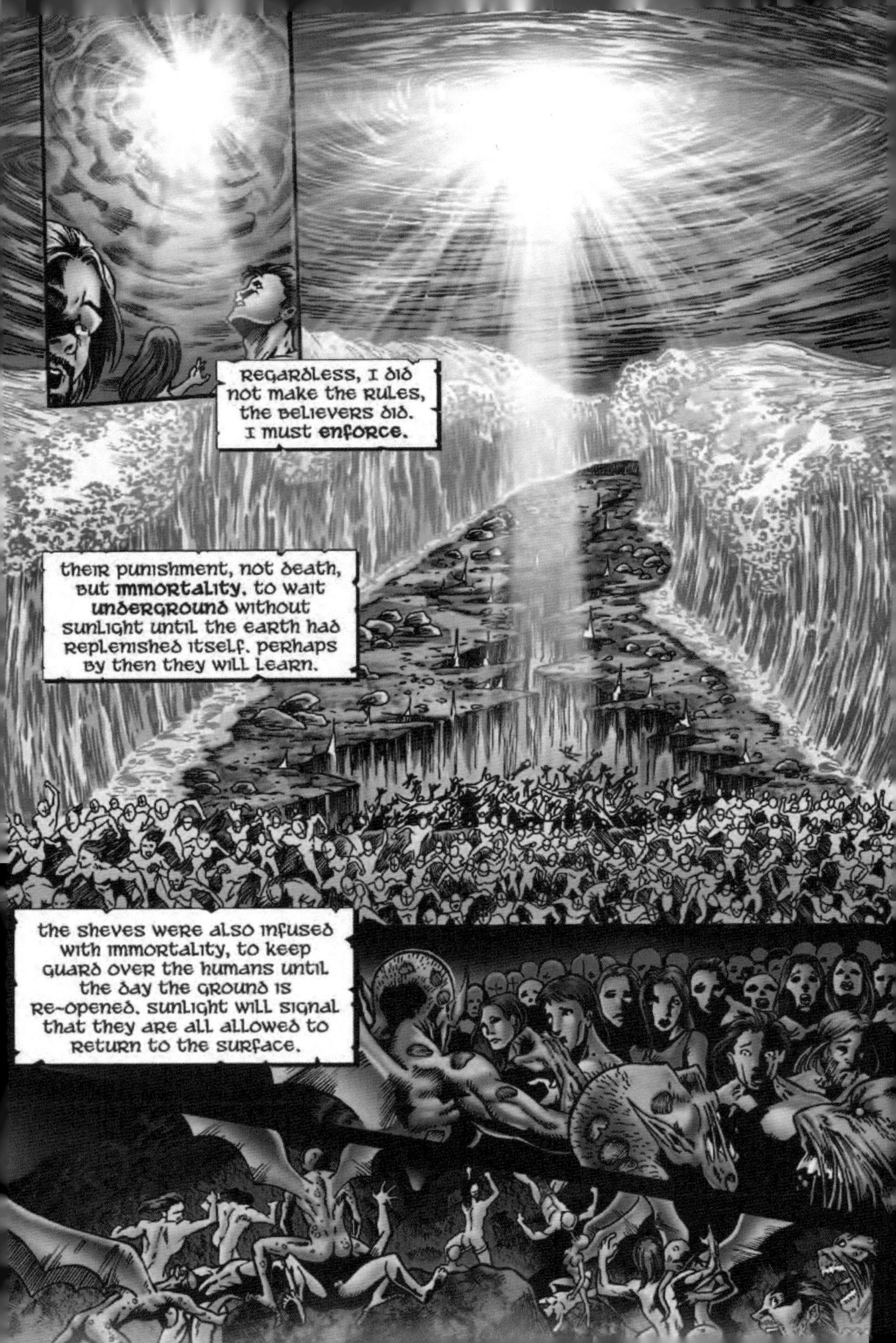
Regardless, I did not make the rules, the believers did. I must enforce.
their punishment, not death, but immortality, to wait underground without sunlight until the earth had replenished itself. perhaps by then they will learn.
the sheves were also infused with immortality, to keep guard over the humans until the day the ground is re-opened. sunlight will signal that they are all allowed to return to the surface.

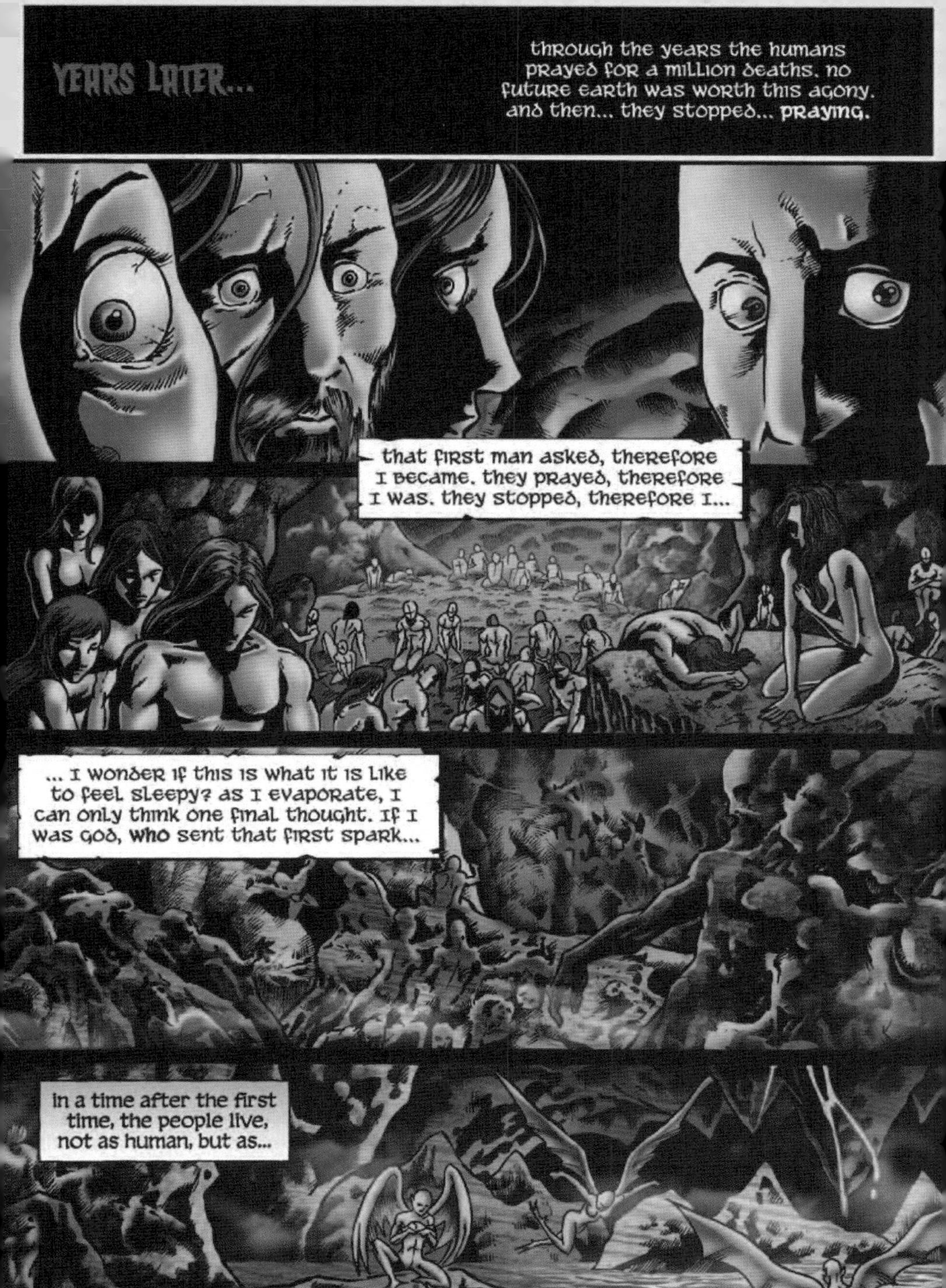
YEARS LATER...
through the years the humans prayed for a million deaths. no future earth was worth this agony. and then... they stopped... praying.
that first man asked, therefore I became. they prayed, therefore I was. they stopped, therefore I...
... I wonder if this is what it is like to feel sleepy? as I evaporate, I can only think one final thought. If I was god, who sent that first spark...
in a time after the first time, the people live, not as human, but as...
Carbon!

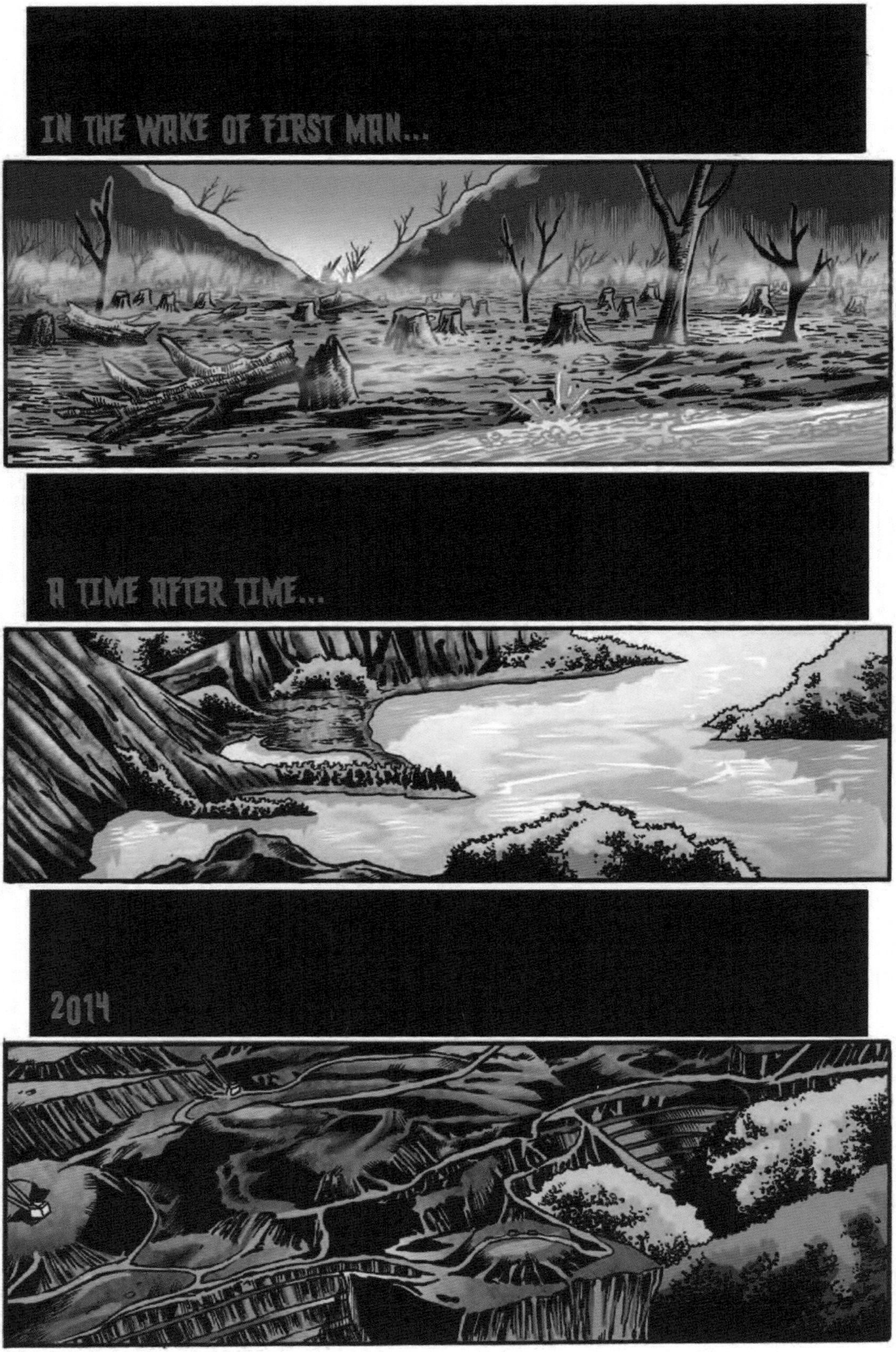
IN THE WAKE OF FIRST MAN...
A TIME AFTER TIME...
2014

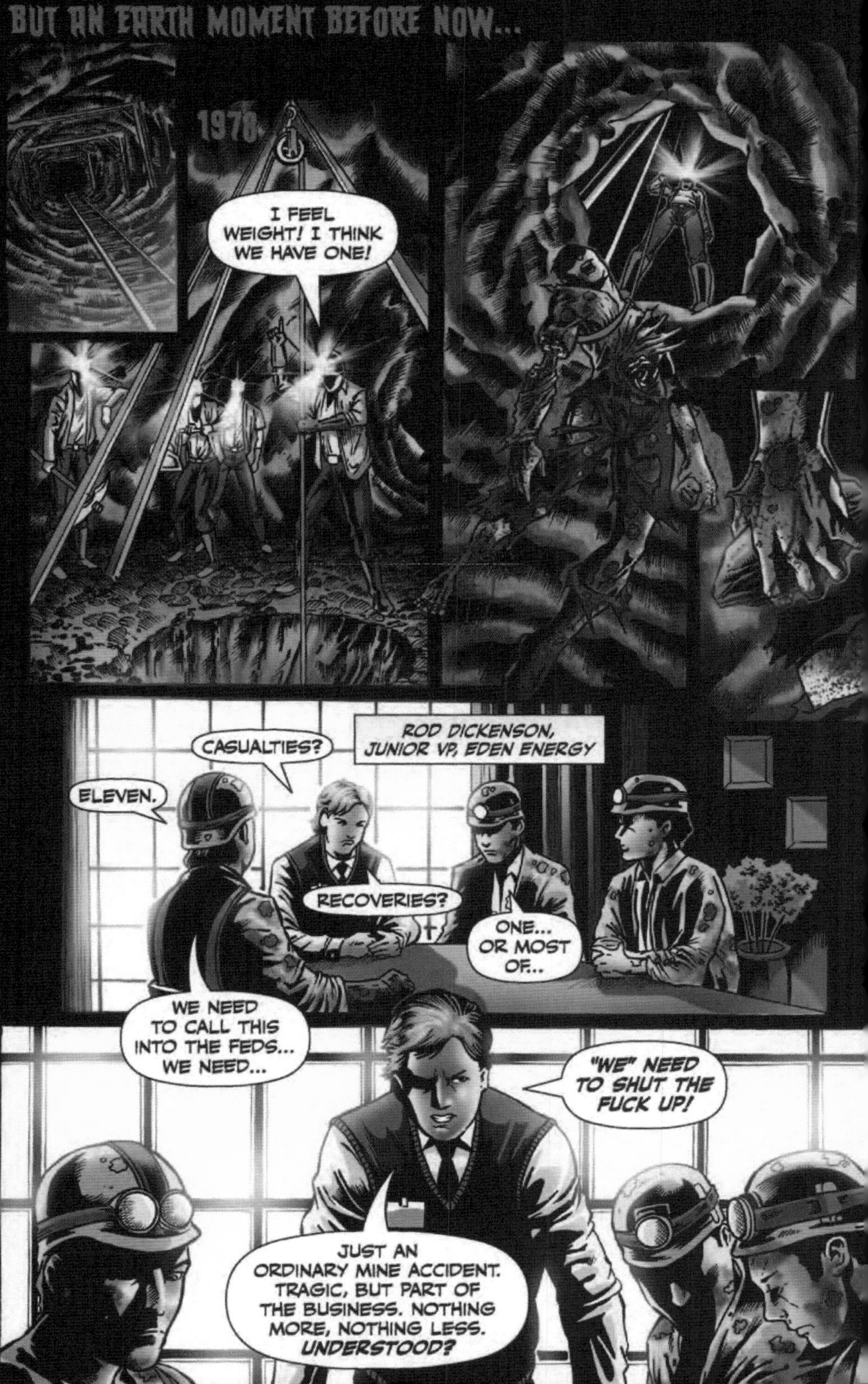
BUT AN EARTH MOMENT BEFORE NOW...
1978
I FEEL WEIGHT! I THINK WE HAVE ONE!
ROD DICKENSON, JUNIOR VP, EDEN ENERGY
CASUALTIES?
ELEVEN.
RECOVERIES?
ONE... OR MOST OF...
WE NEED TO CALL THIS INTO THE FEDS... WE NEED...
"WE" NEED TO SHUT THE FUCK UP!
JUST AN ORDINARY MINE ACCIDENT. TRAGIC, BUT PART OF THE BUSINESS. NOTHING MORE, NOTHING LESS. UNDERSTOOD?

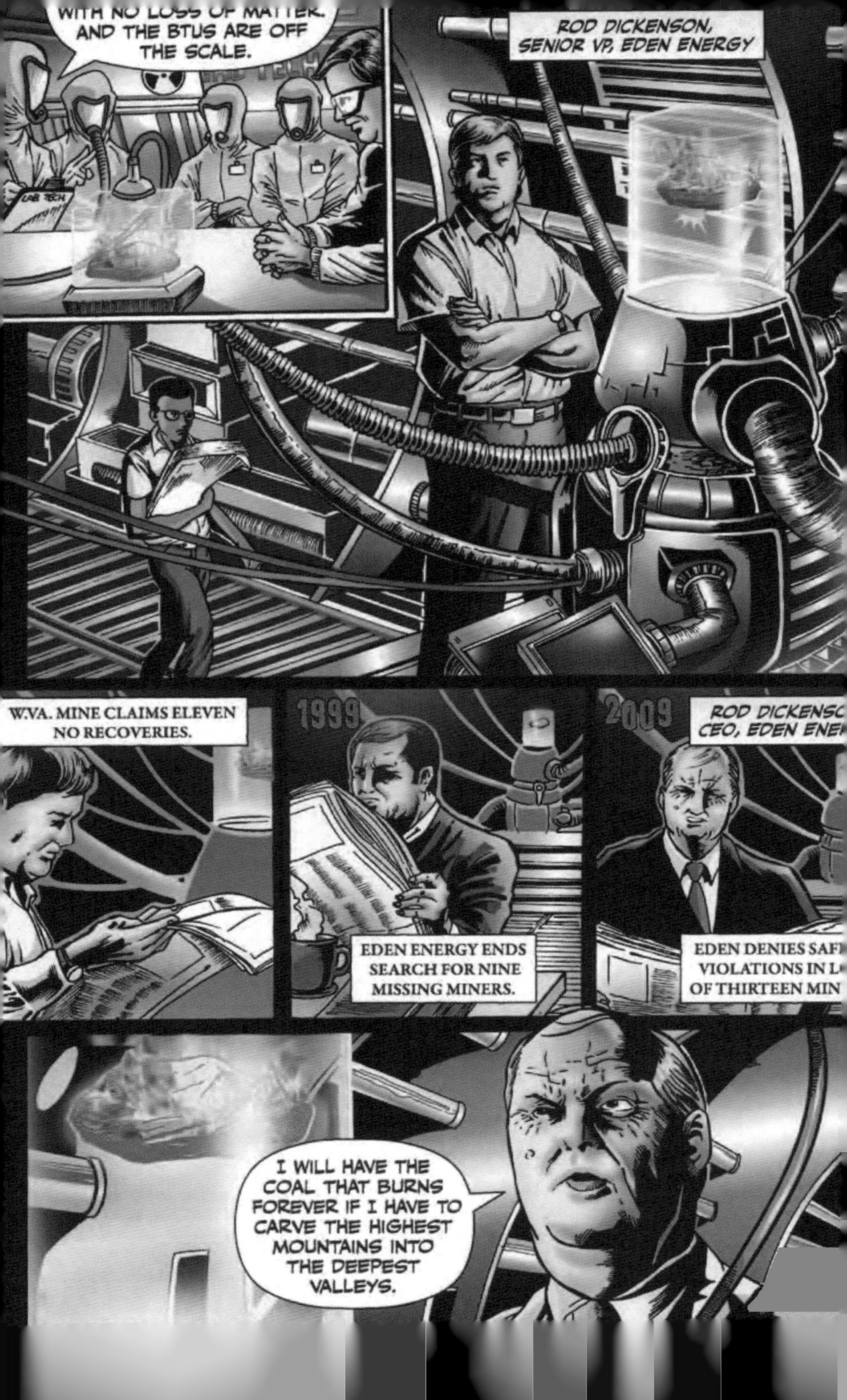
WITH NO LOSS OF MATTER.
AND THE BTUS ARE OFF THE SCALE.
LAB TECH
ROD DICKENSON, SENIOR VP, EDEN ENERGY
W.VA. MINE CLAIMS ELEVEN NO RECOVERIES.
1999
EDEN ENERGY ENDS SEARCH FOR NINE MISSING MINERS.
2009
I WILL HAVE THE COAL THAT BURNS FOREVER IF I HAVE TO CARVE THE HIGHEST MOUNTAINS INTO THE DEEPEST VALLEYS.

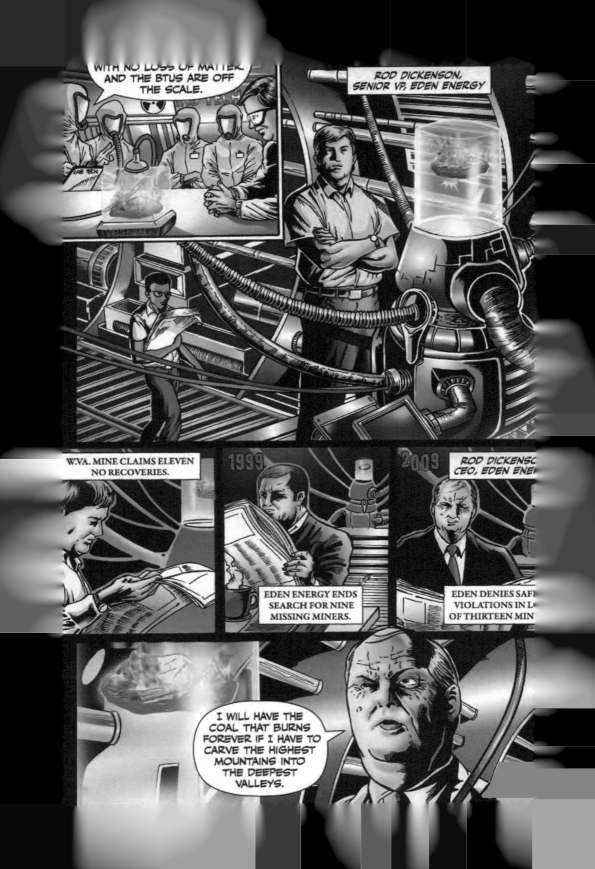

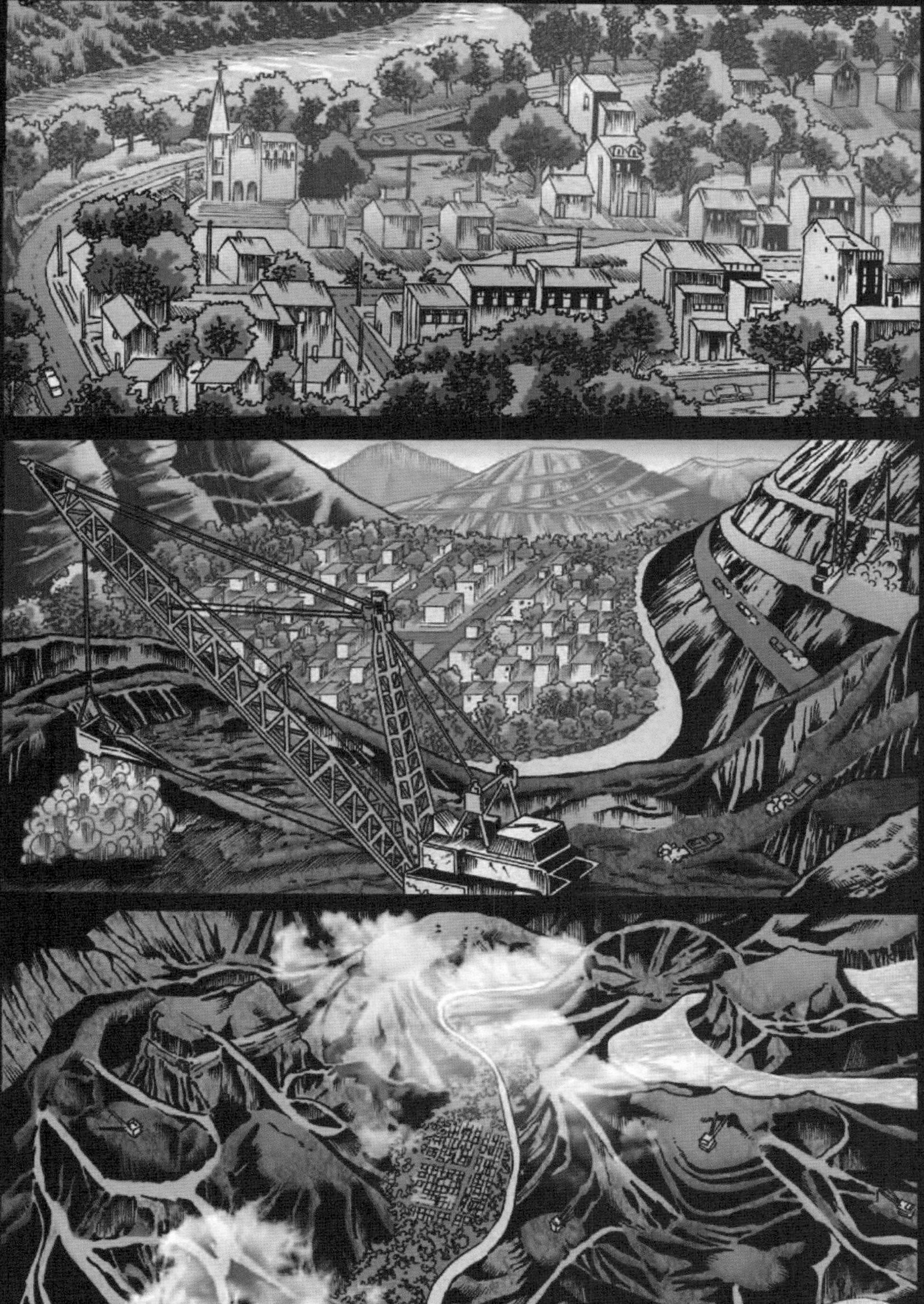

END BOOK 1

BOOK II

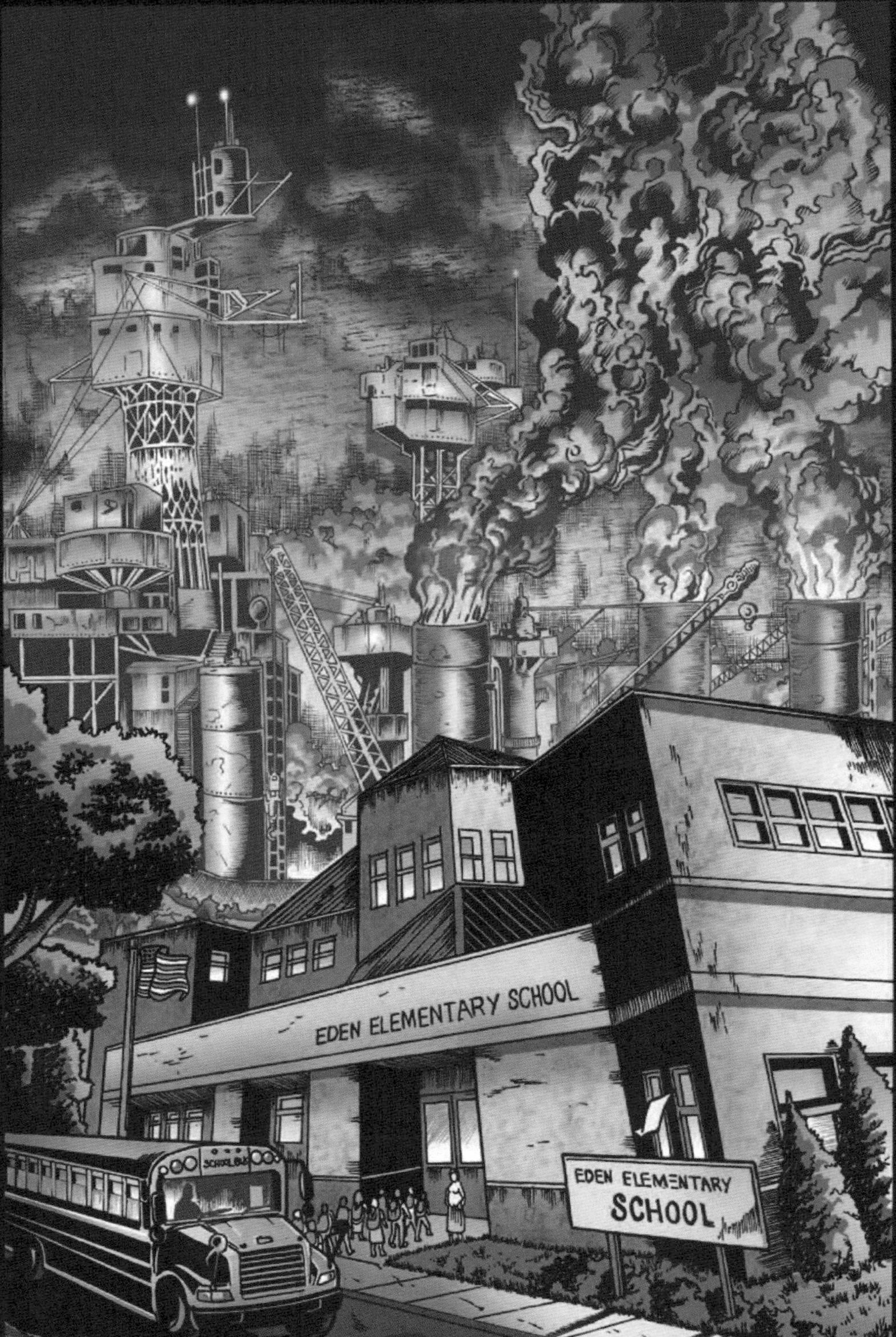
EDEN ELEMENTARY SCHOOL
SCHOOL BUS
EDEN ELEMENTARY
SCHOOL

WHERE'S THE HEAT?

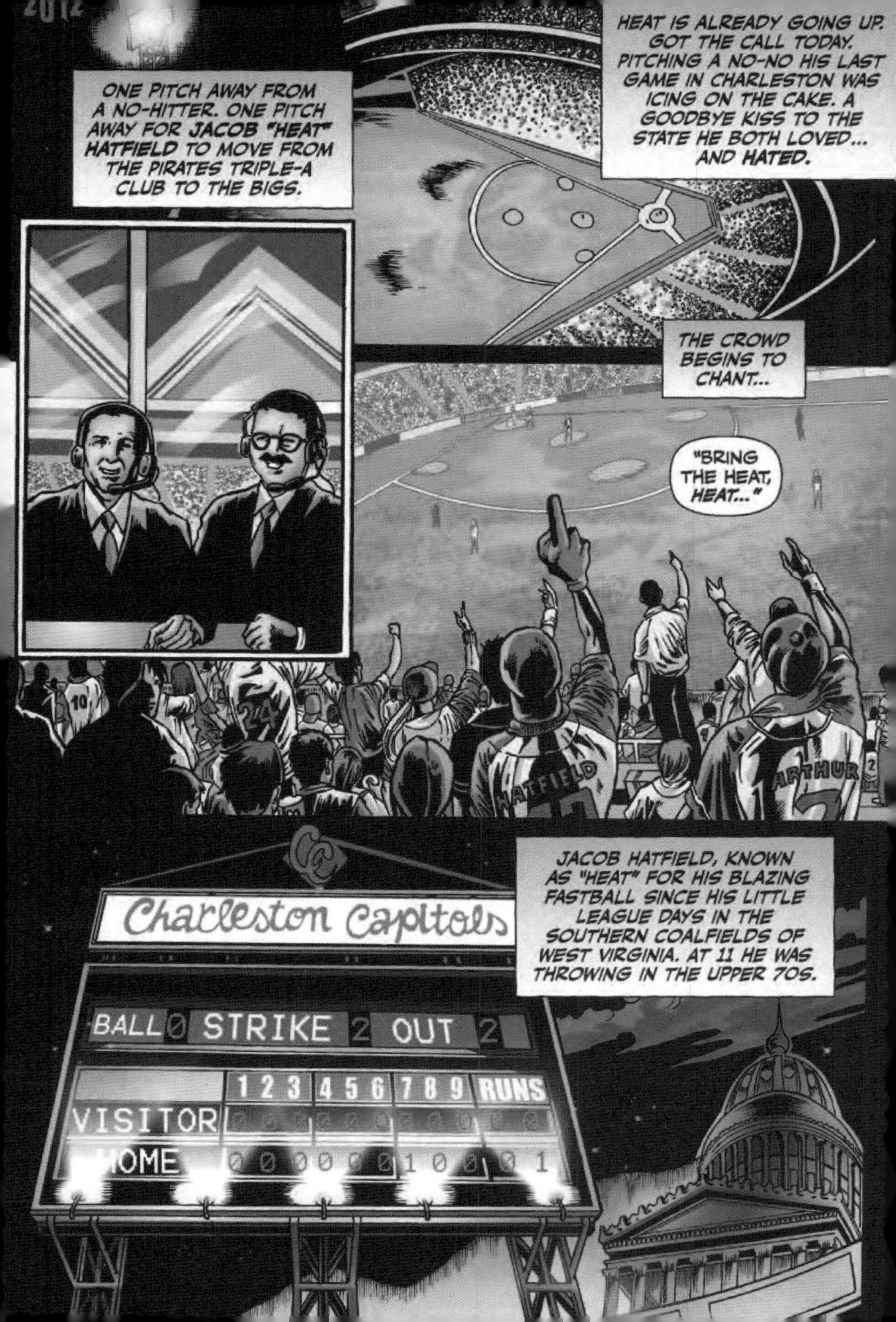
2012
ONE PITCH AWAY FROM A NO-HITTER. ONE PITCH AWAY FOR JACOB "HEAT" HATFIELD TO MOVE FROM THE PIRATES TRIPLE-A CLUB TO THE BIGS.
HEAT IS ALREADY GOING UP. GOT THE CALL TODAY. PITCHING A NO-NO HIS LAST GAME IN CHARLESTON WAS ICING ON THE CAKE. A GOODBYE KISS TO THE STATE HE BOTH LOVED... AND HATED.
THE CROWD BEGINS TO CHANT...
"BRING THE HEAT, HEAT..."
HATFIELD
ARTHUR
JACOB HATFIELD, KNOWN AS "HEAT" FOR HIS BLAZING FASTBALL SINCE HIS LITTLE LEAGUE DAYS IN THE SOUTHERN COALFIELDS OF WEST VIRGINIA. AT 11 HE WAS THROWING IN THE UPPER 70S.
Charleston Capitols
BALL 0 STRIKE 2 OUT 2
1 2 3 4 5 6 7 8 9 RUNS
VISITOR
HOME 0 0 0 0 0 0 1 0 0 0 1

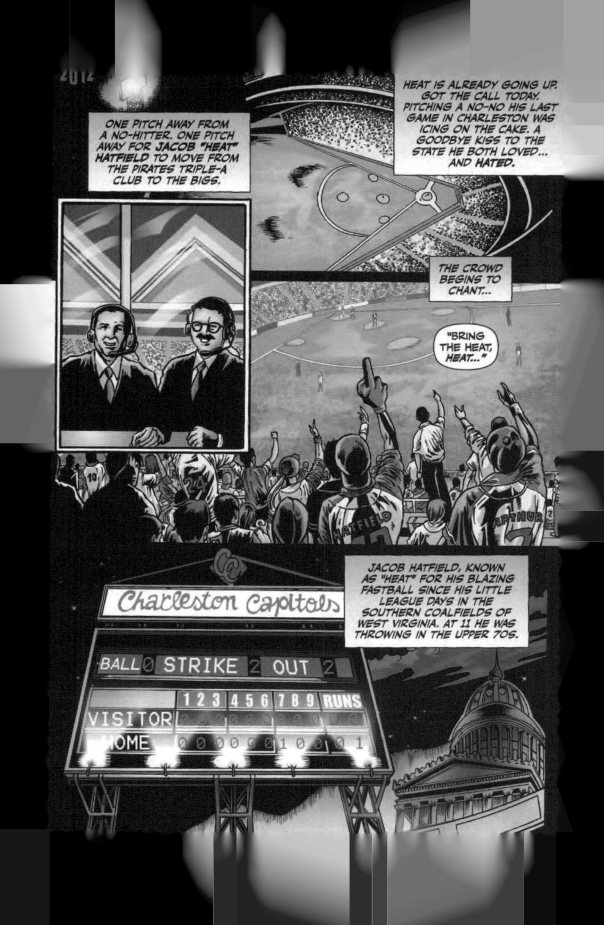

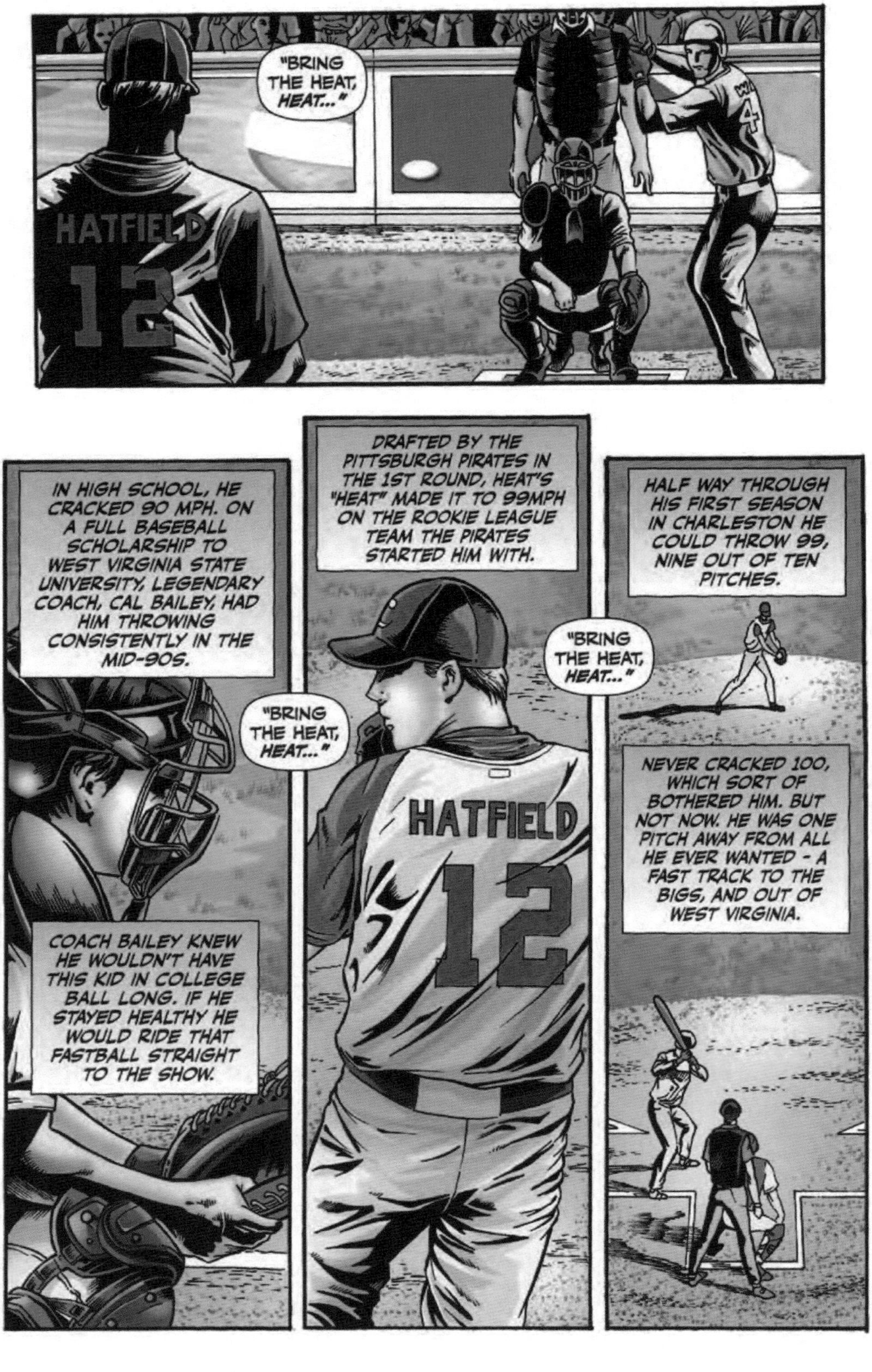
"BRING THE HEAT, HEAT..."
HATFIELD
12
IN HIGH SCHOOL, HE CRACKED 90 MPH. ON A FULL BASEBALL SCHOLARSHIP TO WEST VIRGINIA STATE UNIVERSITY, LEGENDARY COACH, CAL BAILEY, HAD HIM THROWING CONSISTENTLY IN THE MID-90S.
COACH BAILEY KNEW HE WOULDN'T HAVE THIS KID IN COLLEGE BALL LONG. IF HE STAYED HEALTHY HE WOULD RIDE THAT FASTBALL STRAIGHT TO THE SHOW.
DRAFTED BY THE PITTSBURGH PIRATES IN THE 1ST ROUND, HEAT'S "HEAT" MADE IT TO 99MPH ON THE ROOKIE LEAGUE TEAM THE PIRATES STARTED HIM WITH.
"BRING THE HEAT, HEAT..."
HATFIELD
12
HALF WAY THROUGH HIS FIRST SEASON IN CHARLESTON HE COULD THROW 99, NINE OUT OF TEN PITCHES.
"BRING THE HEAT, HEAT..."
NEVER CRACKED 100, WHICH SORT OF BOTHERED HIM. BUT NOT NOW. HE WAS ONE PITCH AWAY FROM ALL HE EVER WANTED - A FAST TRACK TO THE BIGS, AND OUT OF WEST VIRGINIA.

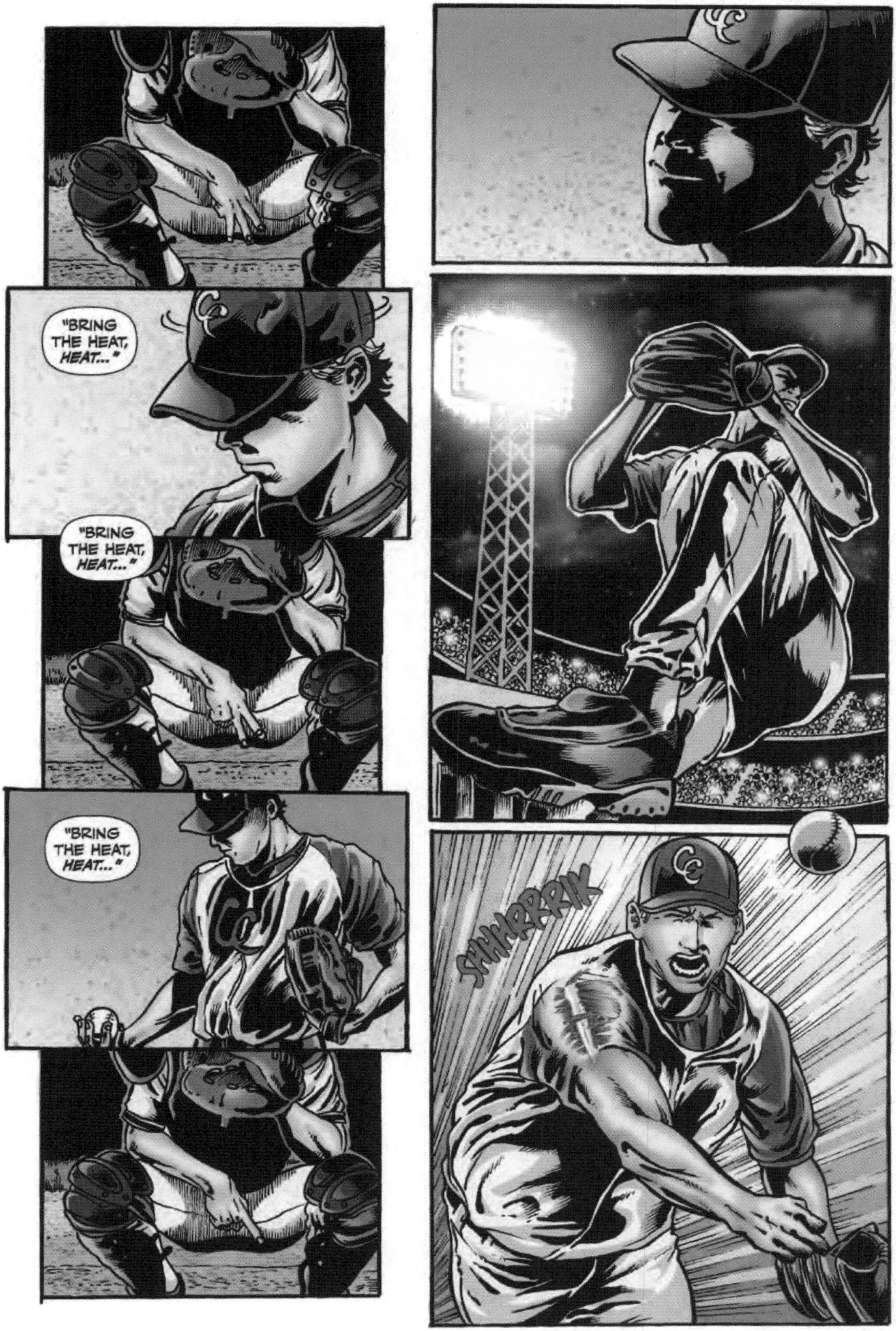
"BRING THE HEAT, HEAT..."
"BRING THE HEAT, HEAT..."
"BRING THE HEAT, HEAT..."
SHHHRRRRIK

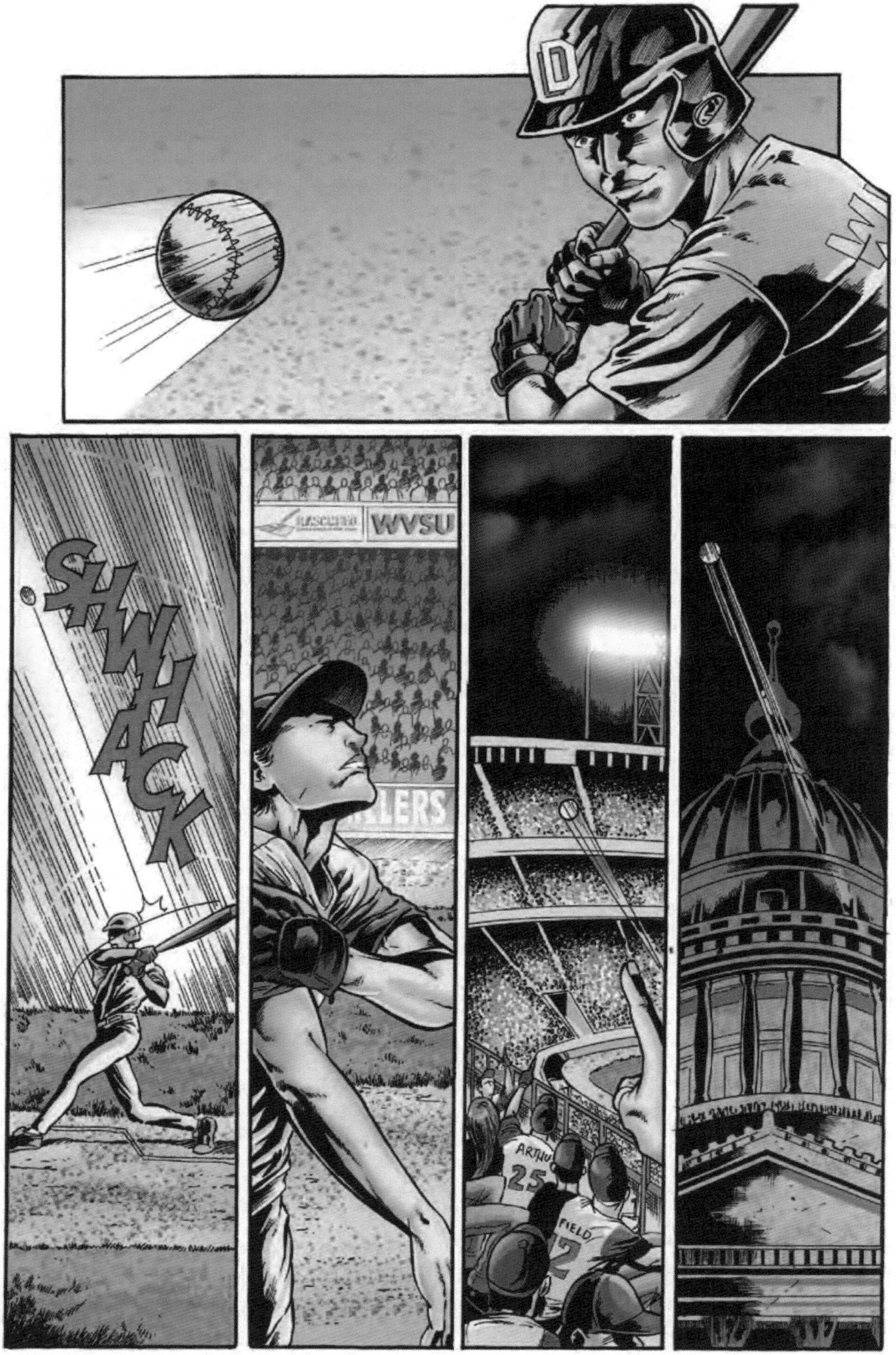
SHWHACK
WVSU

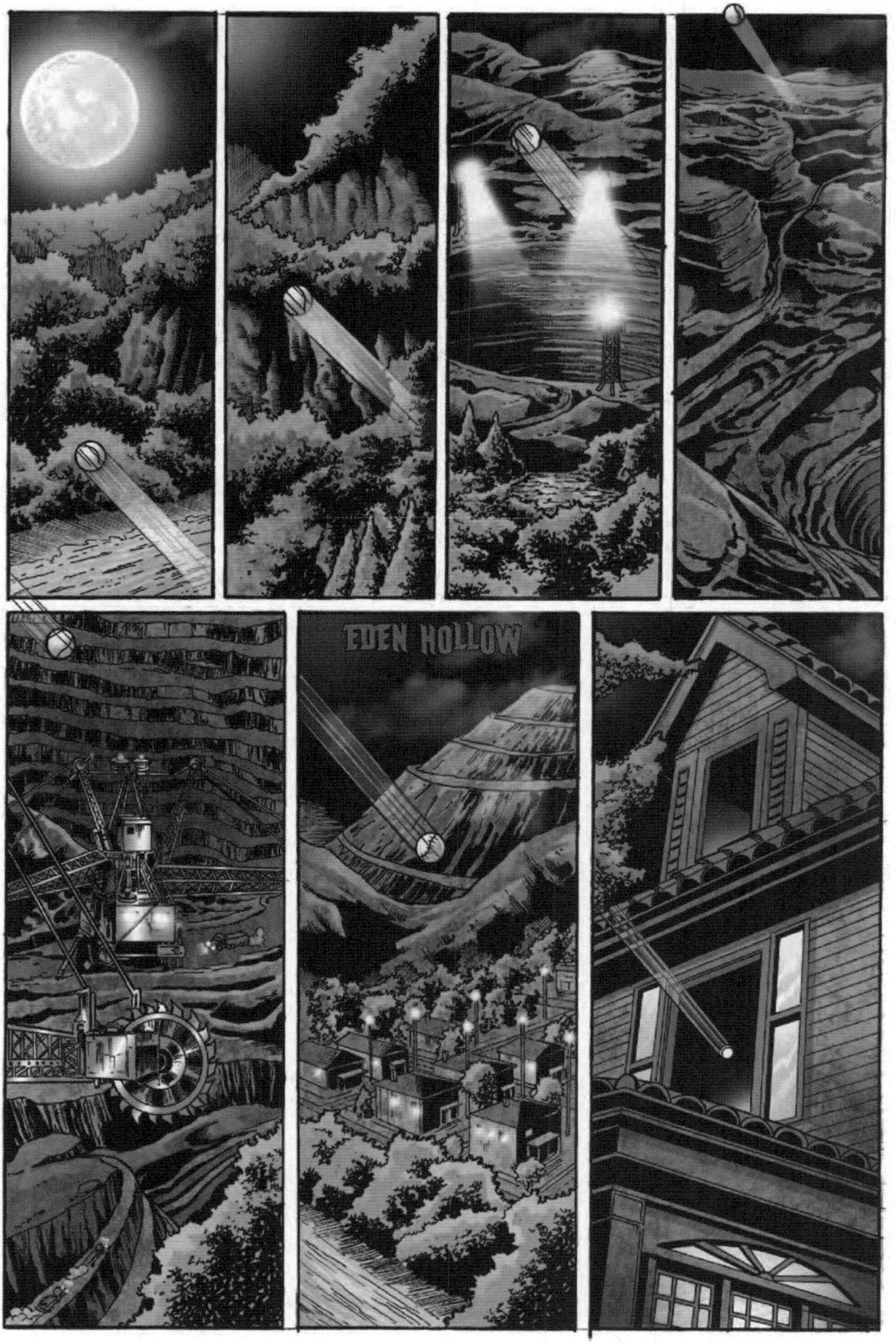
EDEN HOLLOW

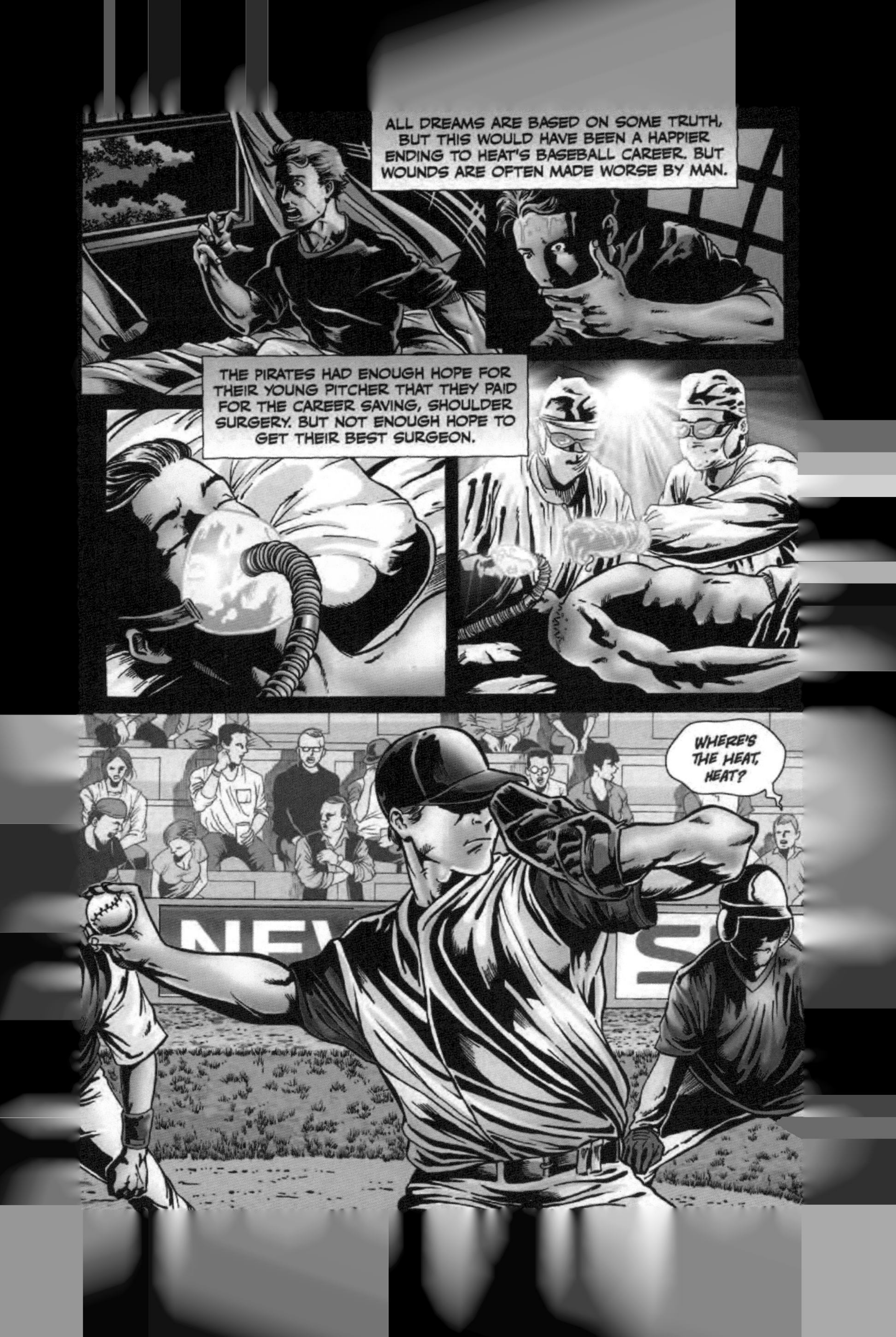
ALL DREAMS ARE BASED ON SOME TRUTH, BUT THIS WOULD HAVE BEEN A HAPPIER ENDING TO HEAT'S BASEBALL CAREER. BUT WOUNDS ARE OFTEN MADE WORSE BY MAN.
THE PIRATES HAD ENOUGH HOPE FOR THEIR YOUNG PITCHER THAT THEY PAID FOR THE CAREER SAVING, SHOULDER SURGERY. BUT NOT ENOUGH HOPE TO GET THEIR BEST SURGEON.
WHERE'S THE HEAT, HEAT?

NO ONE COULD REALLY SAY IF IT WAS THE MAJOR LEAGUE SURGERY WITH A MINOR LEAGUE SURGEON, OR HEAT'S PHYSIOLOGY JUST COULDN'T ACCEPT THE NEW TENDON CONFIGURATIONS, BUT HEAT'S "HEAT" WAS GONE.

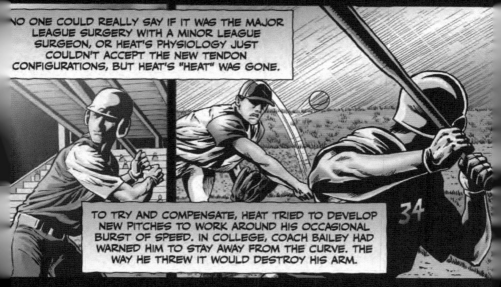

TO TRY AND COMPENSATE, HEAT TRIED TO DEVELOP NEW PITCHES TO WORK AROUND HIS OCCASIONAL BURST OF SPEED. IN COLLEGE, COACH BAILEY HAD WARNED HIM TO STAY AWAY FROM THE CURVE. THE WAY HE THREW IT WOULD DESTROY HIS ARM.

WHERE'S THE HEAT, HEAT?

YOU BUM!

CRACK

BUT MINOR LEAGUE COACHES, AS DESPERATE AS THE PLAYERS TO MOVE UP, DID NOT LOVE THEIR PLAYERS LIKE CAL BAILEY DID.

IN FACT IT WAS ANOTHER COACH THAT QUIETLY SUGGESTED THAT HEAT TRY STEROIDS, OR "THE GAS" AS THE PLAYERS CALLED THE BANNED MIRACLE DRUGS, TO TRY AND RECOVER FASTER.

MANAGER

Lab Results
Positive

AND THAT COACH WAS NOWHERE TO BE FOUND WHEN A RANDOM TEST CAUGHT HEAT'S GAS. A SUSPENSION AT THIS, THE LOWEST LEVEL OF BASEBALL, IS A DEATH SENTENCE. AND SO IT WAS.

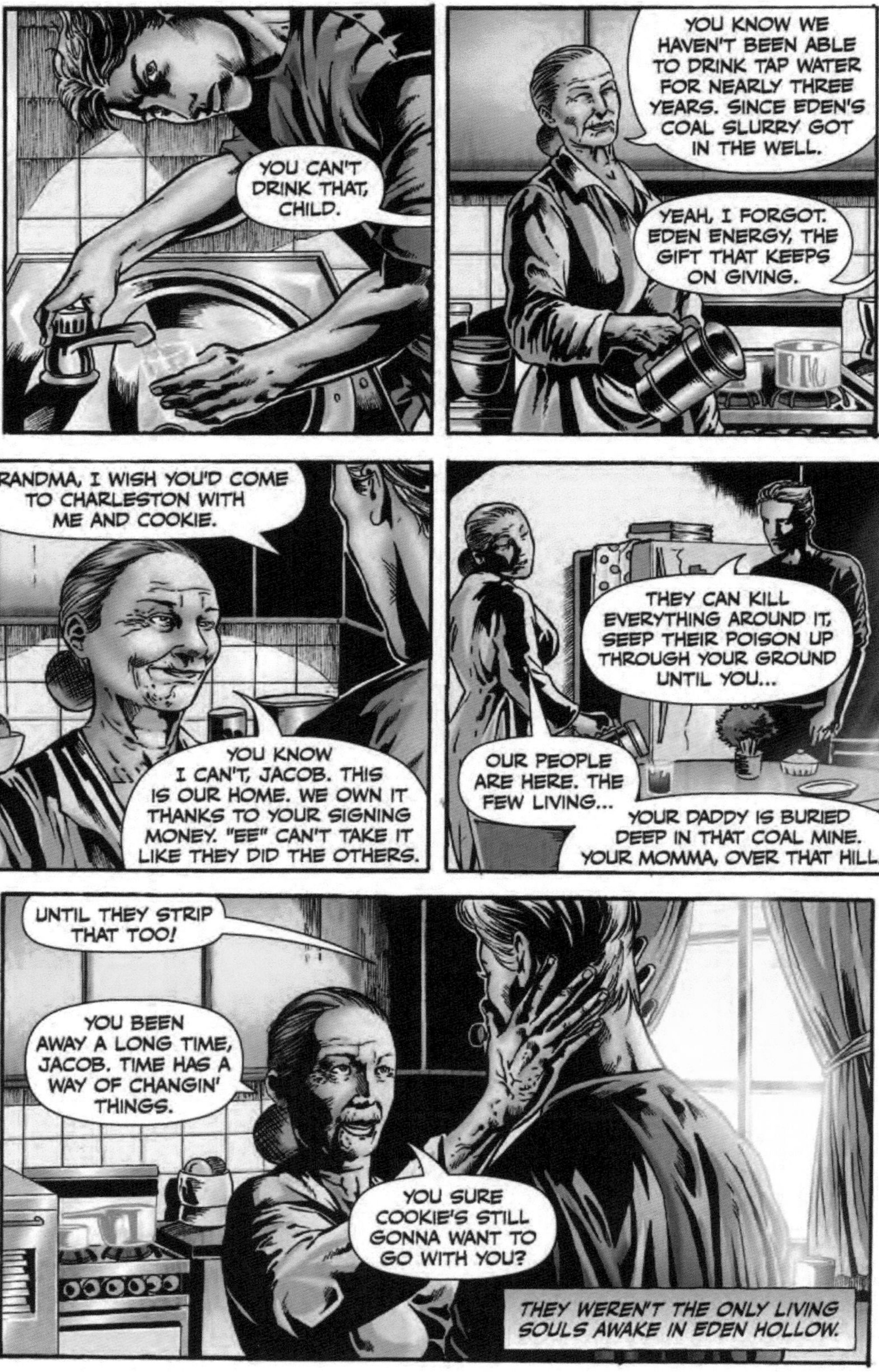
YOU CAN'T DRINK THAT, CHILD.
YOU KNOW WE HAVEN'T BEEN ABLE TO DRINK TAP WATER FOR NEARLY THREE YEARS. SINCE EDEN'S COAL SLURRY GOT IN THE WELL.
YEAH, I FORGOT. EDEN ENERGY, THE GIFT THAT KEEPS ON GIVING.
GRANDMA, I WISH YOU'D COME TO CHARLESTON WITH ME AND COOKIE.
YOU KNOW I CAN'T, JACOB. THIS IS OUR HOME. WE OWN IT THANKS TO YOUR SIGNING MONEY. "EE" CAN'T TAKE IT LIKE THEY DID THE OTHERS.
THEY CAN KILL EVERYTHING AROUND IT, SEEP THEIR POISON UP THROUGH YOUR GROUND UNTIL YOU...
OUR PEOPLE ARE HERE. THE FEW LIVING...
YOUR DADDY IS BURIED DEEP IN THAT COAL MINE. YOUR MOMMA, OVER THAT HILL...
UNTIL THEY STRIP THAT TOO!
YOU BEEN AWAY A LONG TIME, JACOB. TIME HAS A WAY OF CHANGIN' THINGS.
YOU SURE COOKIE'S STILL GONNA WANT TO GO WITH YOU?
THEY WEREN'T THE ONLY LIVING SOULS AWAKE IN EDEN HOLLOW.

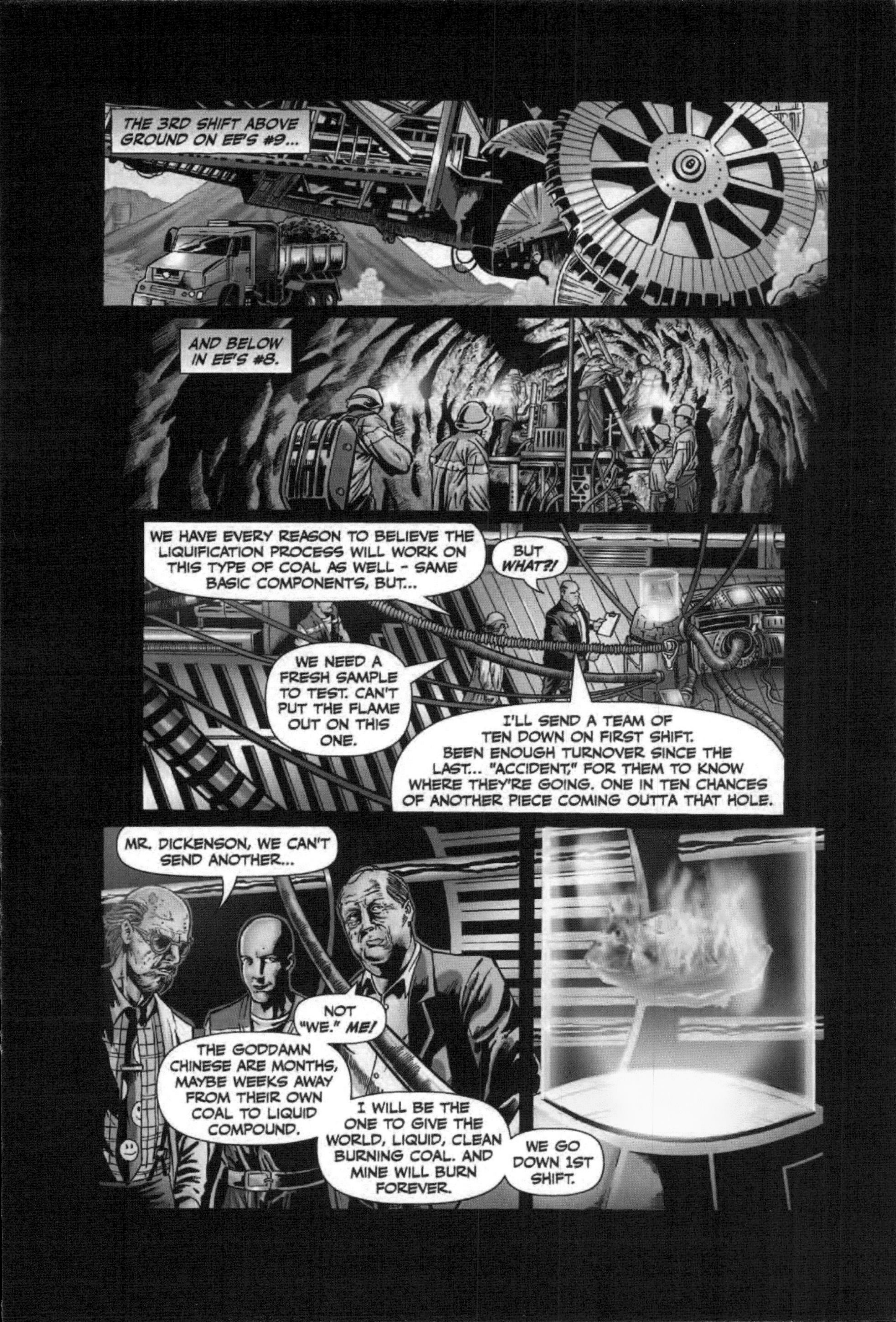
THE 3RD SHIFT ABOVE GROUND ON EE'S #9...
AND BELOW IN EE'S #8.
WE HAVE EVERY REASON TO BELIEVE THE LIQUIFICATION PROCESS WILL WORK ON THIS TYPE OF COAL AS WELL - SAME BASIC COMPONENTS, BUT...
BUT *WHAT?!*
WE NEED A FRESH SAMPLE TO TEST. CAN'T PUT THE FLAME OUT ON THIS ONE.
I'LL SEND A TEAM OF TEN DOWN ON FIRST SHIFT. BEEN ENOUGH TURNOVER SINCE THE LAST... "ACCIDENT," FOR THEM TO KNOW WHERE THEY'RE GOING. ONE IN TEN CHANCES OF ANOTHER PIECE COMING OUTTA THAT HOLE.
MR. DICKENSON, WE CAN'T SEND ANOTHER...
NOT "WE." *ME!*
THE GODDAMN CHINESE ARE MONTHS, MAYBE WEEKS AWAY FROM THEIR OWN COAL TO LIQUID COMPOUND.
I WILL BE THE ONE TO GIVE THE WORLD, LIQUID, CLEAN BURNING COAL. AND MINE WILL BURN FOREVER.
WE GO DOWN 1ST SHIFT.

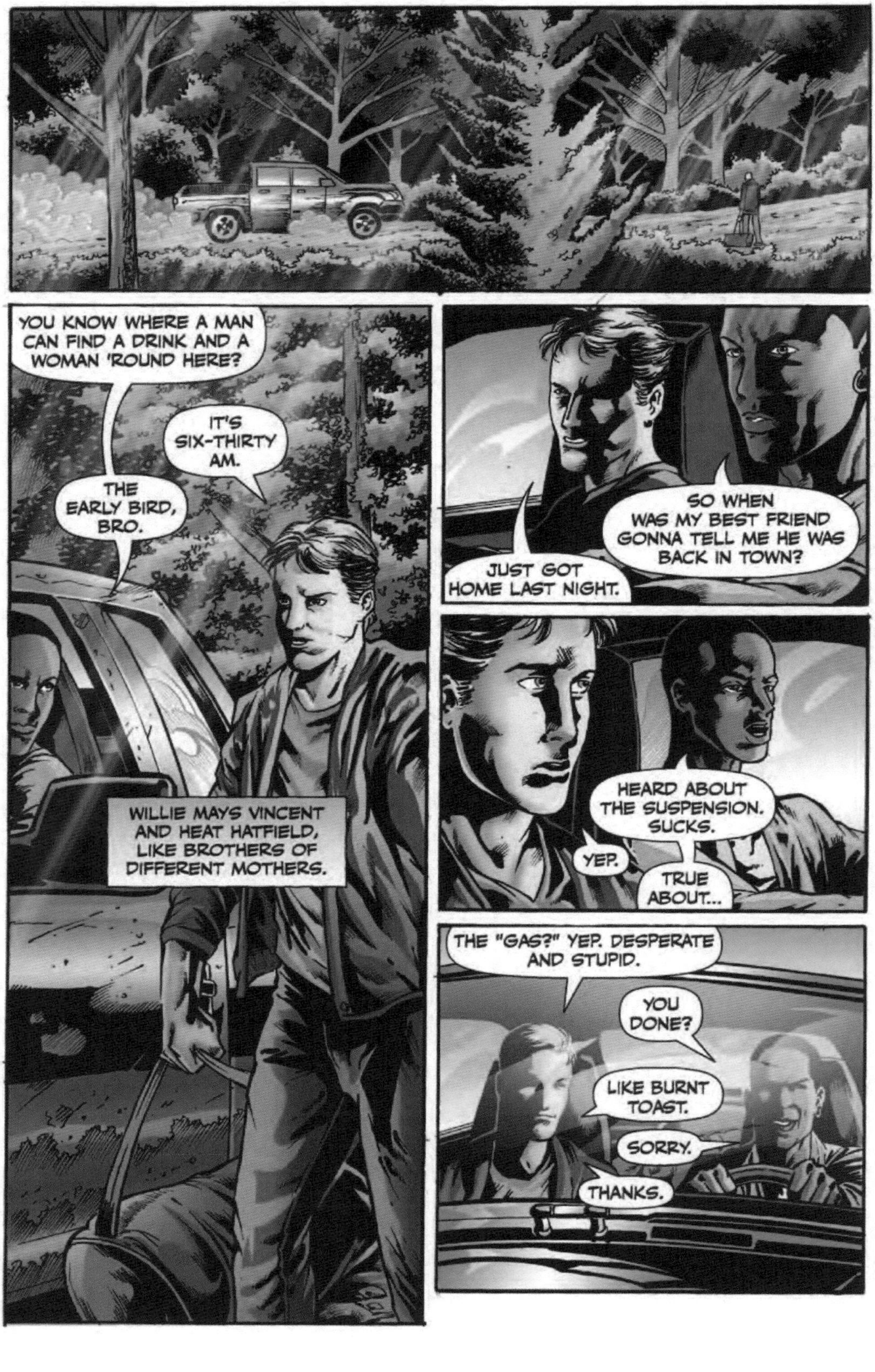
YOU KNOW WHERE A MAN CAN FIND A DRINK AND A WOMAN 'ROUND HERE?
IT'S SIX-THIRTY AM.
THE EARLY BIRD, BRO.
WILLIE MAYS VINCENT AND HEAT HATFIELD, LIKE BROTHERS OF DIFFERENT MOTHERS.
SO WHEN WAS MY BEST FRIEND GONNA TELL ME HE WAS BACK IN TOWN?
JUST GOT HOME LAST NIGHT.
HEARD ABOUT THE SUSPENSION. SUCKS.
YEP.
TRUE ABOUT...
THE "GAS?" YEP. DESPERATE AND STUPID.
YOU DONE?
LIKE BURNT TOAST.
SORRY.
THANKS.

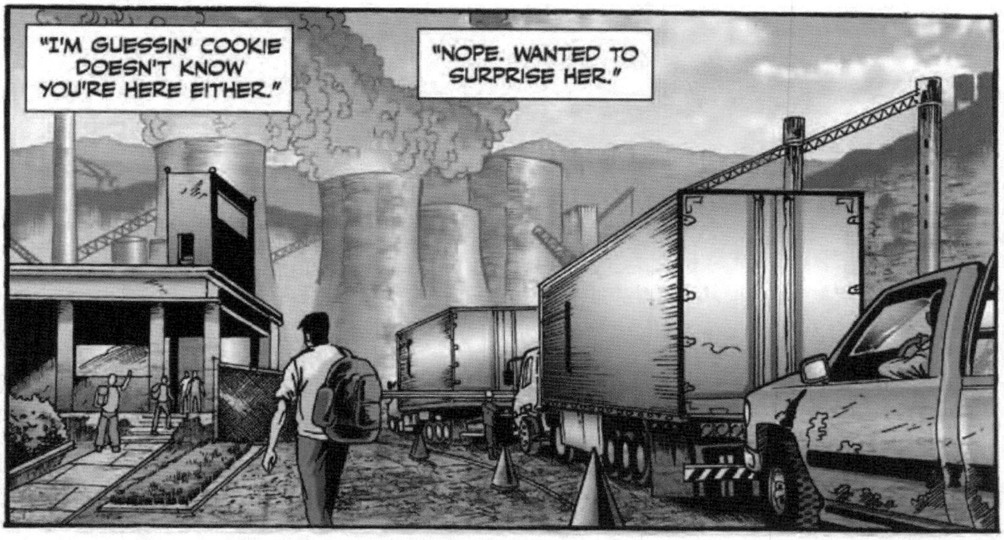
"I'M GUESSIN' COOKIE DOESN'T KNOW YOU'RE HERE EITHER."
"NOPE. WANTED TO SURPRISE HER."

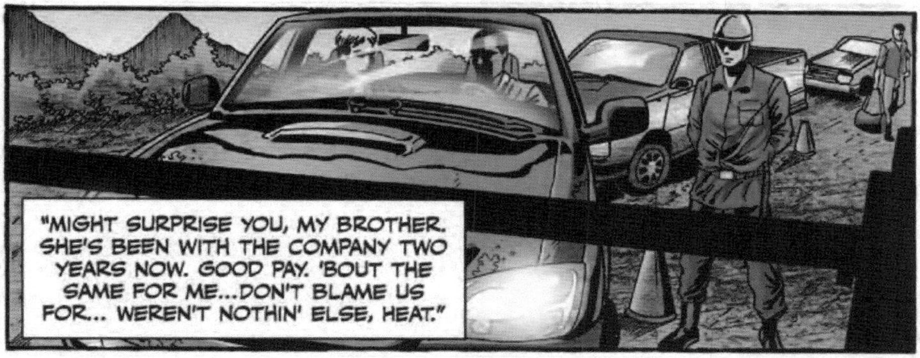
"MIGHT SURPRISE YOU, MY BROTHER. SHE'S BEEN WITH THE COMPANY TWO YEARS NOW. GOOD PAY. 'BOUT THE SAME FOR ME...DON'T BLAME US FOR... WEREN'T NOTHIN' ELSE, HEAT."

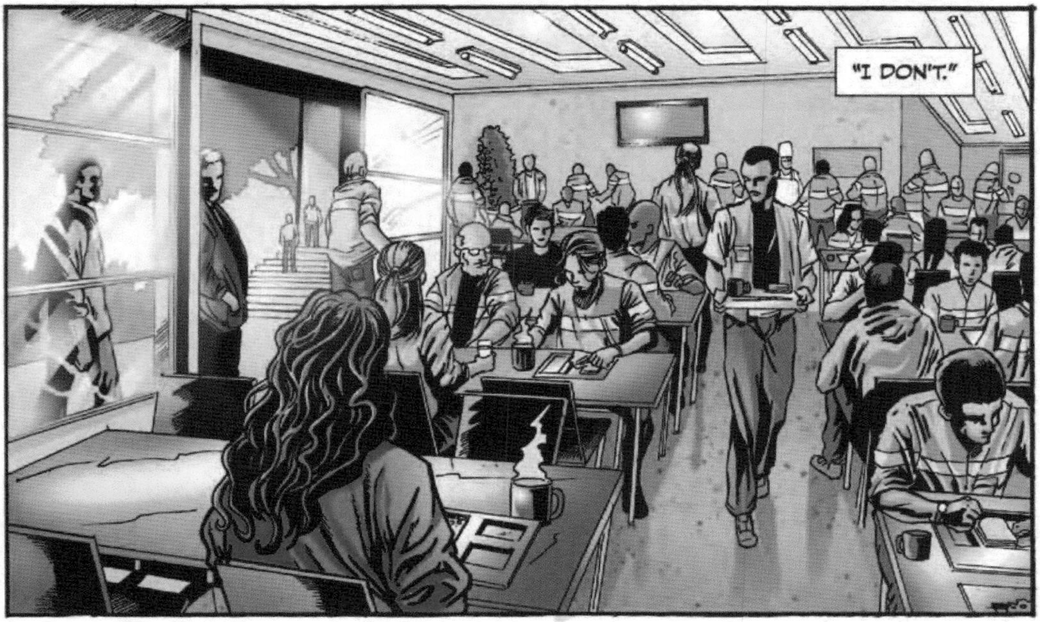
"I DON'T."

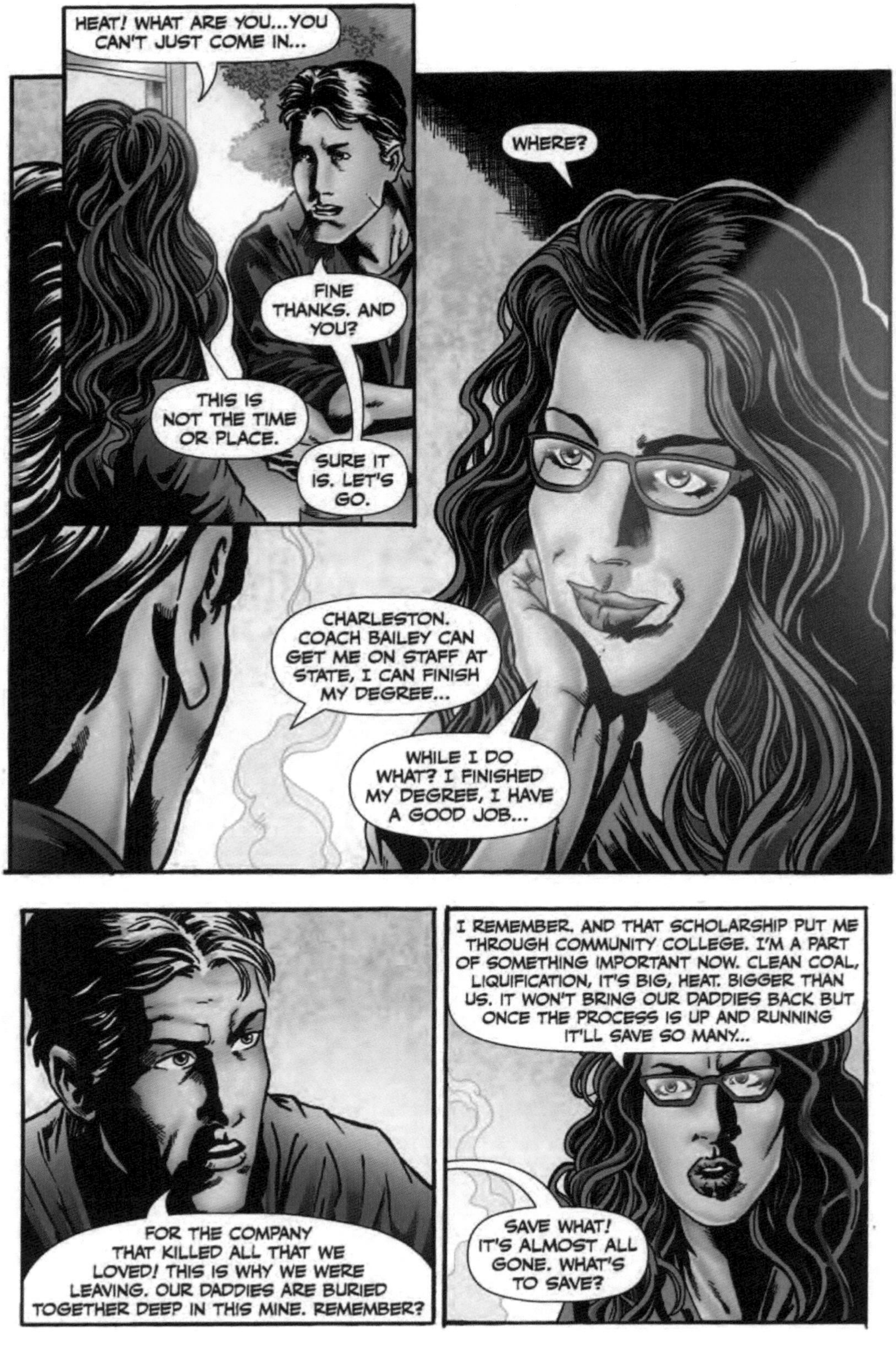
HEAT! WHAT ARE YOU...YOU CAN'T JUST COME IN...
FINE THANKS. AND YOU?
THIS IS NOT THE TIME OR PLACE.
SURE IT IS. LET'S GO.
WHERE?
CHARLESTON. COACH BAILEY CAN GET ME ON STAFF AT STATE, I CAN FINISH MY DEGREE...
WHILE I DO WHAT? I FINISHED MY DEGREE, I HAVE A GOOD JOB...
FOR THE COMPANY THAT KILLED ALL THAT WE LOVED! THIS IS WHY WE WERE LEAVING. OUR DADDIES ARE BURIED TOGETHER DEEP IN THIS MINE. REMEMBER?
I REMEMBER. AND THAT SCHOLARSHIP PUT ME THROUGH COMMUNITY COLLEGE. I'M A PART OF SOMETHING IMPORTANT NOW. CLEAN COAL, LIQUIFICATION, IT'S BIG, HEAT. BIGGER THAN US. IT WON'T BRING OUR DADDIES BACK BUT ONCE THE PROCESS IS UP AND RUNNING IT'LL SAVE SO MANY...
SAVE WHAT! IT'S ALMOST ALL GONE. WHAT'S TO SAVE?

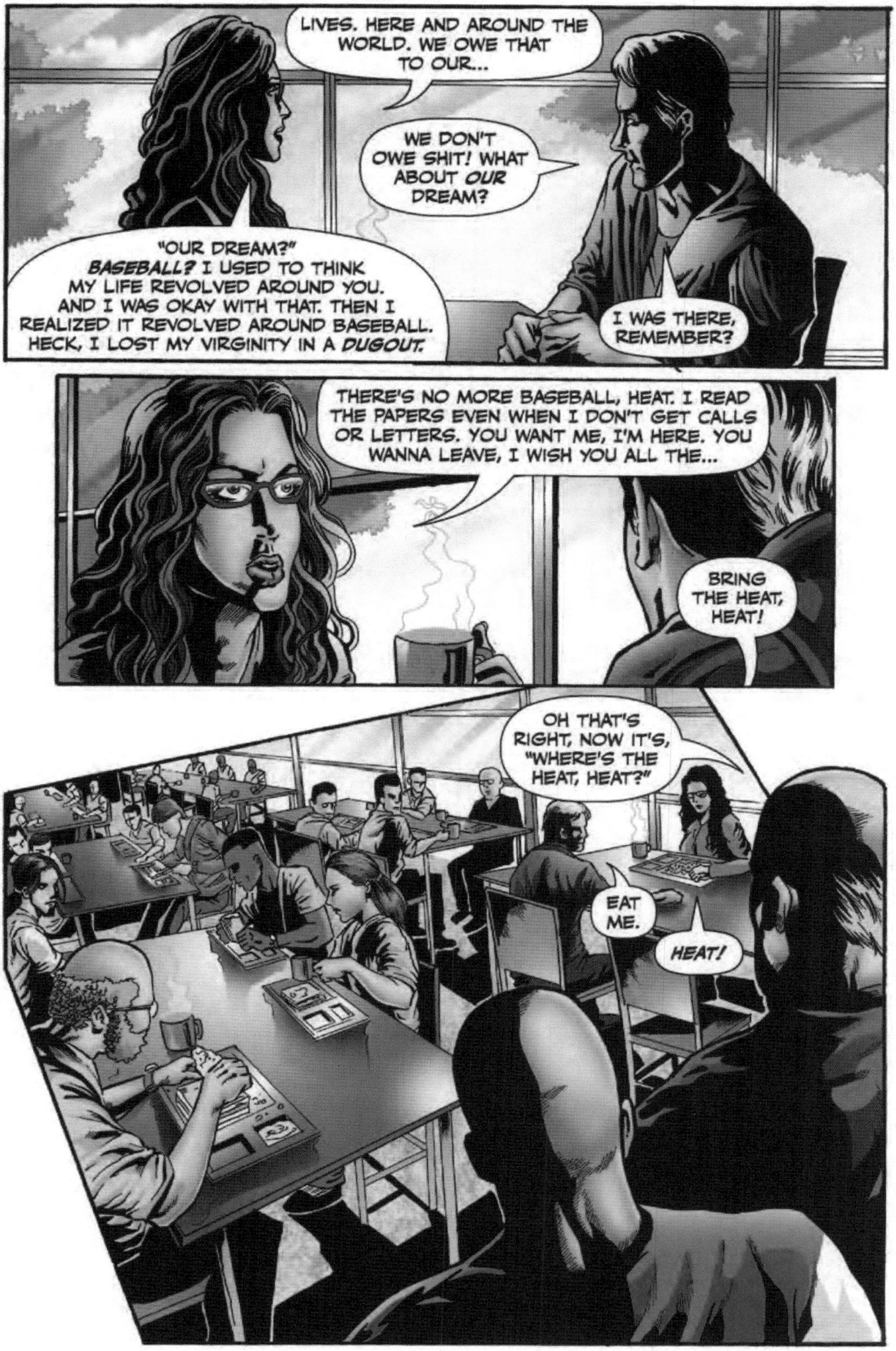

LIVES. HERE AND AROUND THE WORLD. WE OWE THAT TO OUR...
WE DON'T OWE SHIT! WHAT ABOUT *OUR* DREAM?
"OUR DREAM?" *BASEBALL?* I USED TO THINK MY LIFE REVOLVED AROUND YOU. AND I WAS OKAY WITH THAT. THEN I REALIZED IT REVOLVED AROUND BASEBALL. HECK, I LOST MY VIRGINITY IN A *DUGOUT.*
I WAS THERE, REMEMBER?
THERE'S NO MORE BASEBALL, HEAT. I READ THE PAPERS EVEN WHEN I DON'T GET CALLS OR LETTERS. YOU WANT ME, I'M HERE. YOU WANNA LEAVE, I WISH YOU ALL THE...
BRING THE HEAT, HEAT!
OH THAT'S RIGHT, NOW IT'S, "WHERE'S THE HEAT, HEAT?"
EAT ME.
HEAT!

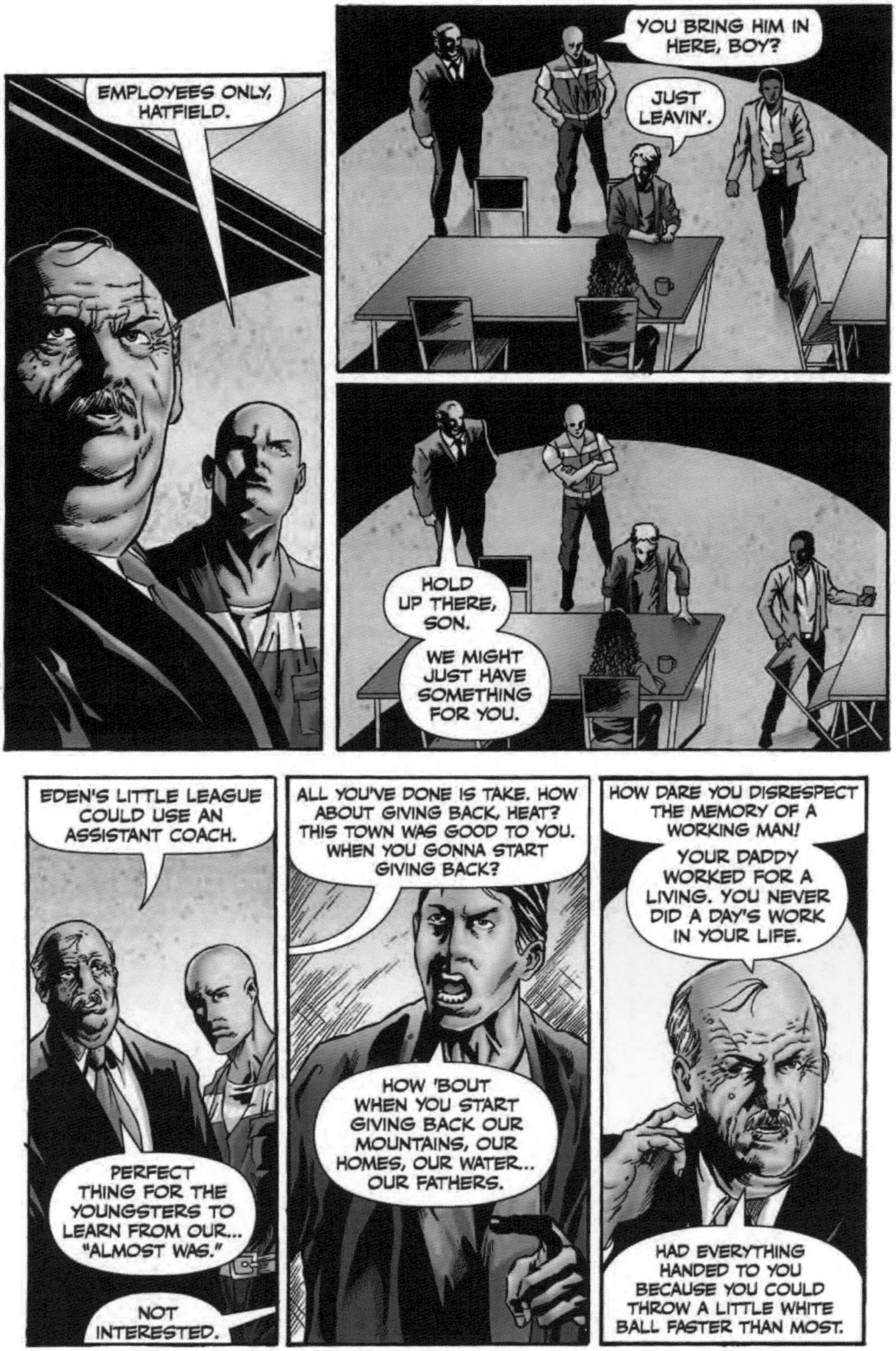

EMPLOYEES ONLY, HATFIELD.
YOU BRING HIM IN HERE, BOY?
JUST LEAVIN'.
HOLD UP THERE, SON.
WE MIGHT JUST HAVE SOMETHING FOR YOU.
EDEN'S LITTLE LEAGUE COULD USE AN ASSISTANT COACH.
PERFECT THING FOR THE YOUNGSTERS TO LEARN FROM OUR... "ALMOST WAS."
NOT INTERESTED.
ALL YOU'VE DONE IS TAKE. HOW ABOUT GIVING BACK, HEAT? THIS TOWN WAS GOOD TO YOU. WHEN YOU GONNA START GIVING BACK?
HOW 'BOUT WHEN YOU START GIVING BACK OUR MOUNTAINS, OUR HOMES, OUR WATER.. OUR FATHERS.
HOW DARE YOU DISRESPECT THE MEMORY OF A WORKING MAN!
YOUR DADDY WORKED FOR A LIVING. YOU NEVER DID A DAY'S WORK IN YOUR LIFE.
HAD EVERYTHING HANDED TO YOU BECAUSE YOU COULD THROW A LITTLE WHITE BALL FASTER THAN MOST.

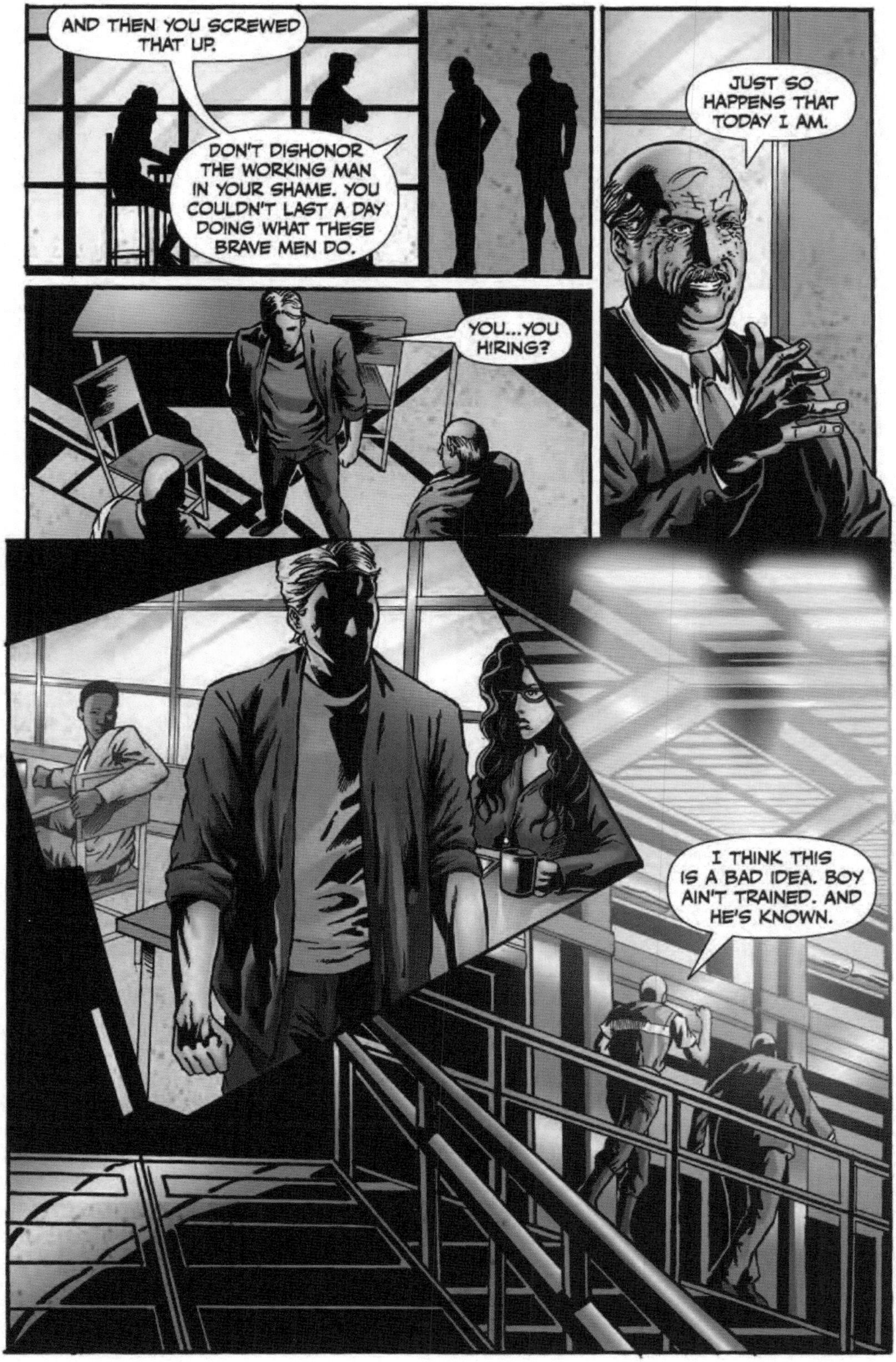
AND THEN YOU SCREWED THAT UP.
DON'T DISHONOR THE WORKING MAN IN YOUR SHAME. YOU COULDN'T LAST A DAY DOING WHAT THESE BRAVE MEN DO.
YOU...YOU HIRING?
JUST SO HAPPENS THAT TODAY I AM.
I THINK THIS IS A BAD IDEA. BOY AIN'T TRAINED. AND HE'S KNOWN.

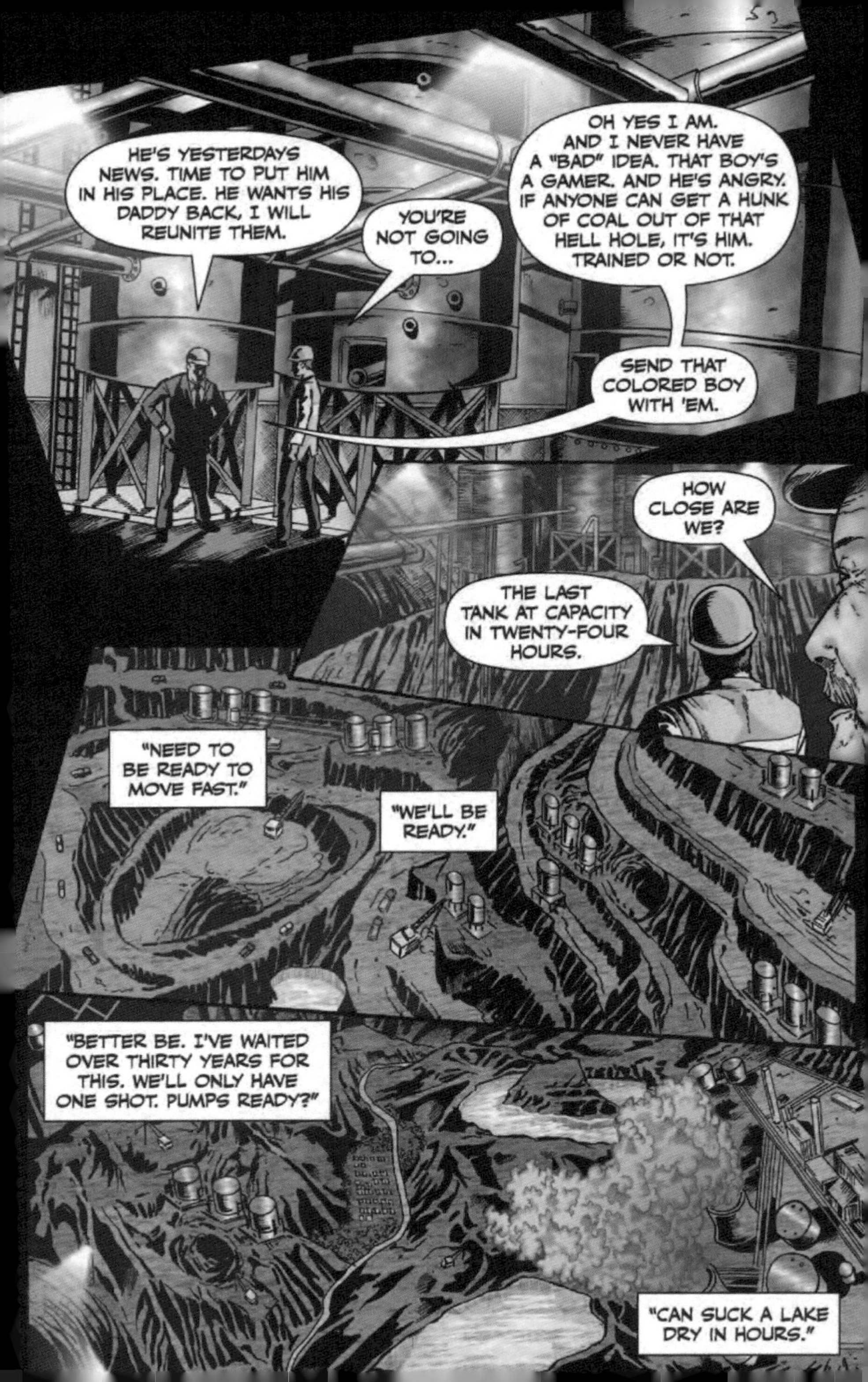
HE'S YESTERDAYS NEWS. TIME TO PUT HIM IN HIS PLACE. HE WANTS HIS DADDY BACK, I WILL REUNITE THEM.
YOU'RE NOT GOING TO...
OH YES I AM. AND I NEVER HAVE A "BAD" IDEA. THAT BOY'S A GAMER. AND HE'S ANGRY. IF ANYONE CAN GET A HUNK OF COAL OUT OF THAT HELL HOLE, IT'S HIM. TRAINED OR NOT.
SEND THAT COLORED BOY WITH 'EM.
HOW CLOSE ARE WE?
THE LAST TANK AT CAPACITY IN TWENTY-FOUR HOURS.
"NEED TO BE READY TO MOVE FAST."
"WE'LL BE READY."
"BETTER BE. I'VE WAITED OVER THIRTY YEARS FOR THIS. WE'LL ONLY HAVE ONE SHOT. PUMPS READY?"
"CAN SUCK A LAKE DRY IN HOURS."

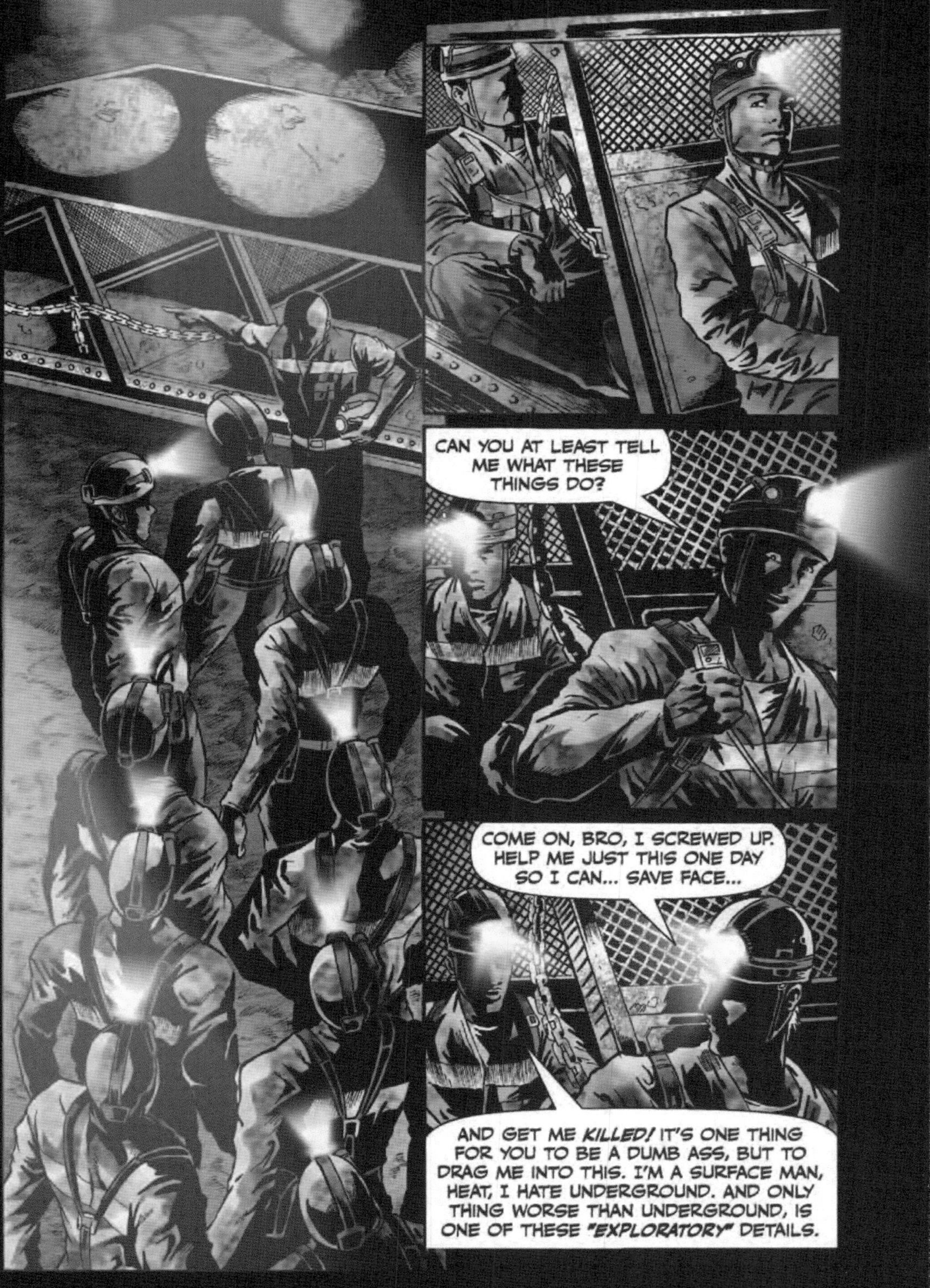
CAN YOU AT LEAST TELL ME WHAT THESE THINGS DO?
COME ON, BRO, I SCREWED UP. HELP ME JUST THIS ONE DAY SO I CAN... SAVE FACE...
AND GET ME KILLED! IT'S ONE THING FOR YOU TO BE A DUMB ASS, BUT TO DRAG ME INTO THIS. I'M A SURFACE MAN, HEAT, I HATE UNDERGROUND. AND ONLY THING WORSE THAN UNDERGROUND, IS ONE OF THESE "EXPLORATORY" DETAILS.

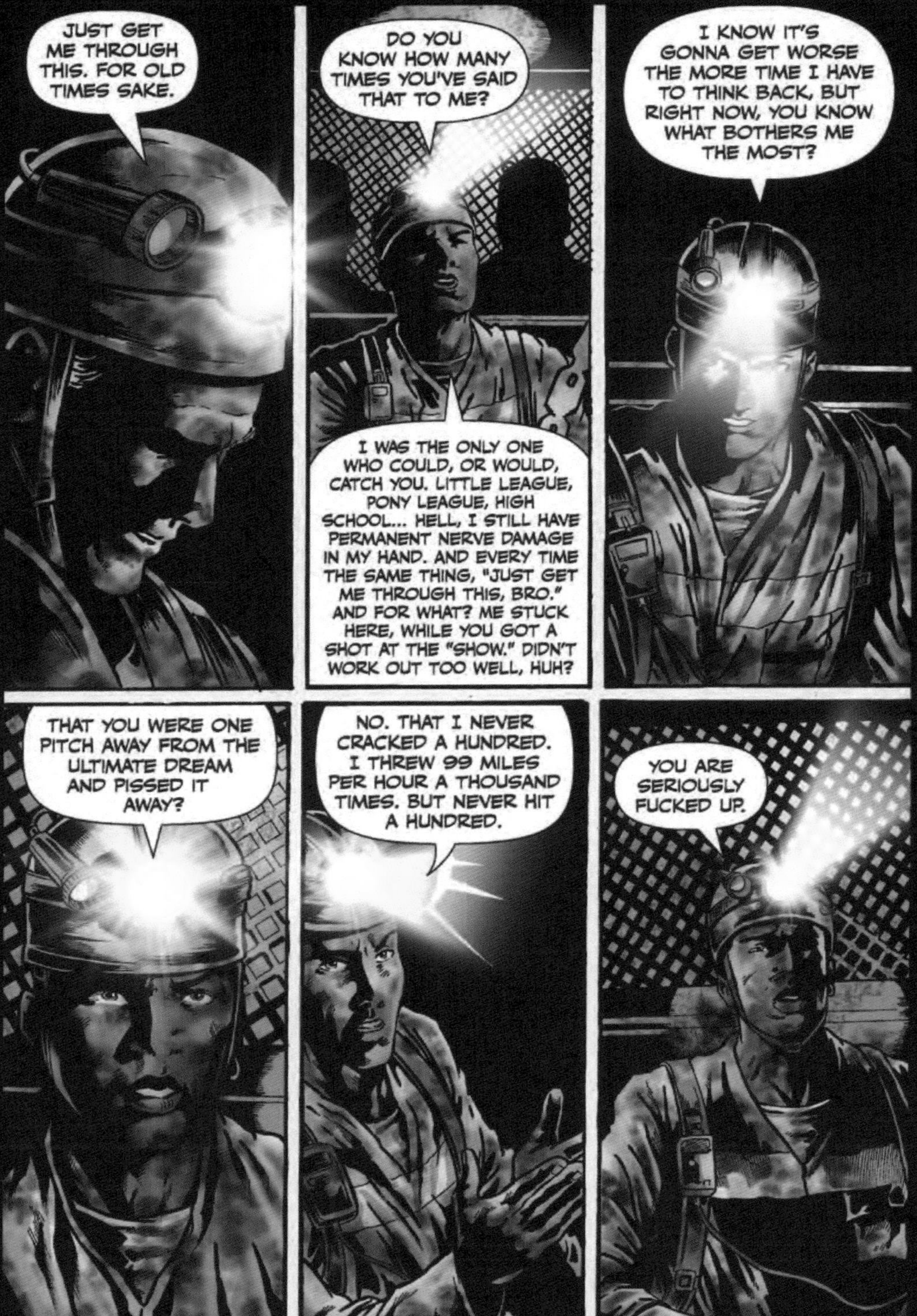
JUST GET ME THROUGH THIS. FOR OLD TIMES SAKE.
DO YOU KNOW HOW MANY TIMES YOU'VE SAID THAT TO ME?
I WAS THE ONLY ONE WHO COULD, OR WOULD, CATCH YOU. LITTLE LEAGUE, PONY LEAGUE, HIGH SCHOOL... HELL, I STILL HAVE PERMANENT NERVE DAMAGE IN MY HAND. AND EVERY TIME THE SAME THING, "JUST GET ME THROUGH THIS, BRO." AND FOR WHAT? ME STUCK HERE, WHILE YOU GOT A SHOT AT THE "SHOW." DIDN'T WORK OUT TOO WELL, HUH?
I KNOW IT'S GONNA GET WORSE THE MORE TIME I HAVE TO THINK BACK, BUT RIGHT NOW, YOU KNOW WHAT BOTHERS ME THE MOST?
THAT YOU WERE ONE PITCH AWAY FROM THE ULTIMATE DREAM AND PISSED IT AWAY?
NO. THAT I NEVER CRACKED A HUNDRED. I THREW 99 MILES PER HOUR A THOUSAND TIMES. BUT NEVER HIT A HUNDRED.
YOU ARE SERIOUSLY FUCKED UP.

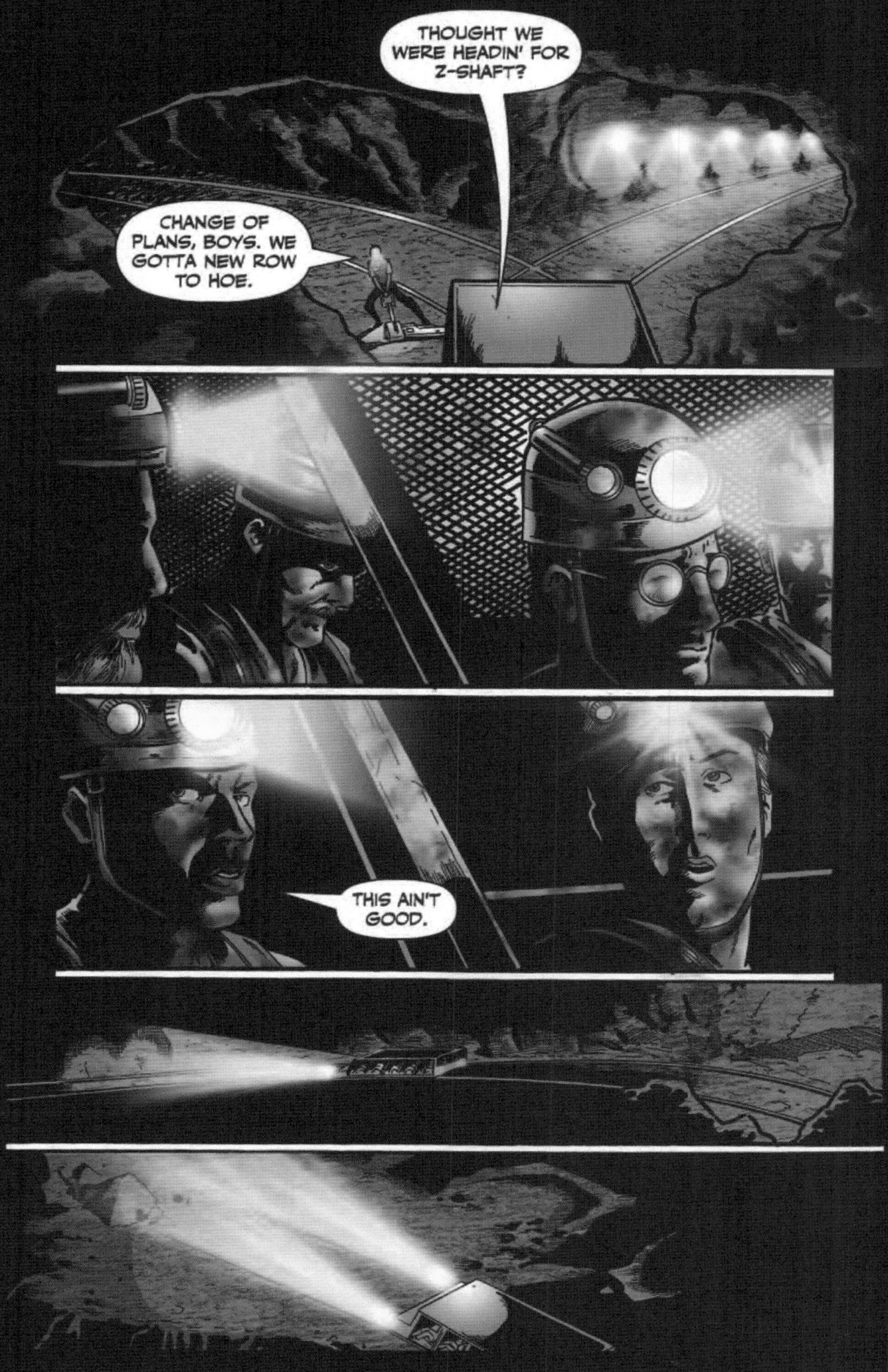
THOUGHT WE WERE HEADIN' FOR Z-SHAFT?
CHANGE OF PLANS, BOYS. WE GOTTA NEW ROW TO HOE.
THIS AIN'T GOOD.

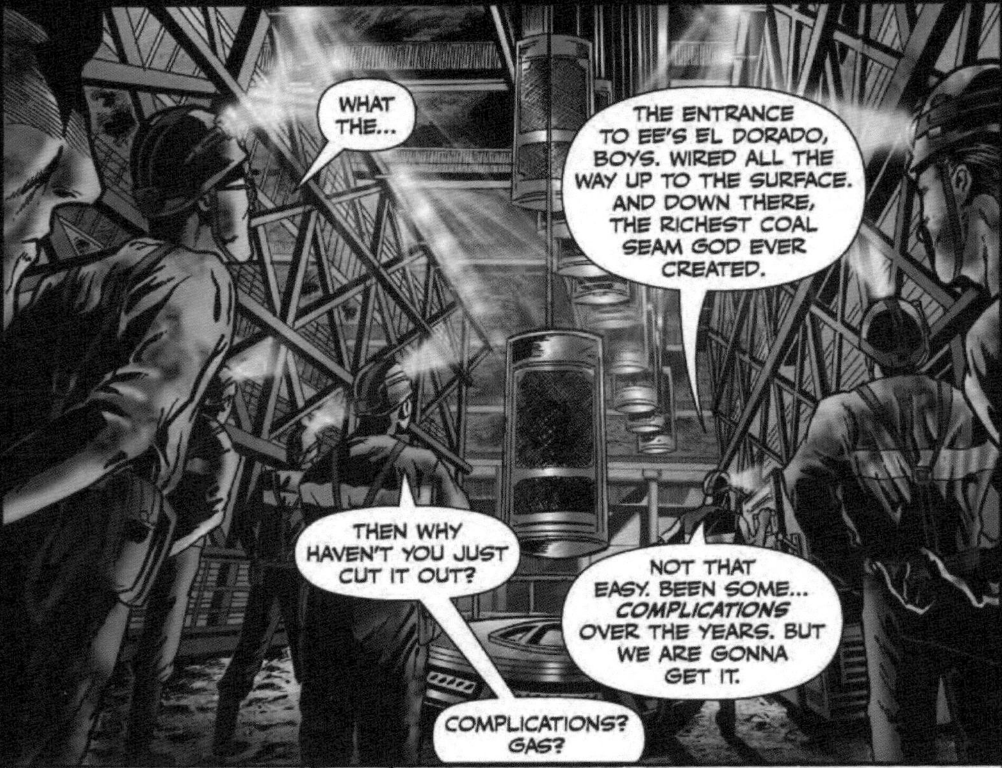
WHAT THE...
THE ENTRANCE TO EE'S EL DORADO, BOYS. WIRED ALL THE WAY UP TO THE SURFACE. AND DOWN THERE, THE RICHEST COAL SEAM GOD EVER CREATED.
THEN WHY HAVEN'T YOU JUST CUT IT OUT?
NOT THAT EASY. BEEN SOME... *COMPLICATIONS* OVER THE YEARS. BUT WE ARE GONNA GET IT.
COMPLICATIONS? GAS?

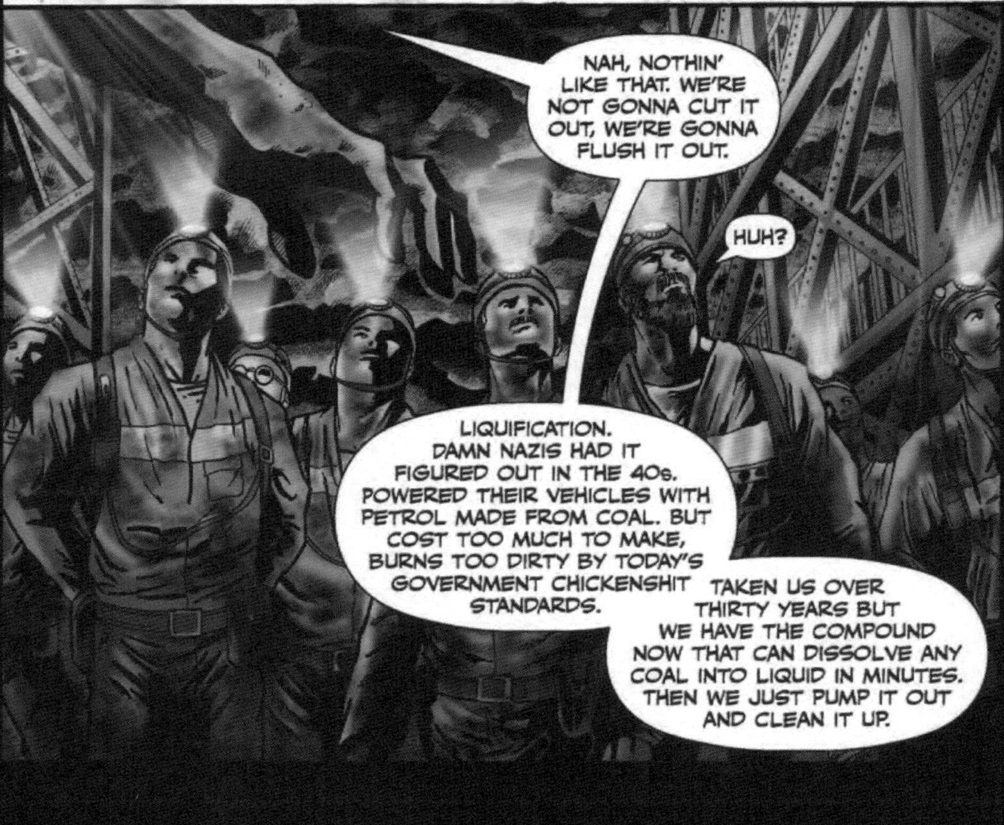
NAH, NOTHIN' LIKE THAT. WE'RE NOT GONNA CUT IT OUT, WE'RE GONNA FLUSH IT OUT.
HUH?
LIQUIFICATION. DAMN NAZIS HAD IT FIGURED OUT IN THE 40s. POWERED THEIR VEHICLES WITH PETROL MADE FROM COAL. BUT COST TOO MUCH TO MAKE, BURNS TOO DIRTY BY TODAY'S GOVERNMENT CHICKENSHIT STANDARDS.
TAKEN US OVER THIRTY YEARS BUT WE HAVE THE COMPOUND NOW THAT CAN DISSOLVE ANY COAL INTO LIQUID IN MINUTES. THEN WE JUST PUMP IT OUT AND CLEAN IT UP.

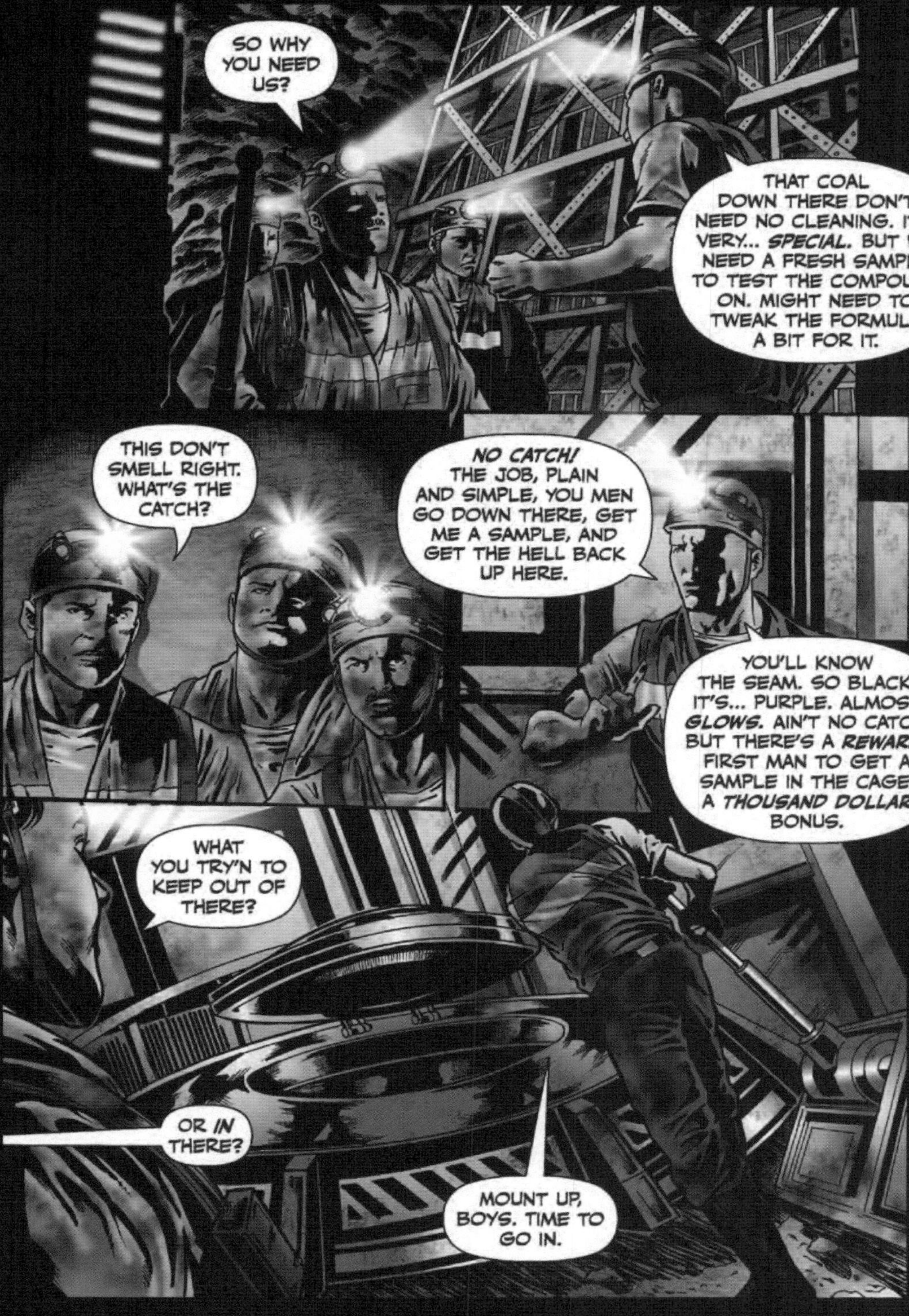
SO WHY YOU NEED US?
THAT COAL DOWN THERE DON'T NEED NO CLEANING. IT'S VERY... *SPECIAL.* BUT WE NEED A FRESH SAMPLE TO TEST THE COMPOUND ON. MIGHT NEED TO TWEAK THE FORMULA A BIT FOR IT.
THIS DON'T SMELL RIGHT. WHAT'S THE CATCH?
NO CATCH! THE JOB, PLAIN AND SIMPLE, YOU MEN GO DOWN THERE, GET ME A SAMPLE, AND GET THE HELL BACK UP HERE.
YOU'LL KNOW THE SEAM. SO BLACK, IT'S... PURPLE. ALMOST *GLOWS.* AIN'T NO CATCH, BUT THERE'S A *REWARD.* FIRST MAN TO GET A SAMPLE IN THE CAGE, A *THOUSAND DOLLAR* BONUS.
WHAT YOU TRY'N TO KEEP OUT OF THERE?
OR *IN* THERE?
MOUNT UP, BOYS. TIME TO GO IN.

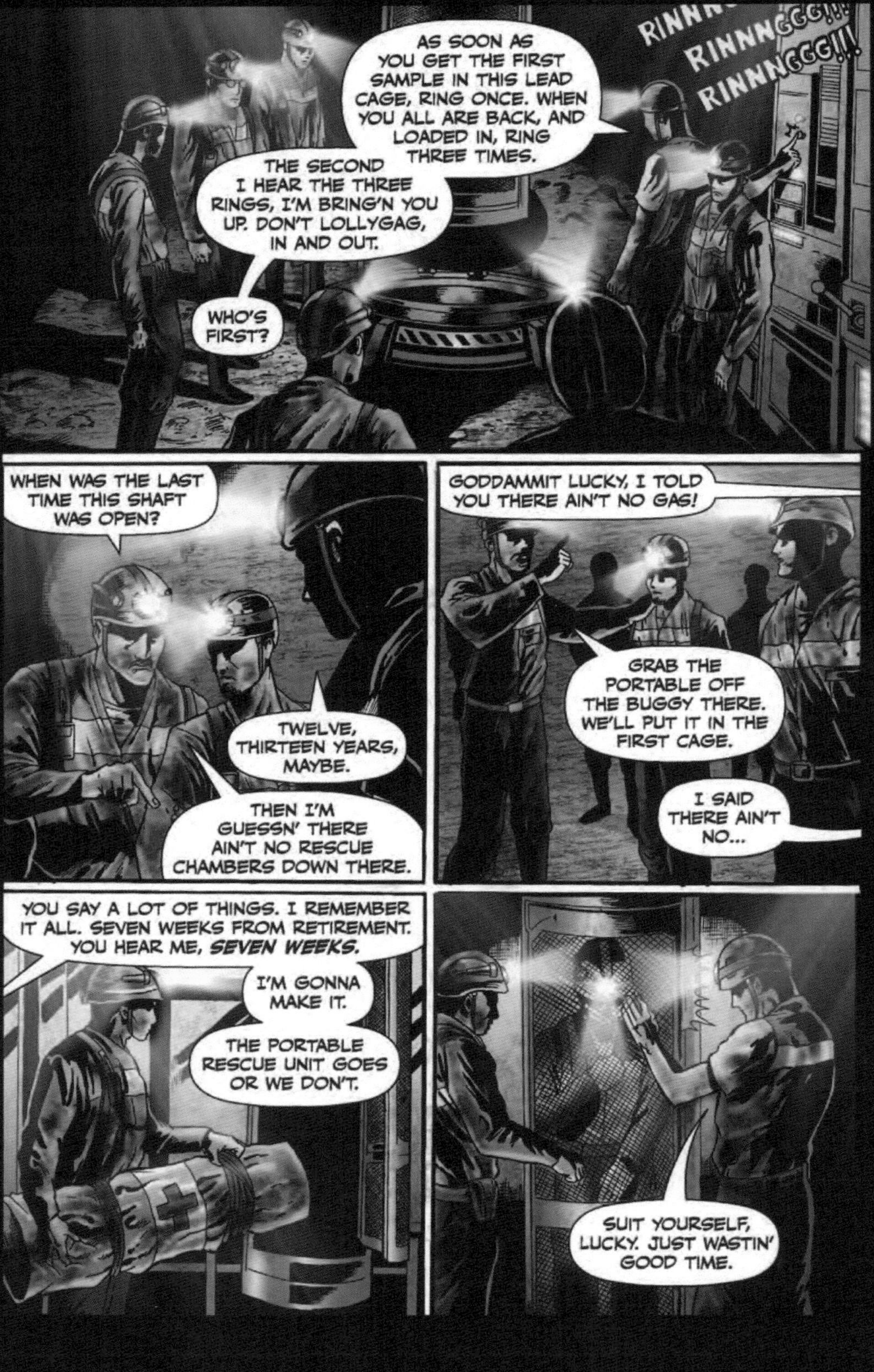
RINNNGGG!!!
RINNNGGG!!!
AS SOON AS YOU GET THE FIRST SAMPLE IN THIS LEAD CAGE, RING ONCE. WHEN YOU ALL ARE BACK, AND LOADED IN, RING THREE TIMES.
THE SECOND I HEAR THE THREE RINGS, I'M BRING'N YOU UP. DON'T LOLLYGAG, IN AND OUT.
WHO'S FIRST?
WHEN WAS THE LAST TIME THIS SHAFT WAS OPEN?
TWELVE, THIRTEEN YEARS, MAYBE.
THEN I'M GUESSN' THERE AIN'T NO RESCUE CHAMBERS DOWN THERE.
GODDAMMIT LUCKY, I TOLD YOU THERE AIN'T NO GAS!
GRAB THE PORTABLE OFF THE BUGGY THERE. WE'LL PUT IT IN THE FIRST CAGE.
I SAID THERE AIN'T NO...
YOU SAY A LOT OF THINGS. I REMEMBER IT ALL. SEVEN WEEKS FROM RETIREMENT. YOU HEAR ME, *SEVEN WEEKS.*
I'M GONNA MAKE IT.
THE PORTABLE RESCUE UNIT GOES OR WE DON'T.
SUIT YOURSELF, LUCKY. JUST WASTIN' GOOD TIME.

GO AHEAD, HEAT. I'LL TAKE THE CABOOSE.

"YOU-ALL COME BACK NOW, YA HEAR."

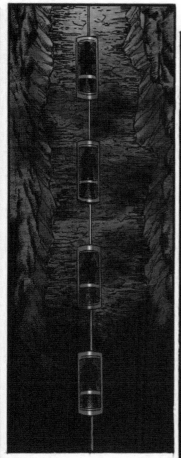

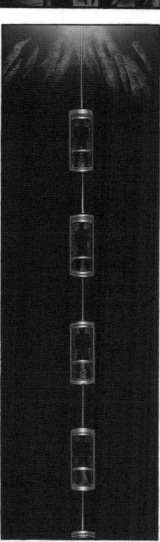

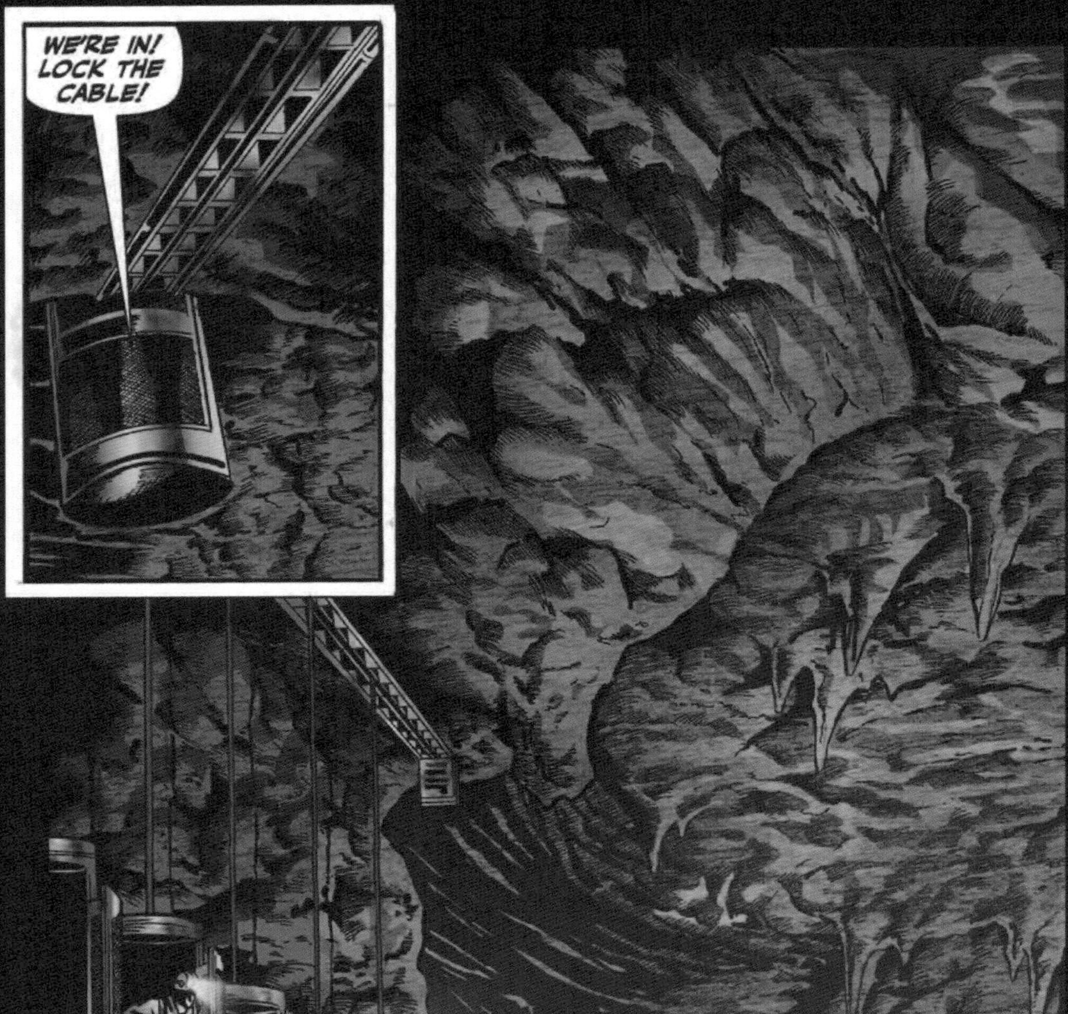
WE'RE IN! LOCK THE CABLE!

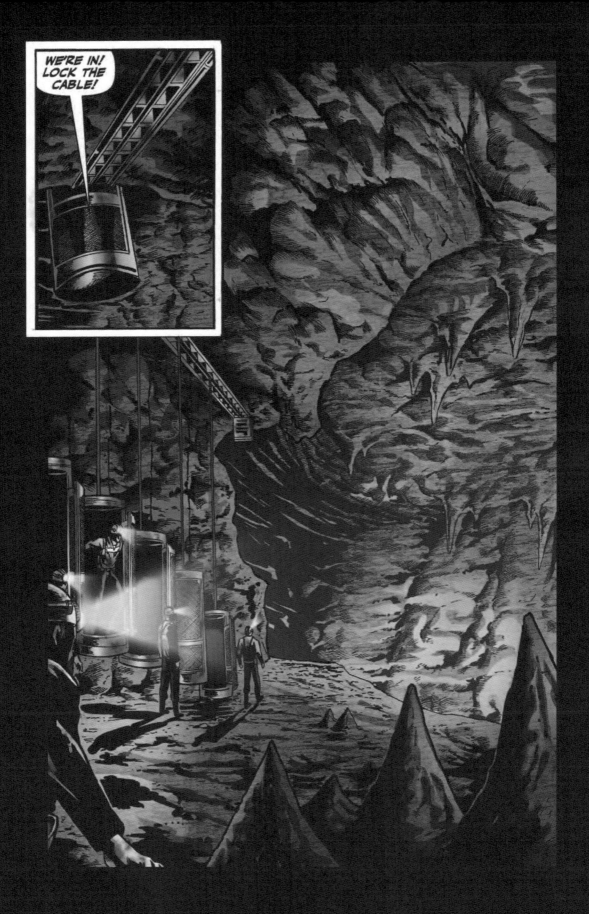

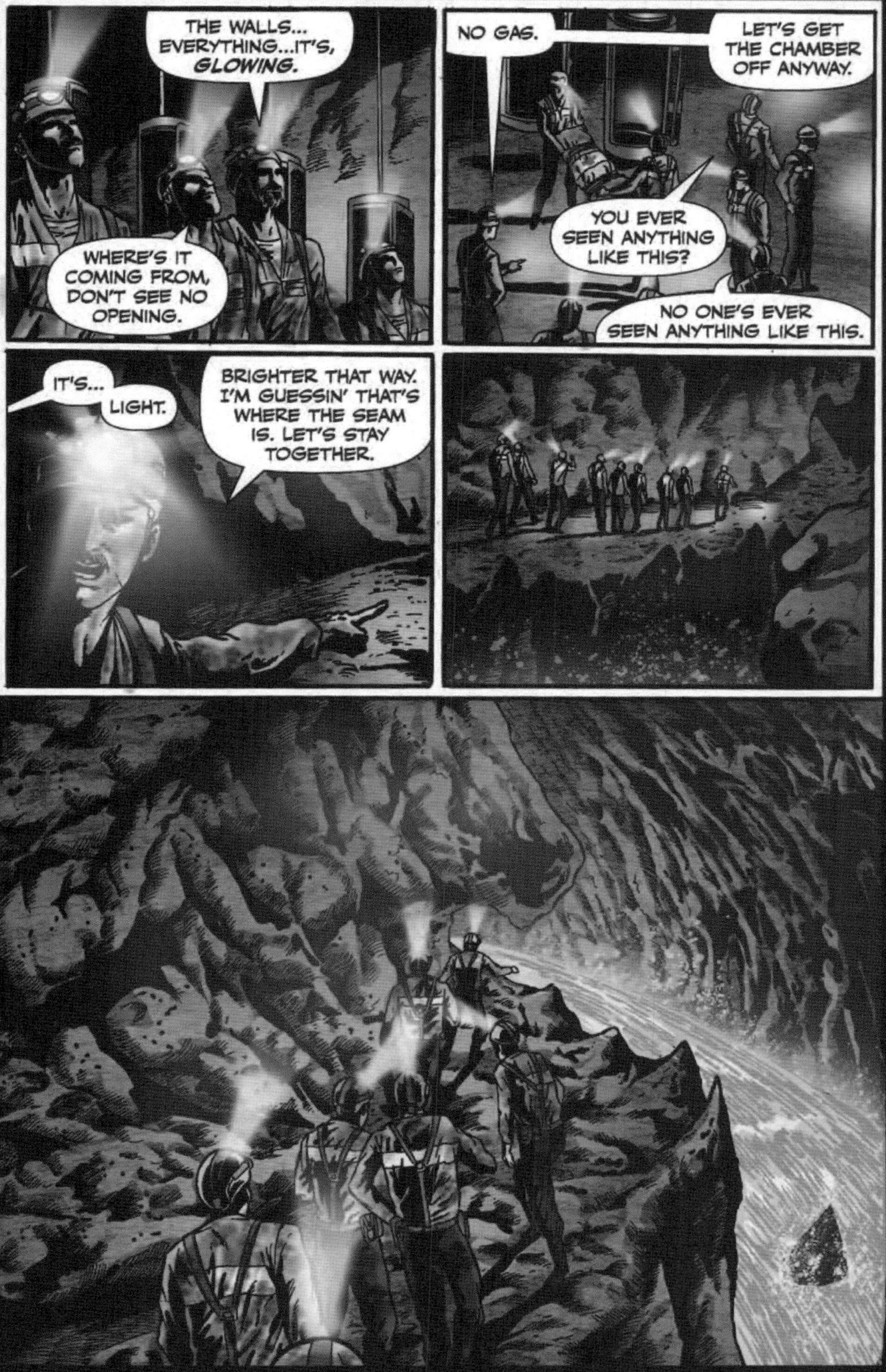

THE WALLS... EVERYTHING...IT'S, GLOWING.
WHERE'S IT COMING FROM, DON'T SEE NO OPENING.
NO GAS.
LET'S GET THE CHAMBER OFF ANYWAY.
YOU EVER SEEN ANYTHING LIKE THIS?
NO ONE'S EVER SEEN ANYTHING LIKE THIS.
IT'S...
LIGHT.
BRIGHTER THAT WAY. I'M GUESSIN' THAT'S WHERE THE SEAM IS. LET'S STAY TOGETHER.

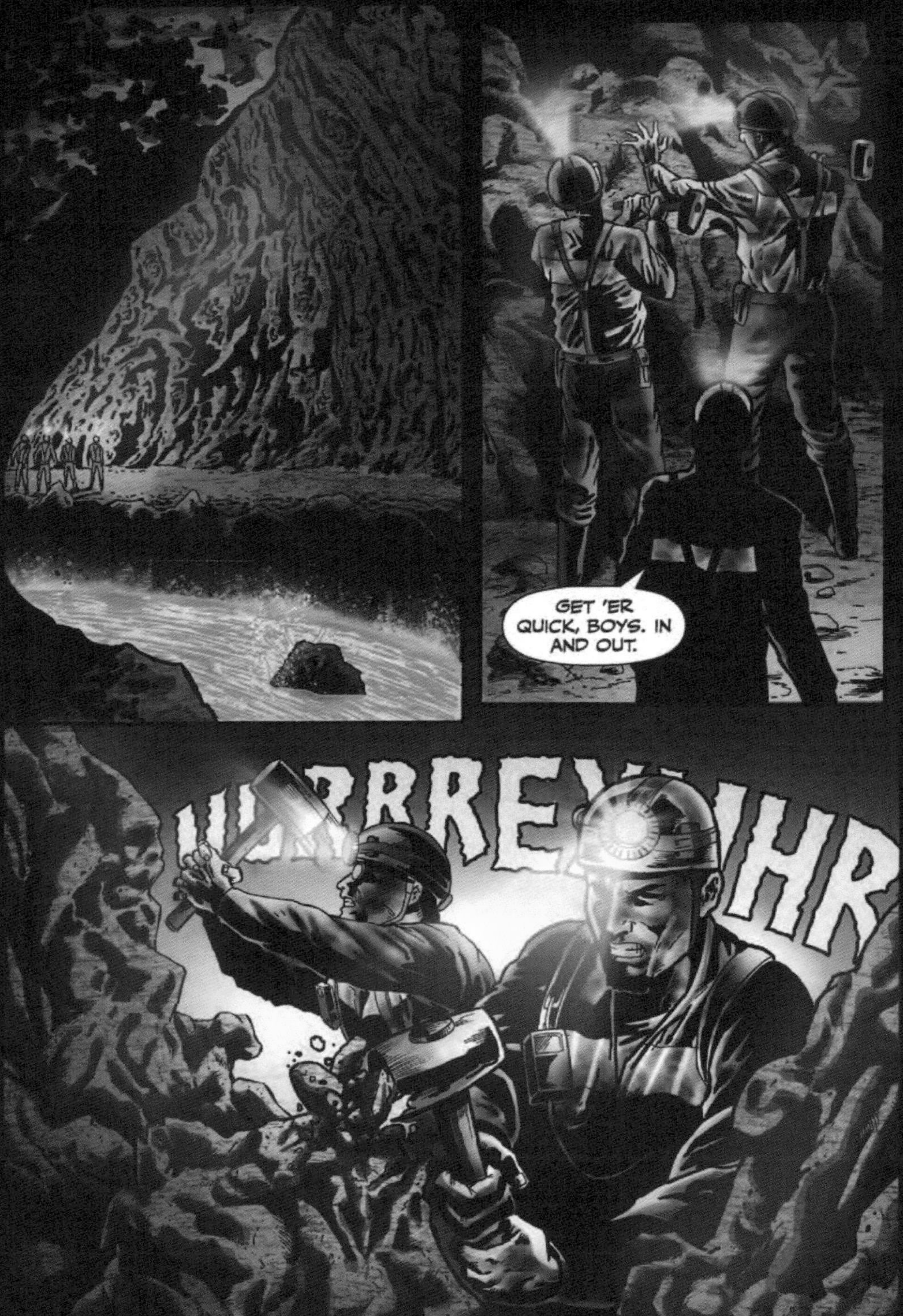
GET 'ER QUICK, BOYS. IN AND OUT.

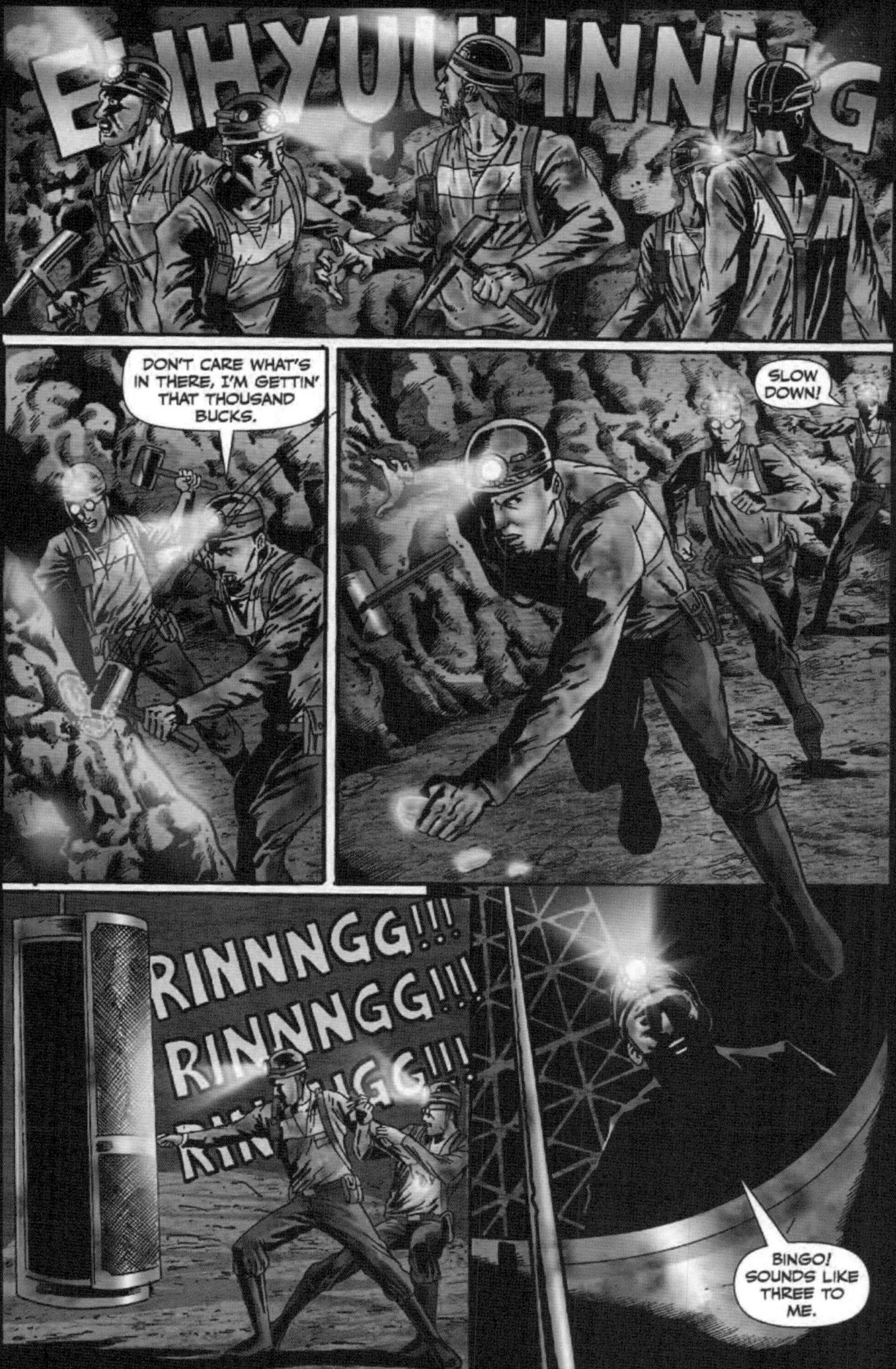
EHHYUUHHNNNG
DON'T CARE WHAT'S IN THERE, I'M GETTIN' THAT THOUSAND BUCKS.
SLOW DOWN!
RINNNGG!!!
RINNNGG!!!
RINNNGG!!!
BINGO! SOUNDS LIKE THREE TO ME.

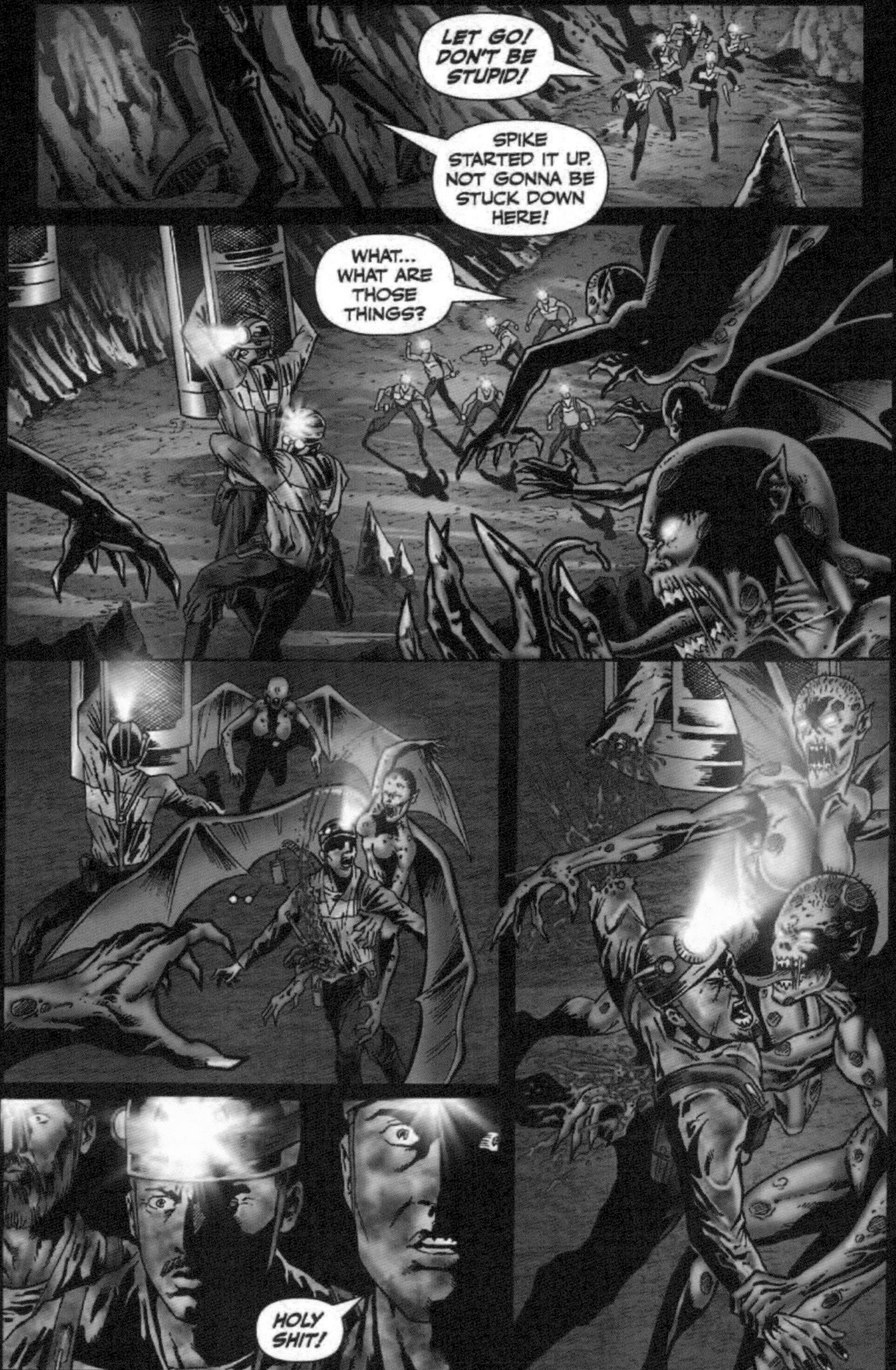
LET GO! DON'T BE STUPID!
SPIKE STARTED IT UP. NOT GONNA BE STUCK DOWN HERE!
WHAT... WHAT ARE THOSE THINGS?
HOLY SHIT!

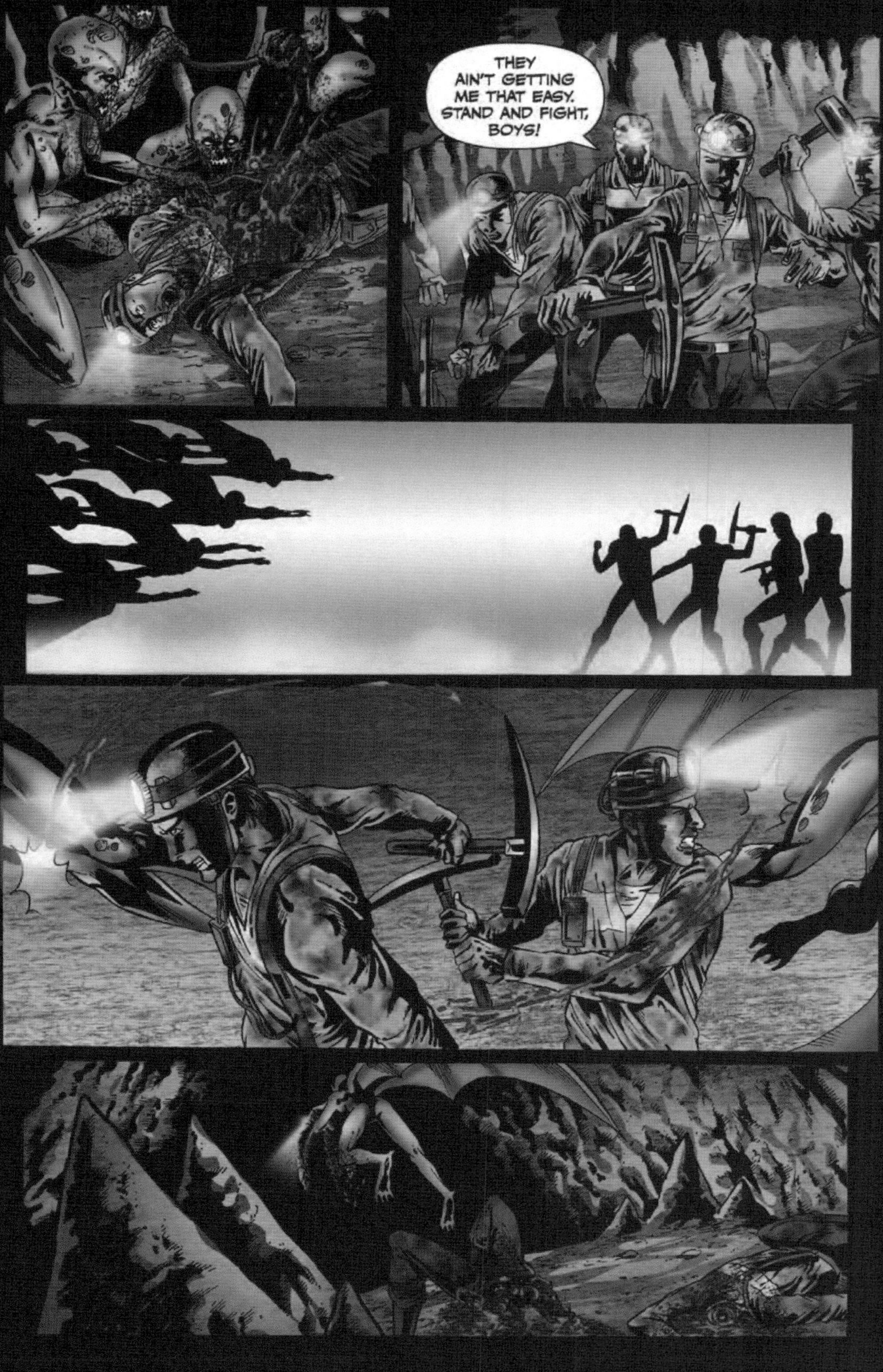
THEY AIN'T GETTING ME THAT EASY. STAND AND FIGHT, BOYS!

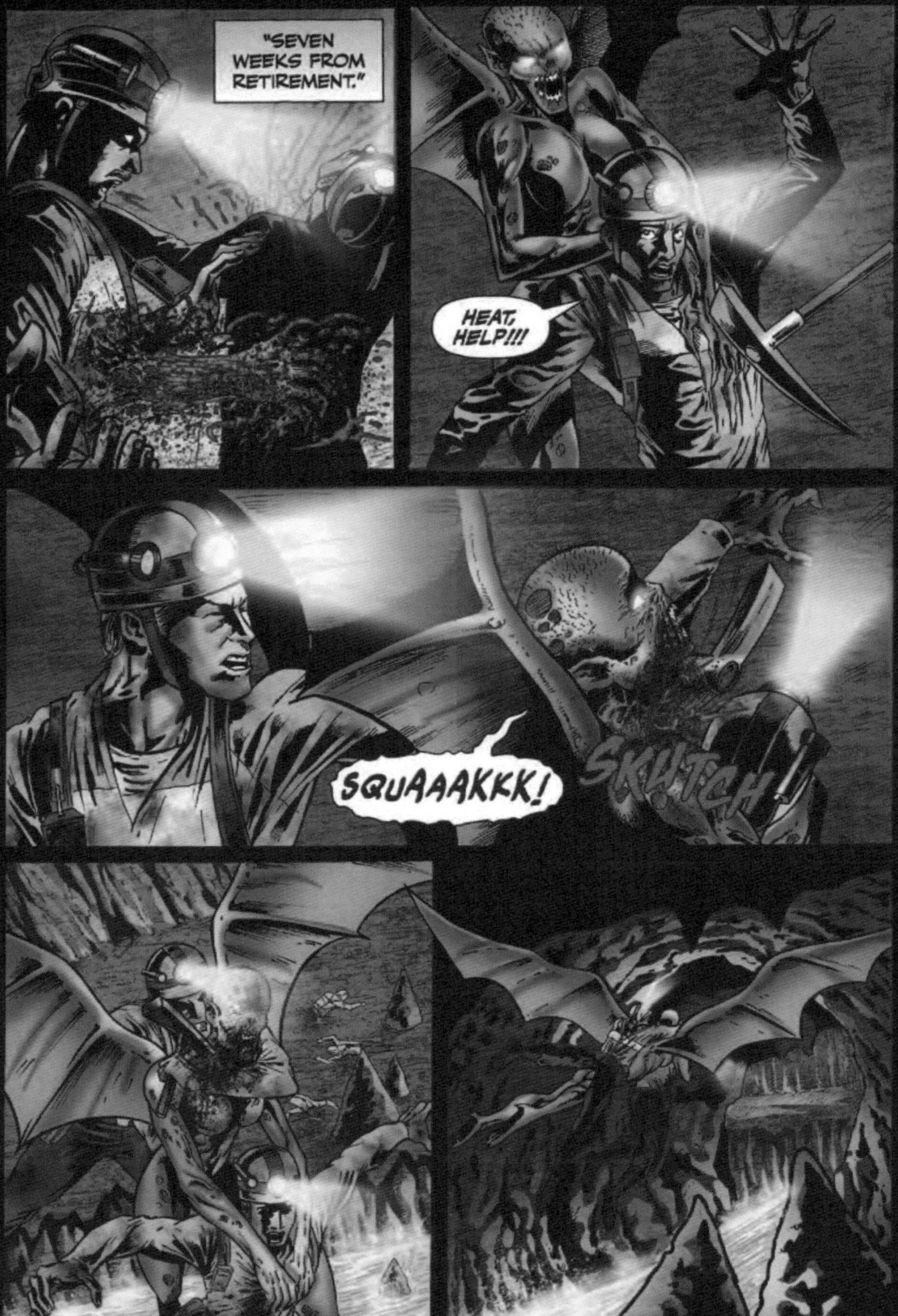
"SEVEN WEEKS FROM RETIREMENT."
HEAT, HELP!!!
SQUAAAKKK!
SKLUTCH

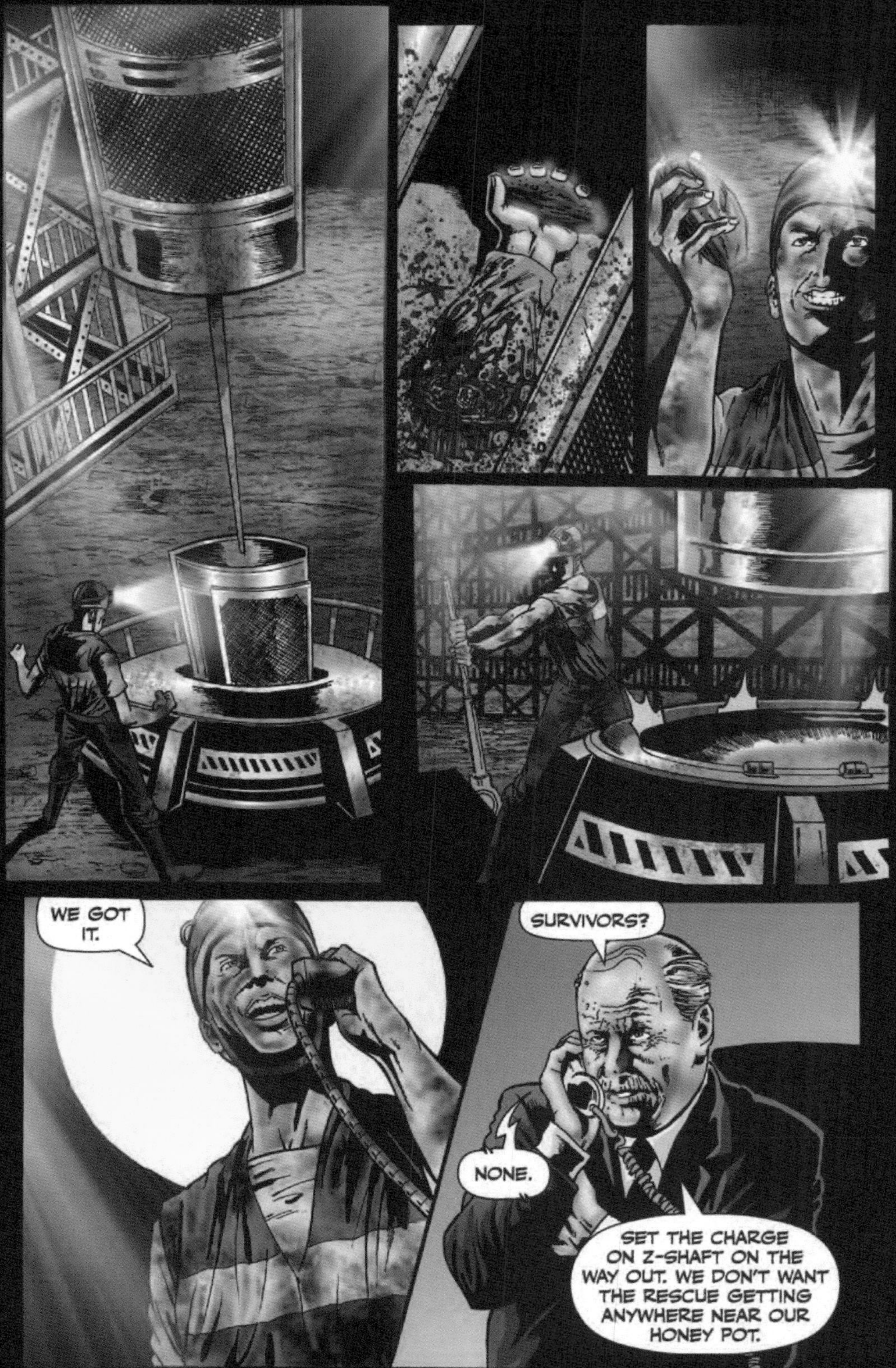
WE GOT IT.
SURVIVORS?
NONE.
SET THE CHARGE ON Z-SHAFT ON THE WAY OUT. WE DON'T WANT THE RESCUE GETTING ANYWHERE NEAR OUR HONEY POT.

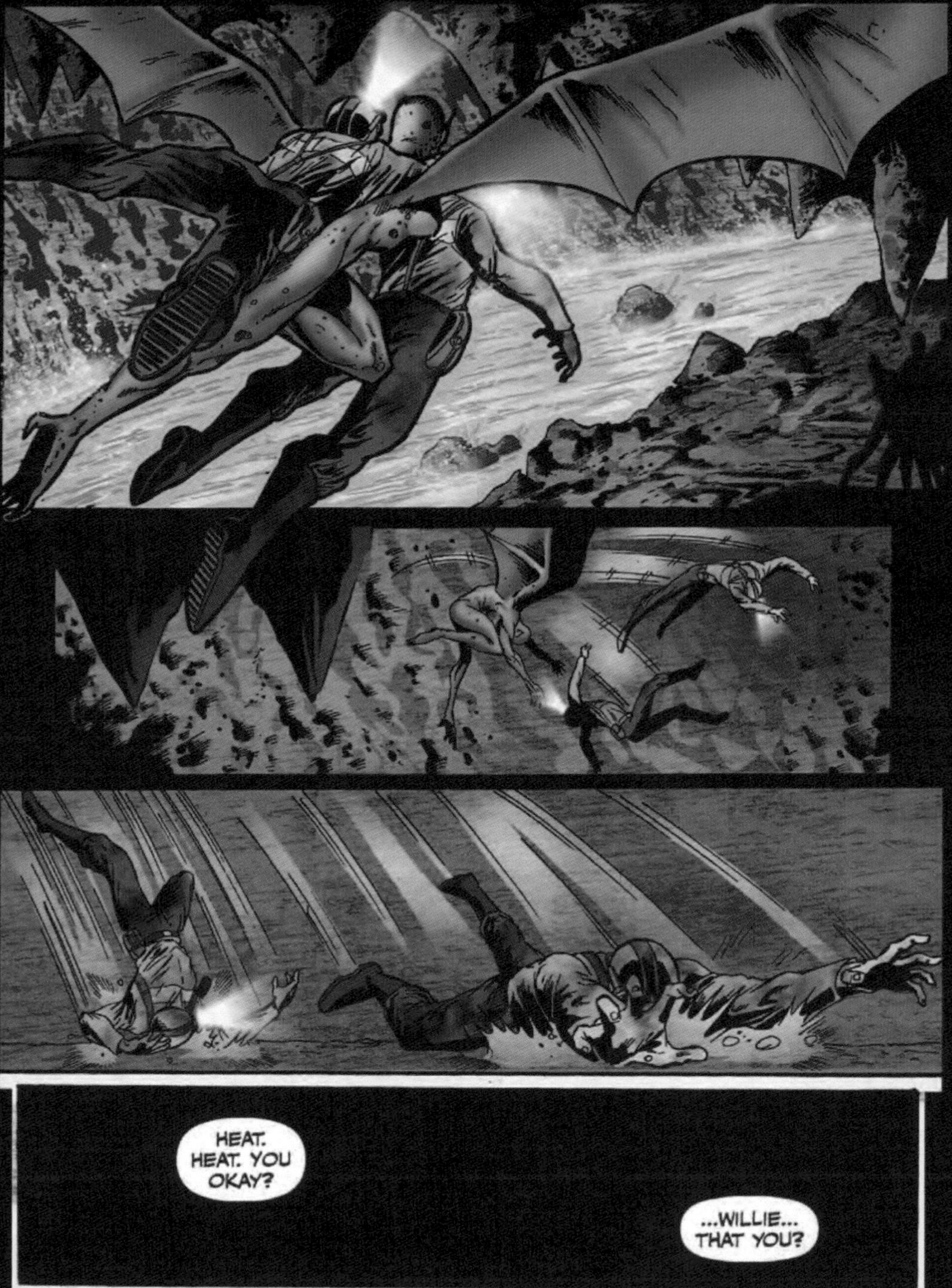
HEAT. HEAT. YOU OKAY?
...WILLIE... THAT YOU?
NO, SON. IT'S YOUR...

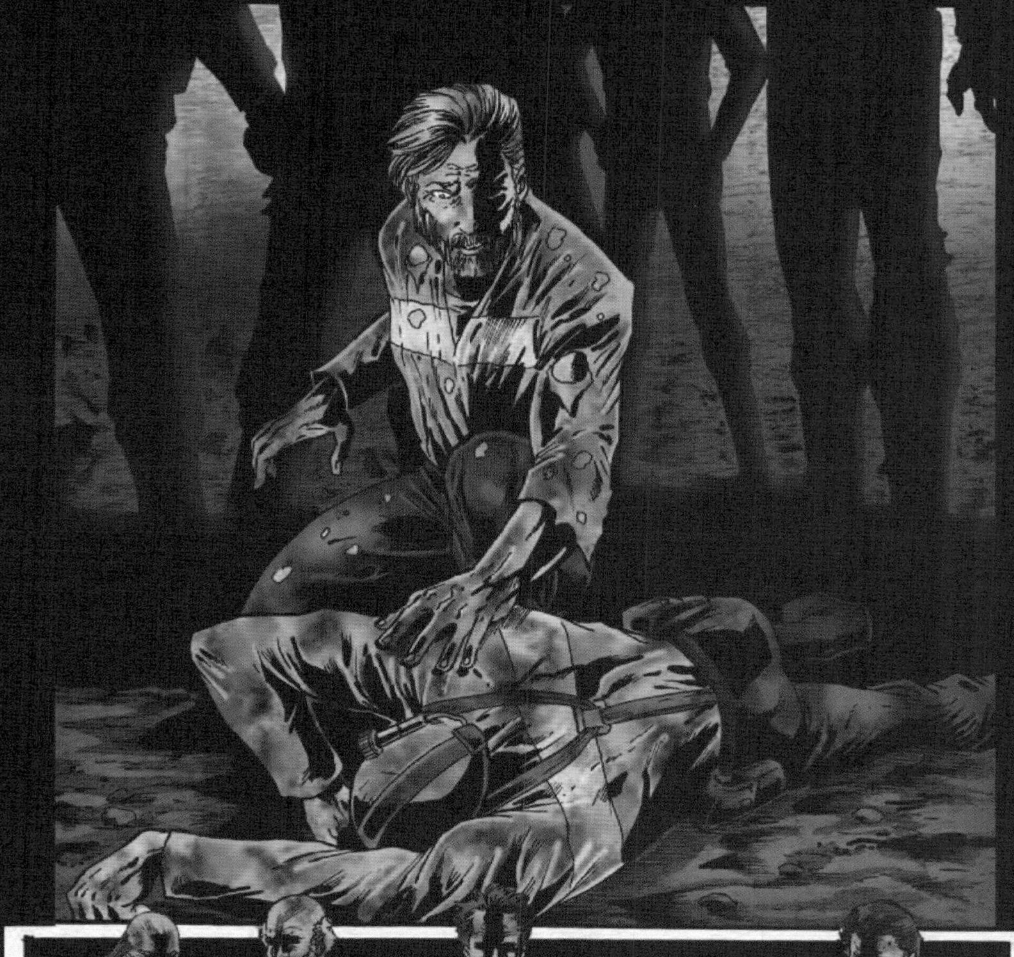
...YOUR
DADDY.

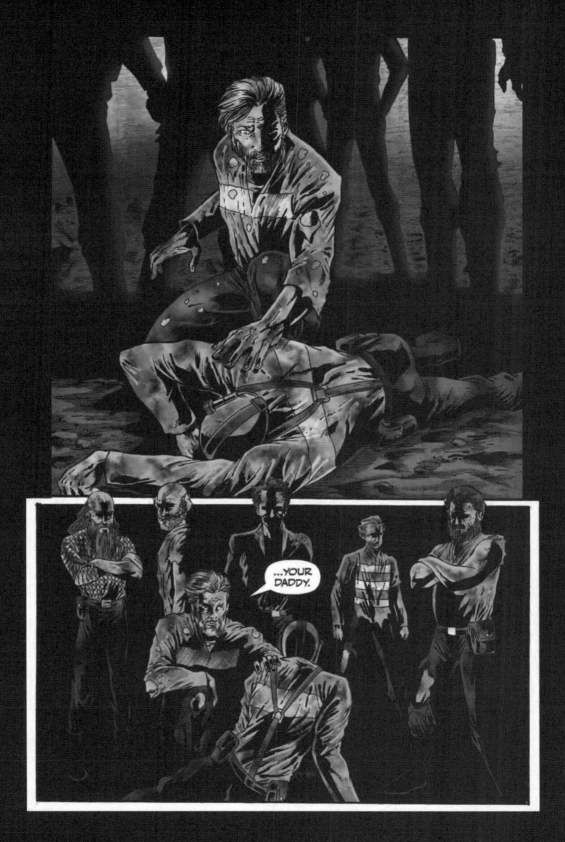

END BOOK II

BOOK III

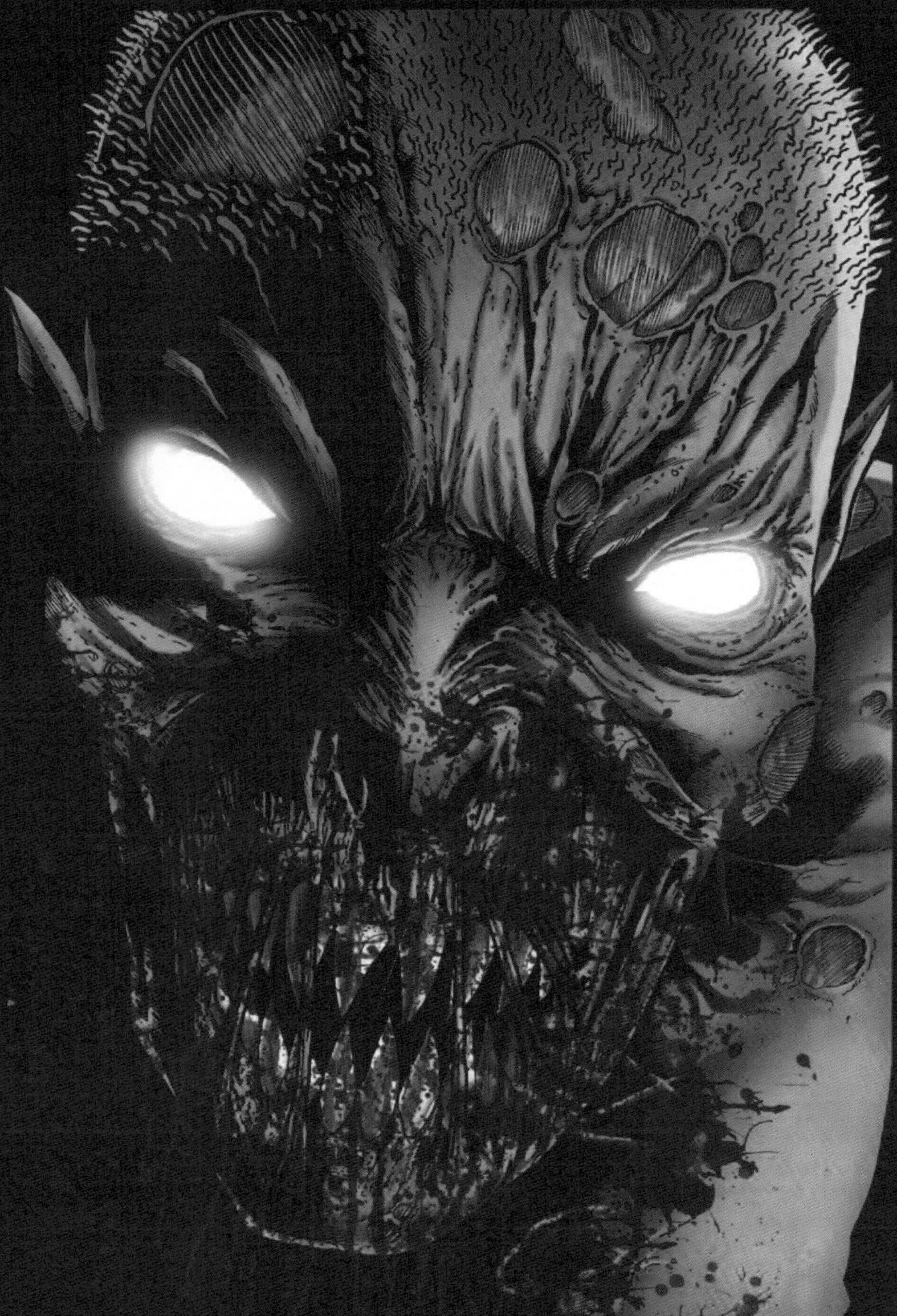

FIRE IN THE HOLE!

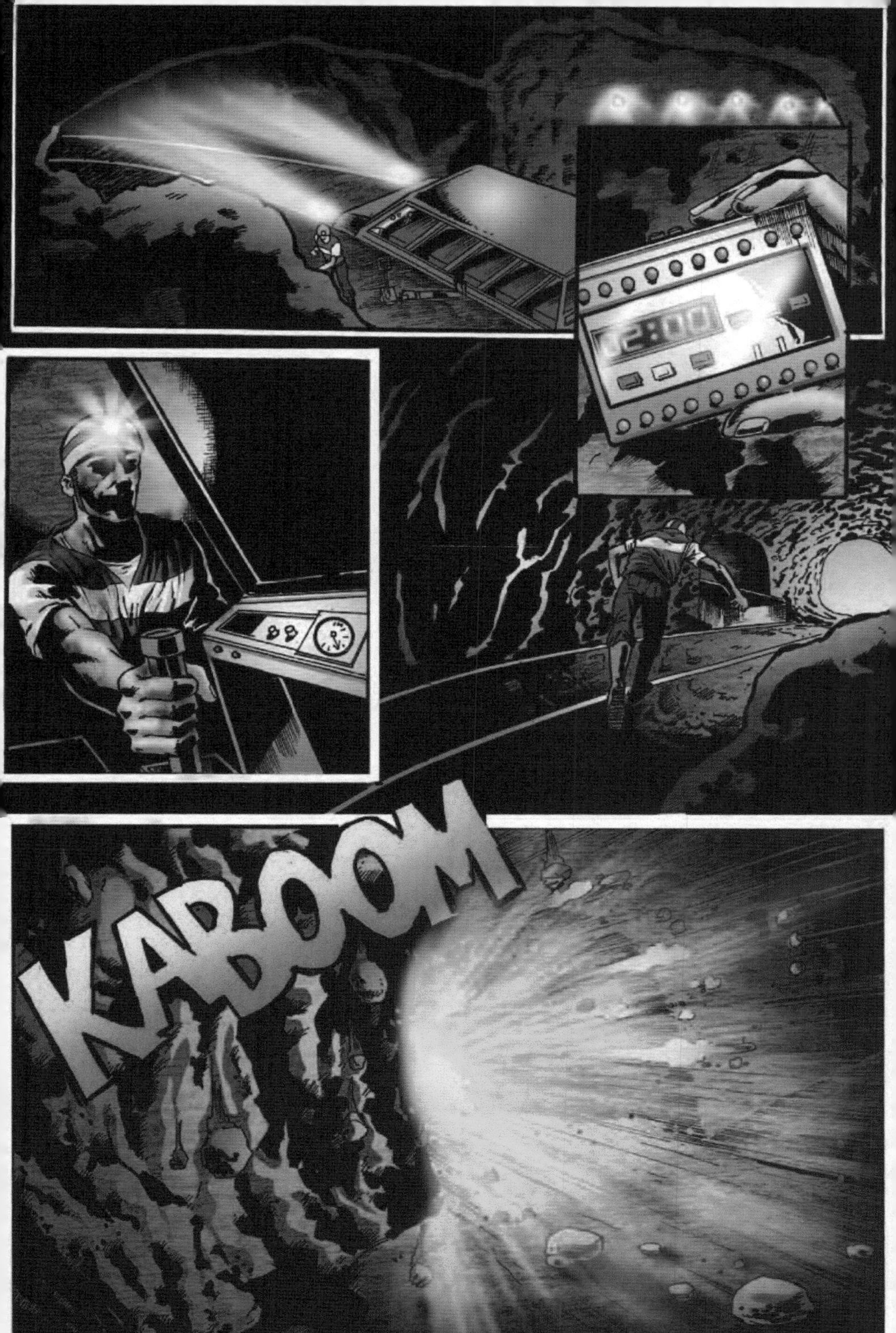
KABOOM

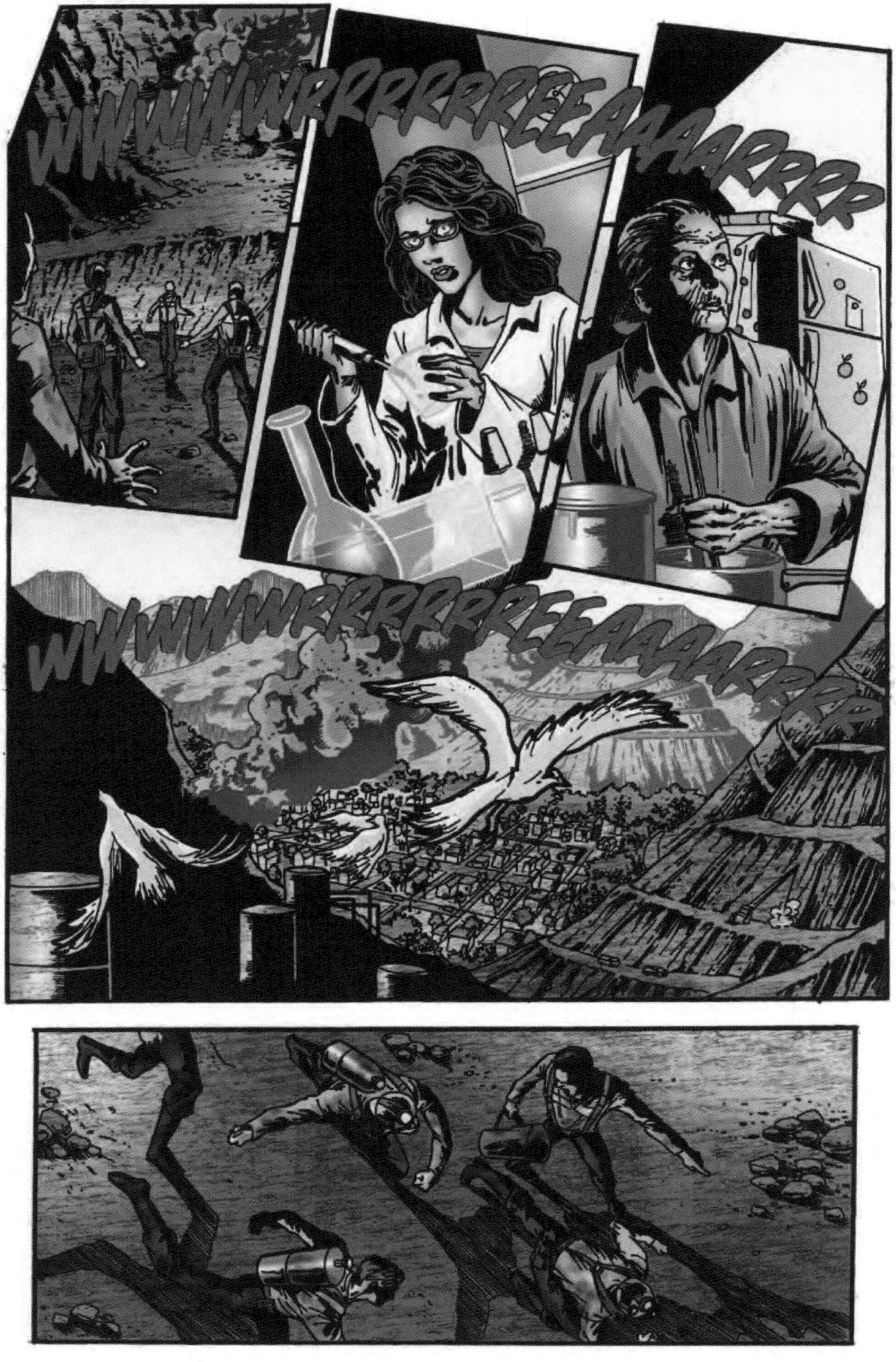
WWWWWWRRRRRRREEAAAAARRRRR
WWWWWWRRRRRRREEAAAAARRRRR

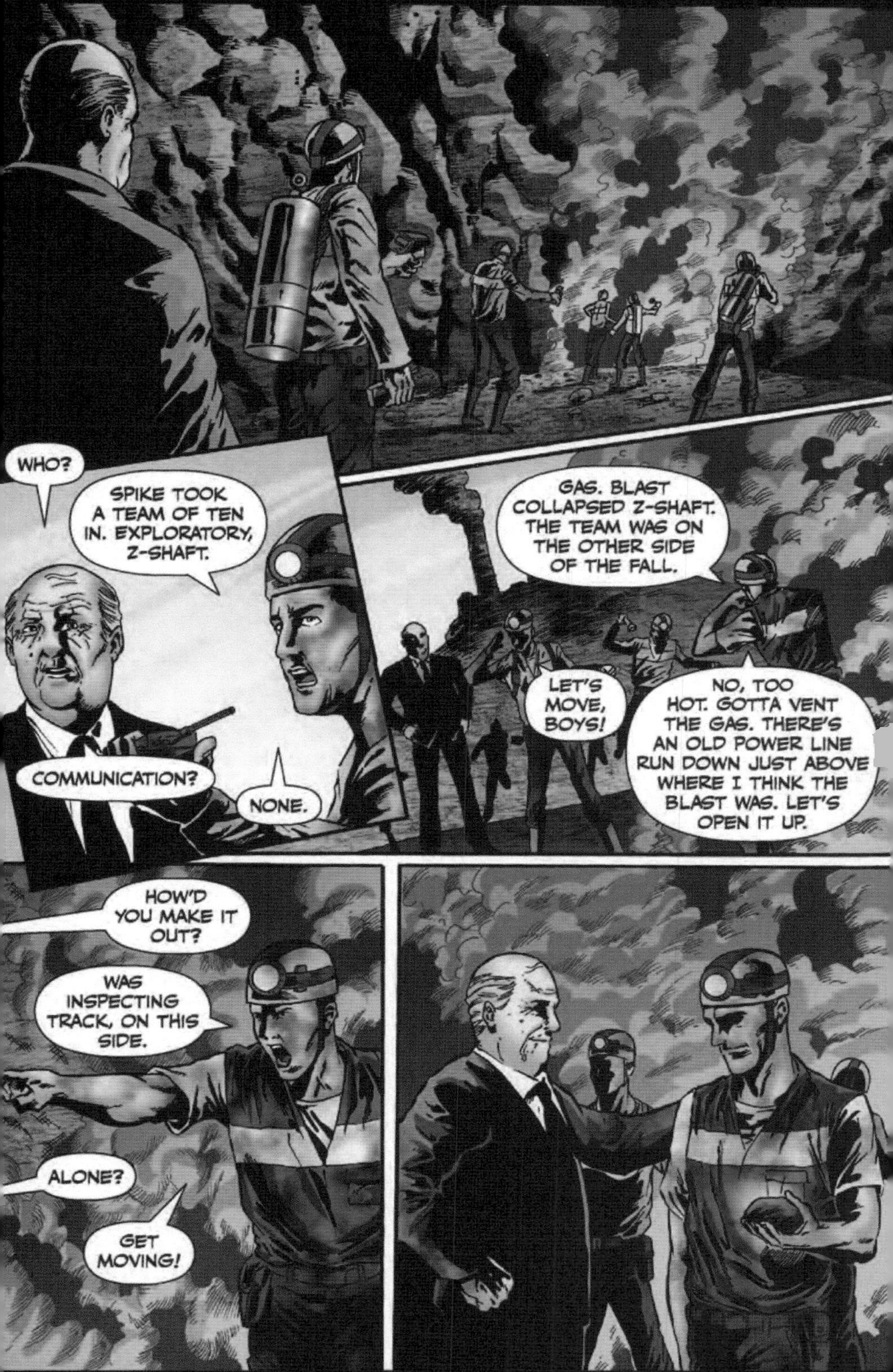
WHO?
SPIKE TOOK A TEAM OF TEN IN. EXPLORATORY, Z-SHAFT.
COMMUNICATION?
NONE.
GAS. BLAST COLLAPSED Z-SHAFT. THE TEAM WAS ON THE OTHER SIDE OF THE FALL.
LET'S MOVE, BOYS!
NO, TOO HOT. GOTTA VENT THE GAS. THERE'S AN OLD POWER LINE RUN DOWN JUST ABOVE WHERE I THINK THE BLAST WAS. LET'S OPEN IT UP.
HOW'D YOU MAKE IT OUT?
WAS INSPECTING TRACK, ON THIS SIDE.
ALONE?
GET MOVING!

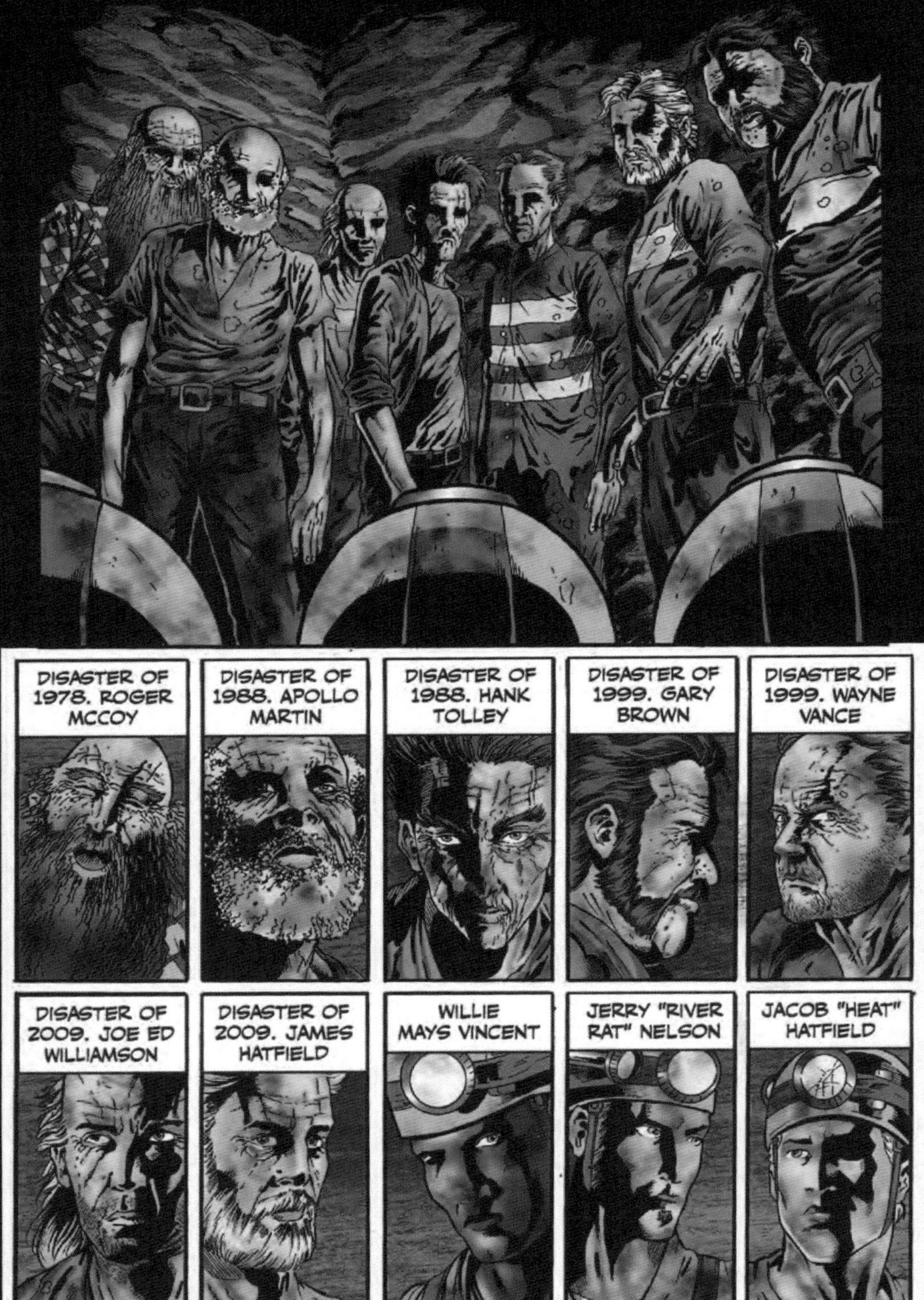

DISASTER OF 1978. ROGER MCCOY
DISASTER OF 1988. APOLLO MARTIN
DISASTER OF 1988. HANK TOLLEY
DISASTER OF 1999. GARY BROWN
DISASTER OF 1999. WAYNE VANCE
DISASTER OF 2009. JOE ED WILLIAMSON
DISASTER OF 2009. JAMES HATFIELD
WILLIE MAYS VINCENT
JERRY "RIVER RAT" NELSON
JACOB "HEAT" HATFIELD

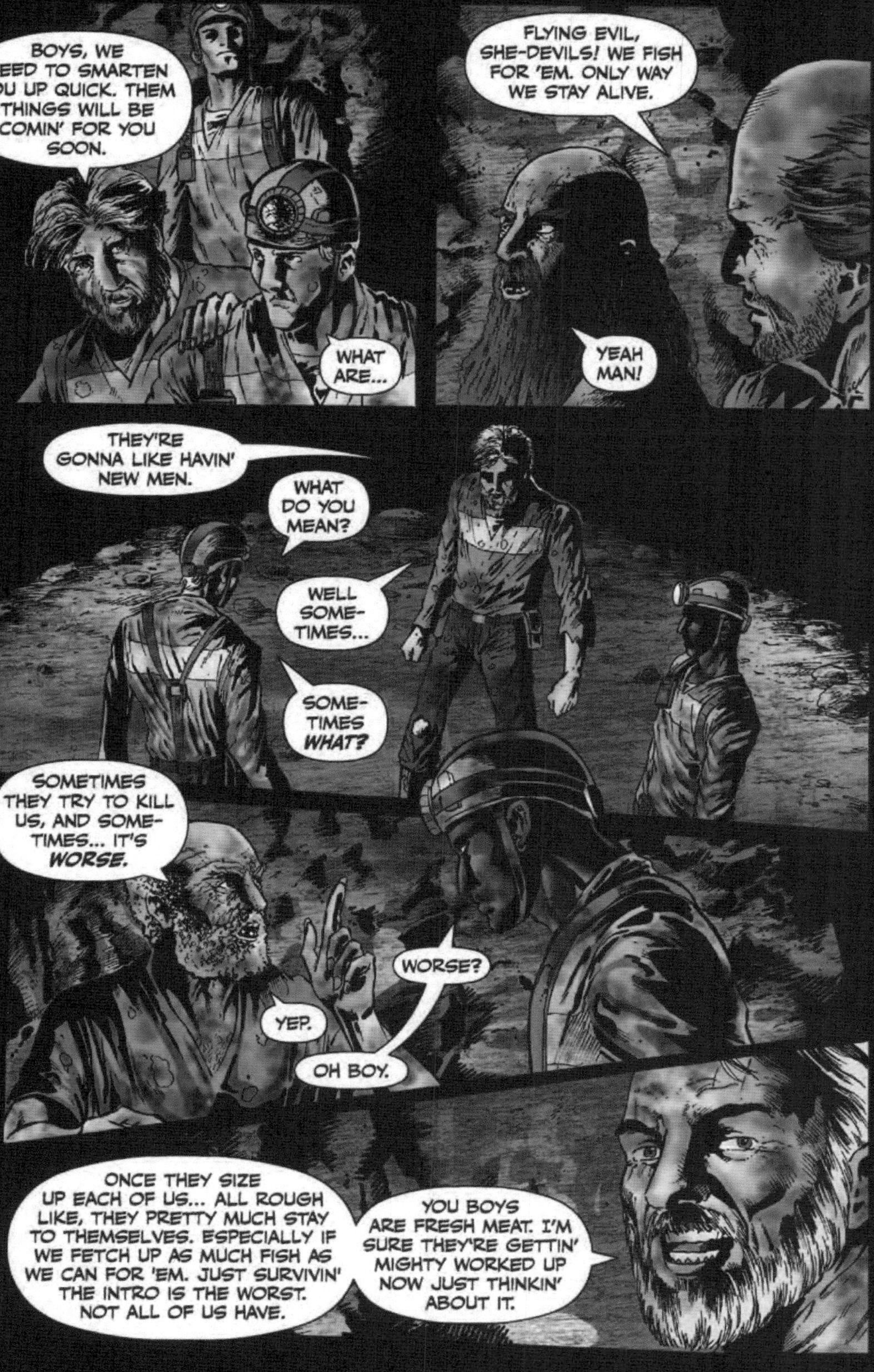
BOYS, WE NEED TO SMARTEN YOU UP QUICK. THEM THINGS WILL BE COMIN' FOR YOU SOON.
WHAT ARE...
FLYING EVIL, SHE-DEVILS! WE FISH FOR 'EM. ONLY WAY WE STAY ALIVE.
YEAH MAN!
THEY'RE GONNA LIKE HAVIN' NEW MEN.
WHAT DO YOU MEAN?
WELL SOME-TIMES...
SOME-TIMES *WHAT?*
SOMETIMES THEY TRY TO KILL US, AND SOME-TIMES... IT'S *WORSE.*
WORSE?
YEP.
OH BOY.
ONCE THEY SIZE UP EACH OF US... ALL ROUGH LIKE, THEY PRETTY MUCH STAY TO THEMSELVES. ESPECIALLY IF WE FETCH UP AS MUCH FISH AS WE CAN FOR 'EM. JUST SURVIVIN' THE INTRO IS THE WORST. NOT ALL OF US HAVE.
YOU BOYS ARE FRESH MEAT. I'M SURE THEY'RE GETTIN' MIGHTY WORKED UP NOW JUST THINKIN' ABOUT IT.

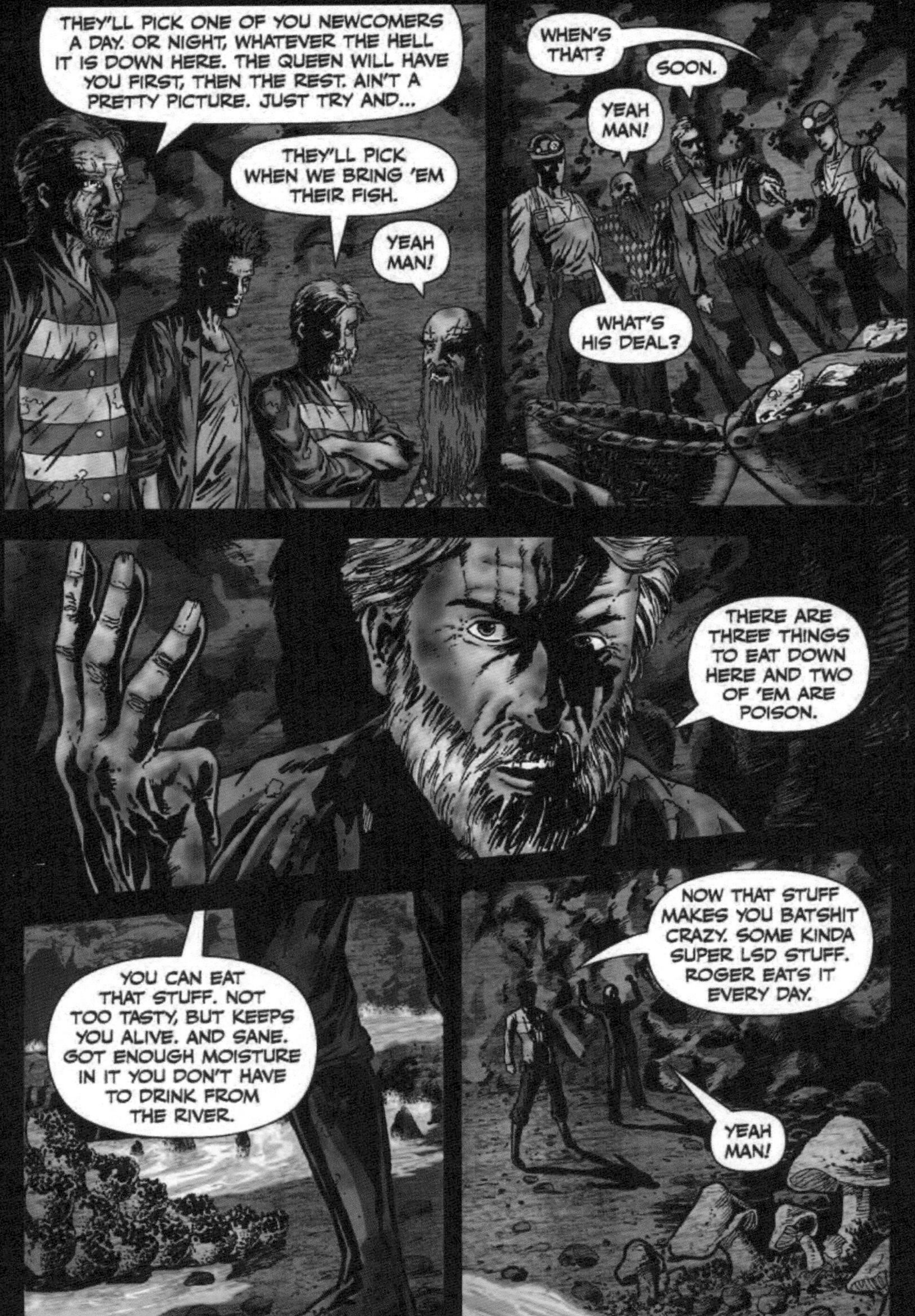
THEY'LL PICK ONE OF YOU NEWCOMERS A DAY. OR NIGHT, WHATEVER THE HELL IT IS DOWN HERE. THE QUEEN WILL HAVE YOU FIRST, THEN THE REST. AIN'T A PRETTY PICTURE. JUST TRY AND...
THEY'LL PICK WHEN WE BRING 'EM THEIR FISH.
YEAH MAN!
WHEN'S THAT?
SOON.
YEAH MAN!
WHAT'S HIS DEAL?
THERE ARE THREE THINGS TO EAT DOWN HERE AND TWO OF 'EM ARE POISON.
YOU CAN EAT THAT STUFF. NOT TOO TASTY, BUT KEEPS YOU ALIVE. AND SANE. GOT ENOUGH MOISTURE IN IT YOU DON'T HAVE TO DRINK FROM THE RIVER.
NOW THAT STUFF MAKES YOU BATSHIT CRAZY. SOME KINDA SUPER LSD STUFF. ROGER EATS IT EVERY DAY.
YEAH MAN!

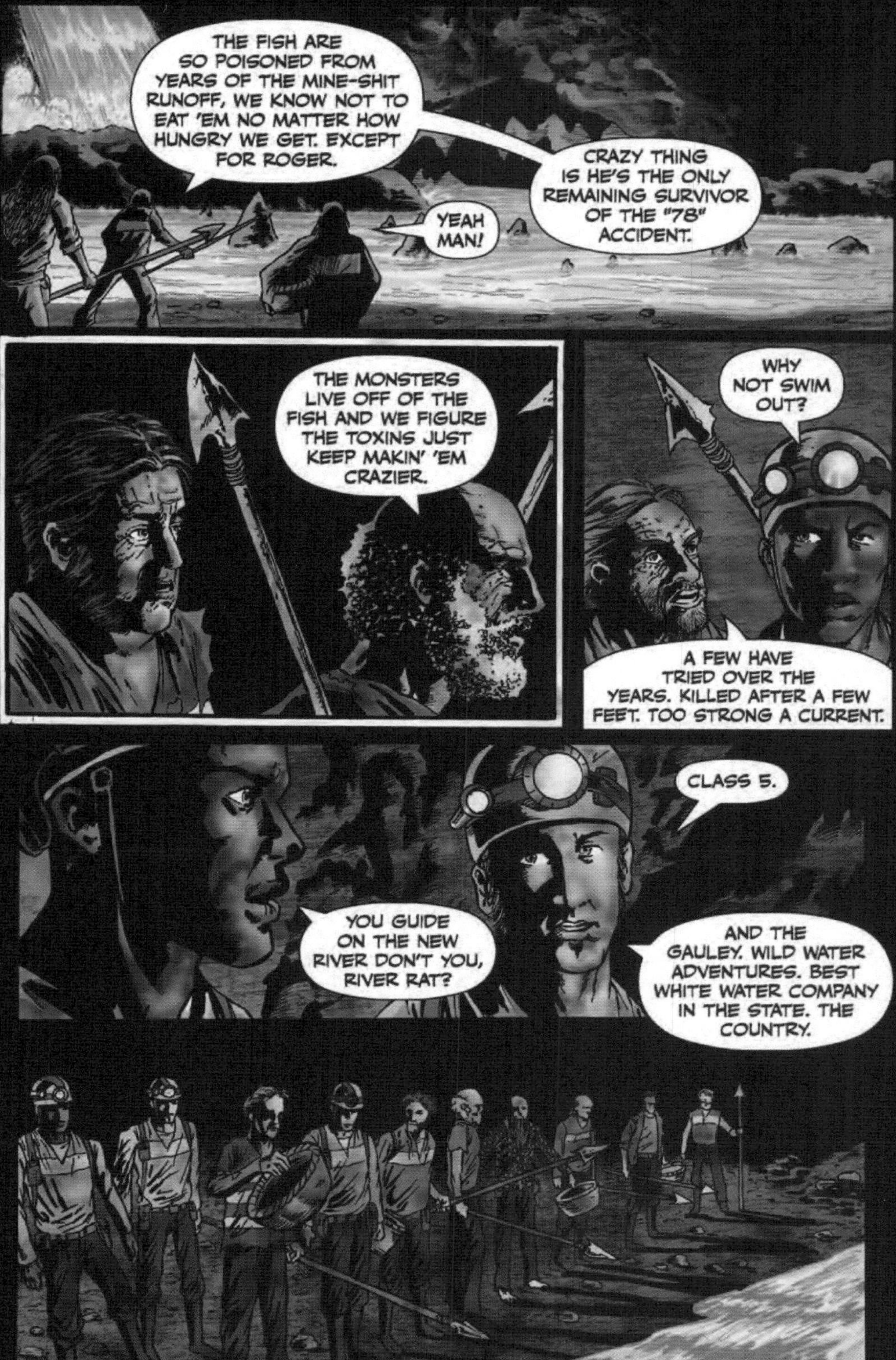
THE FISH ARE SO POISONED FROM YEARS OF THE MINE-SHIT RUNOFF, WE KNOW NOT TO EAT 'EM NO MATTER HOW HUNGRY WE GET. EXCEPT FOR ROGER.
CRAZY THING IS HE'S THE ONLY REMAINING SURVIVOR OF THE "78" ACCIDENT.
YEAH MAN!
THE MONSTERS LIVE OFF OF THE FISH AND WE FIGURE THE TOXINS JUST KEEP MAKIN' 'EM CRAZIER.
WHY NOT SWIM OUT?
A FEW HAVE TRIED OVER THE YEARS. KILLED AFTER A FEW FEET. TOO STRONG A CURRENT.
CLASS 5.
YOU GUIDE ON THE NEW RIVER DON'T YOU, RIVER RAT?
AND THE GAULEY. WILD WATER ADVENTURES. BEST WHITE WATER COMPANY IN THE STATE. THE COUNTRY.

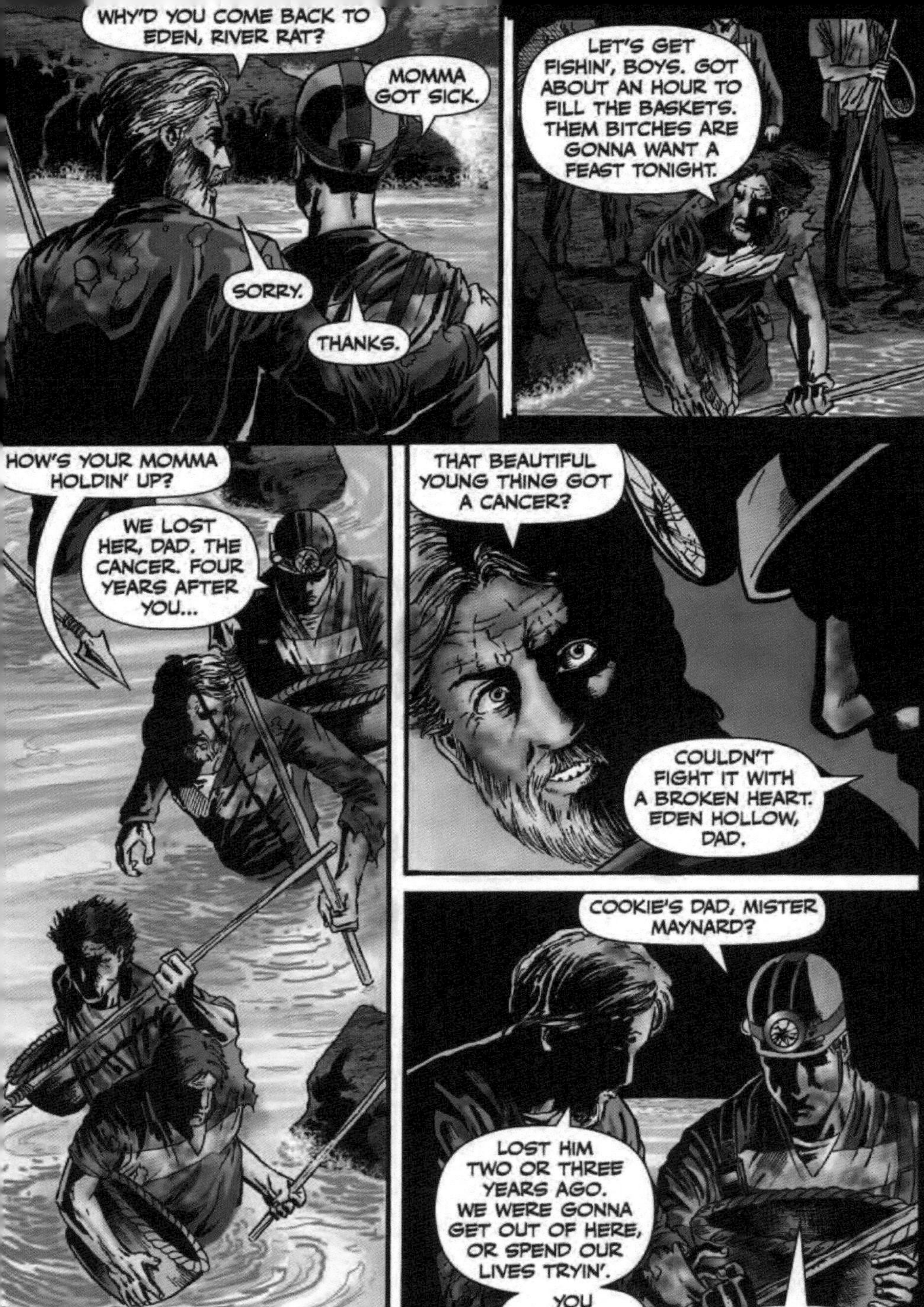
WHY'D YOU COME BACK TO EDEN, RIVER RAT?
MOMMA GOT SICK.
SORRY.
THANKS.
LET'S GET FISHIN', BOYS. GOT ABOUT AN HOUR TO FILL THE BASKETS. THEM BITCHES ARE GONNA WANT A FEAST TONIGHT.
HOW'S YOUR MOMMA HOLDIN' UP?
WE LOST HER, DAD. THE CANCER. FOUR YEARS AFTER YOU...
THAT BEAUTIFUL YOUNG THING GOT A CANCER?
COULDN'T FIGHT IT WITH A BROKEN HEART. EDEN HOLLOW, DAD.
COOKIE'S DAD, MISTER MAYNARD?
LOST HIM TWO OR THREE YEARS AGO. WE WERE GONNA GET OUT OF HERE, OR SPEND OUR LIVES TRYIN'.
YOU AND COOKIE STILL...
NOT SURE. BEEN A PRETTY CRAZY DAY.

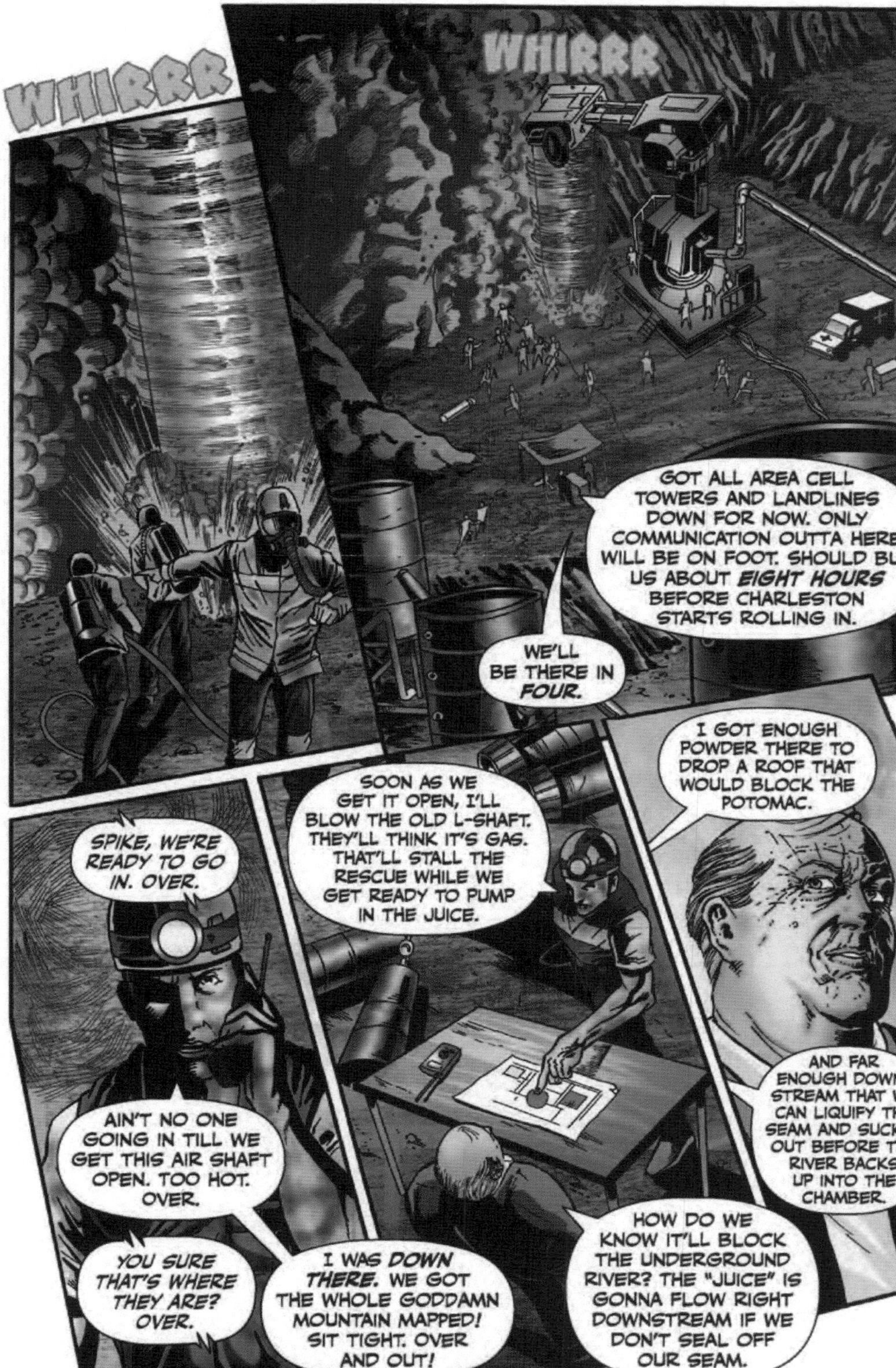
WHIRRR
WHIRRR
GOT ALL AREA CELL TOWERS AND LANDLINES DOWN FOR NOW. ONLY COMMUNICATION OUTTA HERE WILL BE ON FOOT. SHOULD BUY US ABOUT EIGHT HOURS BEFORE CHARLESTON STARTS ROLLING IN.
WE'LL BE THERE IN FOUR.
SPIKE, WE'RE READY TO GO IN. OVER.
AIN'T NO ONE GOING IN TILL WE GET THIS AIR SHAFT OPEN. TOO HOT. OVER.
YOU SURE THAT'S WHERE THEY ARE? OVER.
I WAS DOWN THERE. WE GOT THE WHOLE GODDAMN MOUNTAIN MAPPED! SIT TIGHT. OVER AND OUT!
SOON AS WE GET IT OPEN, I'LL BLOW THE OLD L-SHAFT. THEY'LL THINK IT'S GAS. THAT'LL STALL THE RESCUE WHILE WE GET READY TO PUMP IN THE JUICE.
HOW DO WE KNOW IT'LL BLOCK THE UNDERGROUND RIVER? THE "JUICE" IS GONNA FLOW RIGHT DOWNSTREAM IF WE DON'T SEAL OFF OUR SEAM.
I GOT ENOUGH POWDER THERE TO DROP A ROOF THAT WOULD BLOCK THE POTOMAC.
AND FAR ENOUGH DOWNSTREAM THAT WE CAN LIQUIFY THE SEAM AND SUCK IT OUT BEFORE THE RIVER BACKS UP INTO THE CHAMBER.

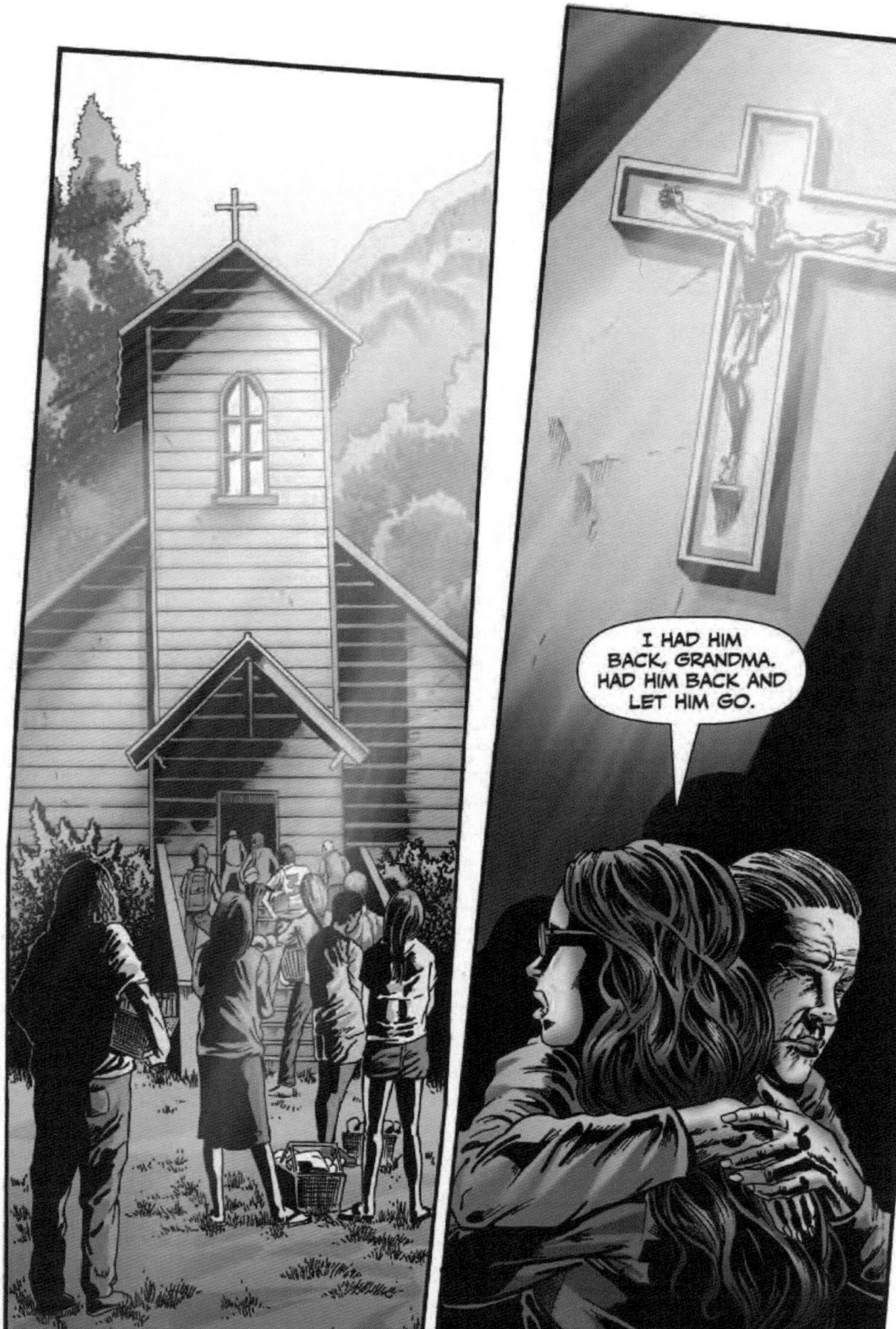
I HAD HIM BACK, GRANDMA. HAD HIM BACK AND LET HIM GO.

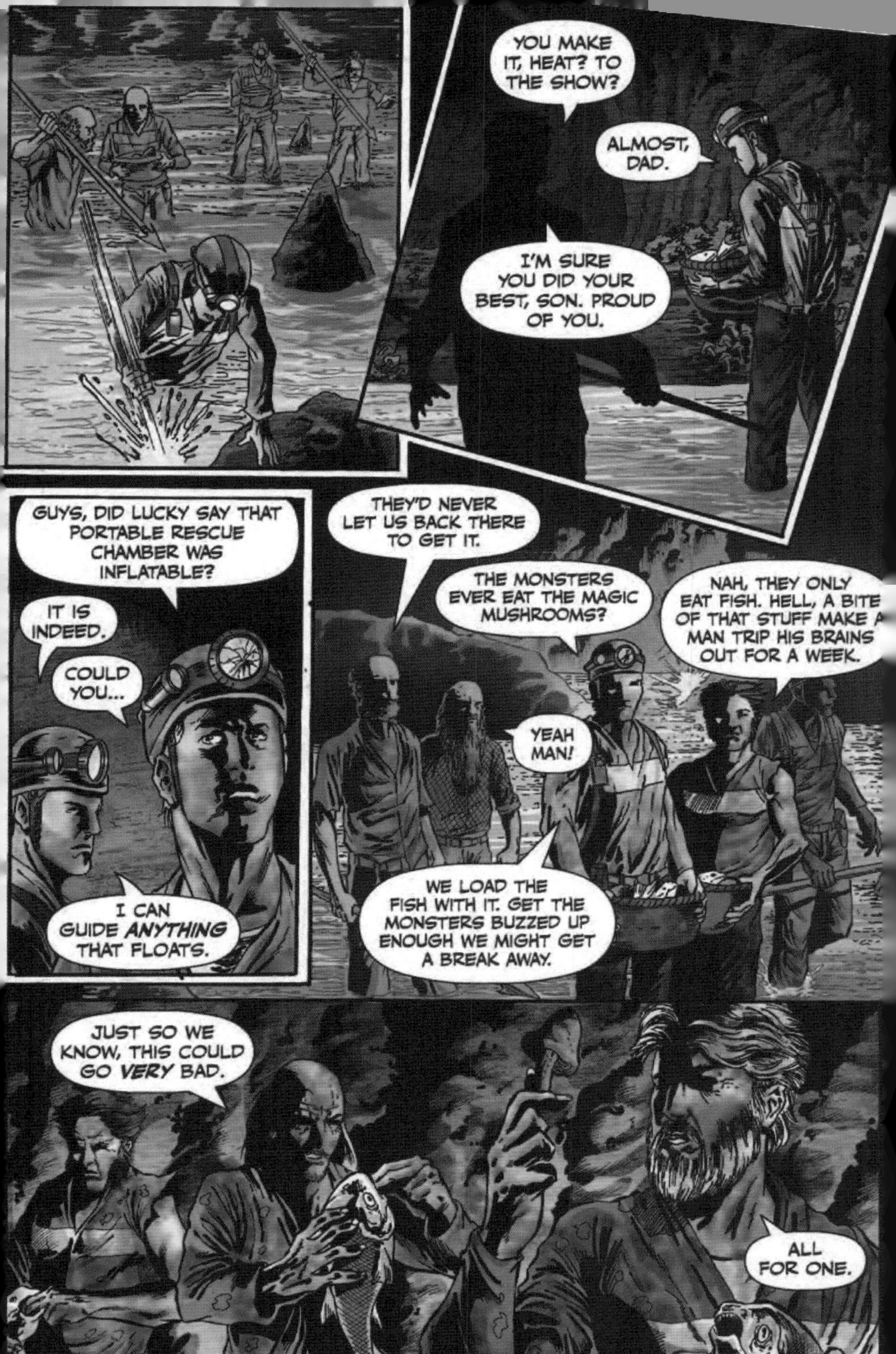
YOU MAKE IT, HEAT? TO THE SHOW?
ALMOST, DAD.
I'M SURE YOU DID YOUR BEST, SON. PROUD OF YOU.
GUYS, DID LUCKY SAY THAT PORTABLE RESCUE CHAMBER WAS INFLATABLE?
IT IS INDEED.
COULD YOU...
I CAN GUIDE *ANYTHING* THAT FLOATS.
THEY'D NEVER LET US BACK THERE TO GET IT.
THE MONSTERS EVER EAT THE MAGIC MUSHROOMS?
NAH, THEY ONLY EAT FISH. HELL, A BITE OF THAT STUFF MAKE A MAN TRIP HIS BRAINS OUT FOR A WEEK.
YEAH MAN!
WE LOAD THE FISH WITH IT. GET THE MONSTERS BUZZED UP ENOUGH WE MIGHT GET A BREAK AWAY.
JUST SO WE KNOW, THIS COULD GO *VERY* BAD.
ALL FOR ONE.

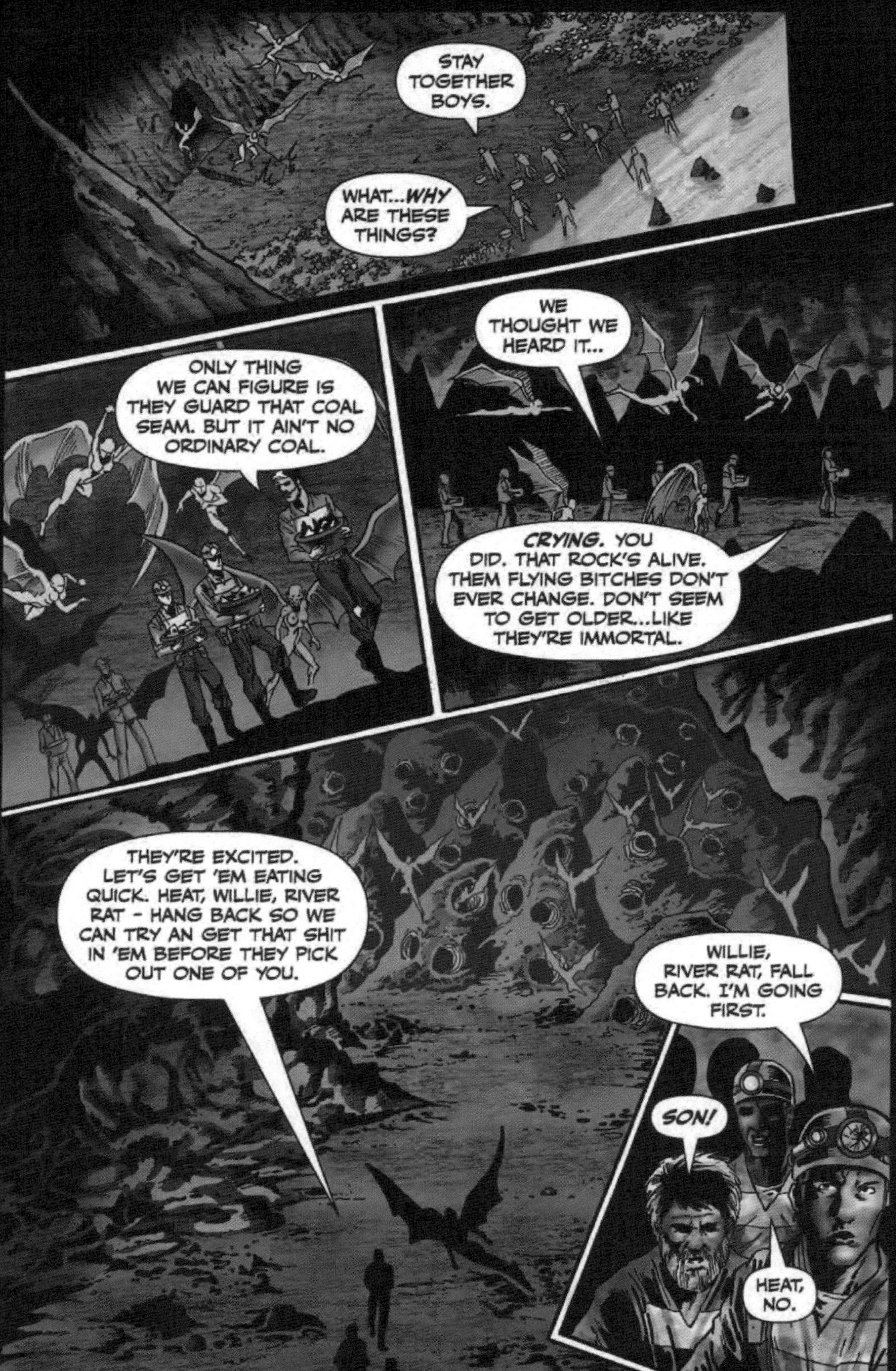
STAY TOGETHER BOYS.
WHAT...*WHY* ARE THESE THINGS?
ONLY THING WE CAN FIGURE IS THEY GUARD THAT COAL SEAM. BUT IT AIN'T NO ORDINARY COAL.
WE THOUGHT WE HEARD IT...
CRYING. YOU DID. THAT ROCK'S ALIVE. THEM FLYING BITCHES DON'T EVER CHANGE. DON'T SEEM TO GET OLDER...LIKE THEY'RE IMMORTAL.
THEY'RE EXCITED. LET'S GET 'EM EATING QUICK. HEAT, WILLIE, RIVER RAT - HANG BACK SO WE CAN TRY AN GET THAT SHIT IN 'EM BEFORE THEY PICK OUT ONE OF YOU.
WILLIE, RIVER RAT, FALL BACK. I'M GOING FIRST.
SON!
HEAT, NO.

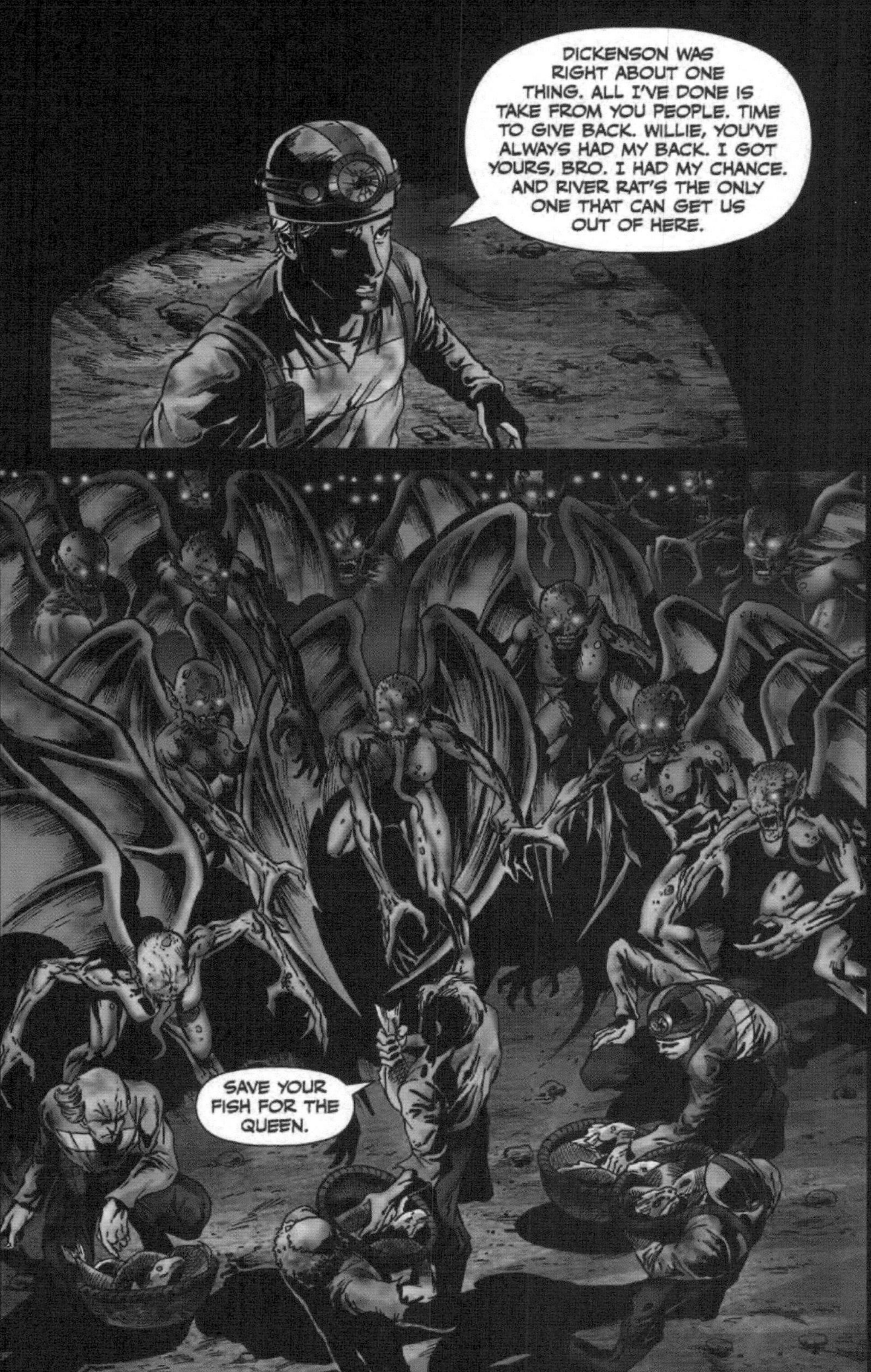
DICKENSON WAS RIGHT ABOUT ONE THING. ALL I'VE DONE IS TAKE FROM YOU PEOPLE. TIME TO GIVE BACK. WILLIE, YOU'VE ALWAYS HAD MY BACK. I GOT YOURS, BRO. I HAD MY CHANCE. AND RIVER RAT'S THE ONLY ONE THAT CAN GET US OUT OF HERE.
SAVE YOUR FISH FOR THE QUEEN.

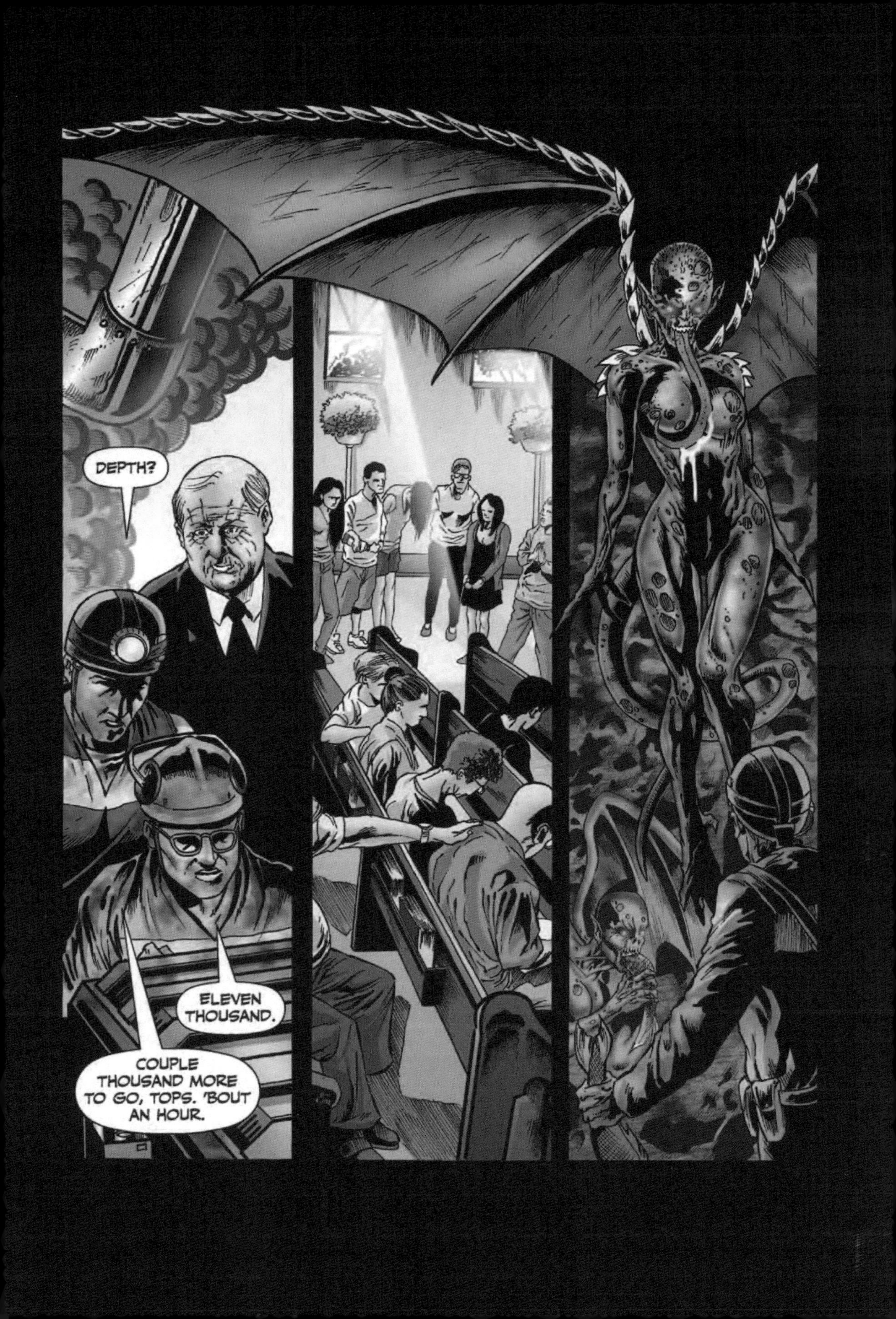
DEPTH?
ELEVEN THOUSAND.
COUPLE THOUSAND MORE TO GO, TOPS. 'BOUT AN HOUR.

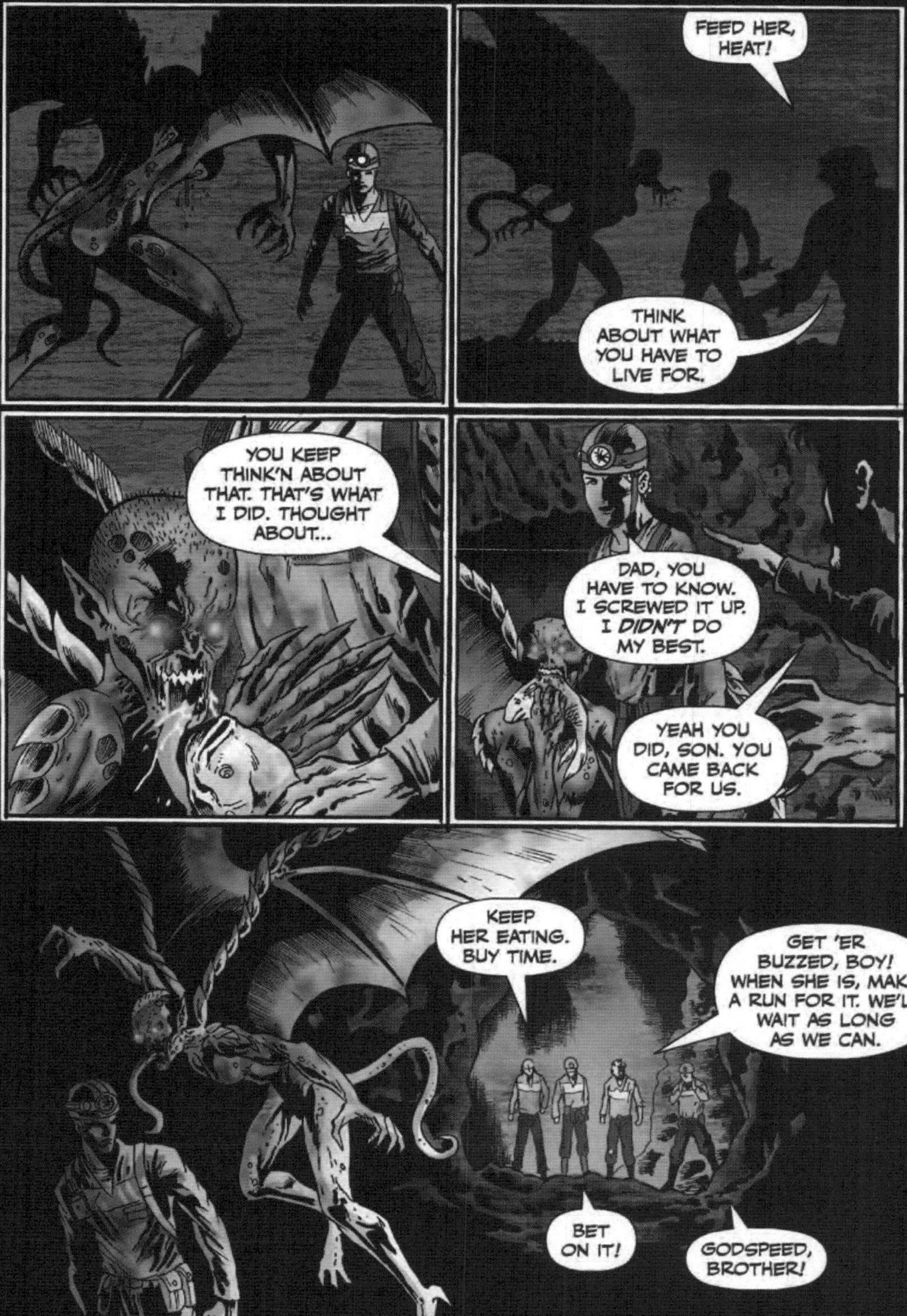
FEED HER, HEAT!
THINK ABOUT WHAT YOU HAVE TO LIVE FOR.
YOU KEEP THINK'N ABOUT THAT. THAT'S WHAT I DID. THOUGHT ABOUT...
DAD, YOU HAVE TO KNOW. I SCREWED IT UP. I *DIDN'T* DO MY BEST.
YEAH YOU DID, SON. YOU CAME BACK FOR US.
KEEP HER EATING. BUY TIME.
GET 'ER BUZZED, BOY! WHEN SHE IS, MAKE A RUN FOR IT. WE'LL WAIT AS LONG AS WE CAN.
BET ON IT!
GODSPEED, BROTHER!

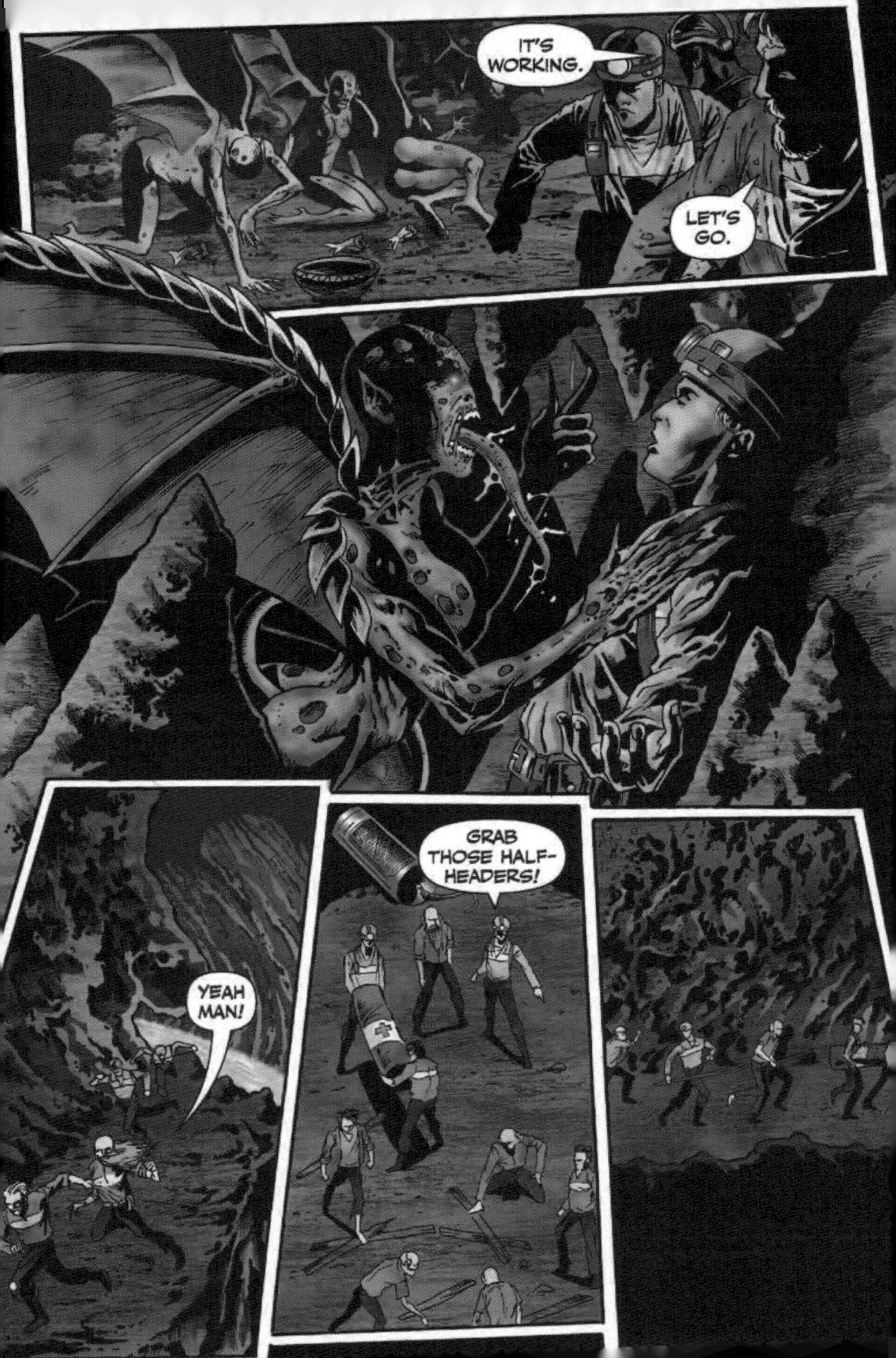
IT'S WORKING.
LET'S GO.
YEAH MAN!
GRAB THOSE HALF-HEADERS!

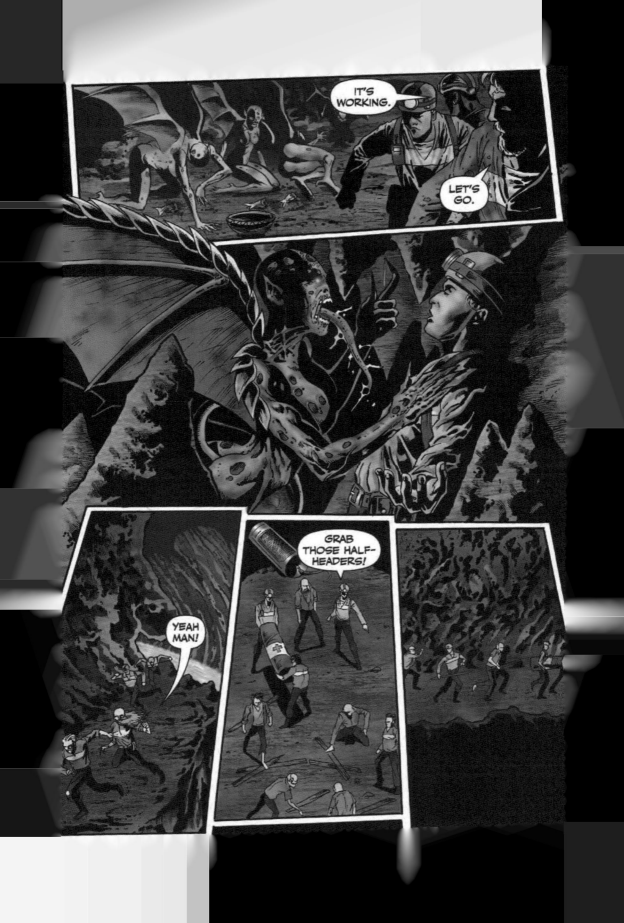

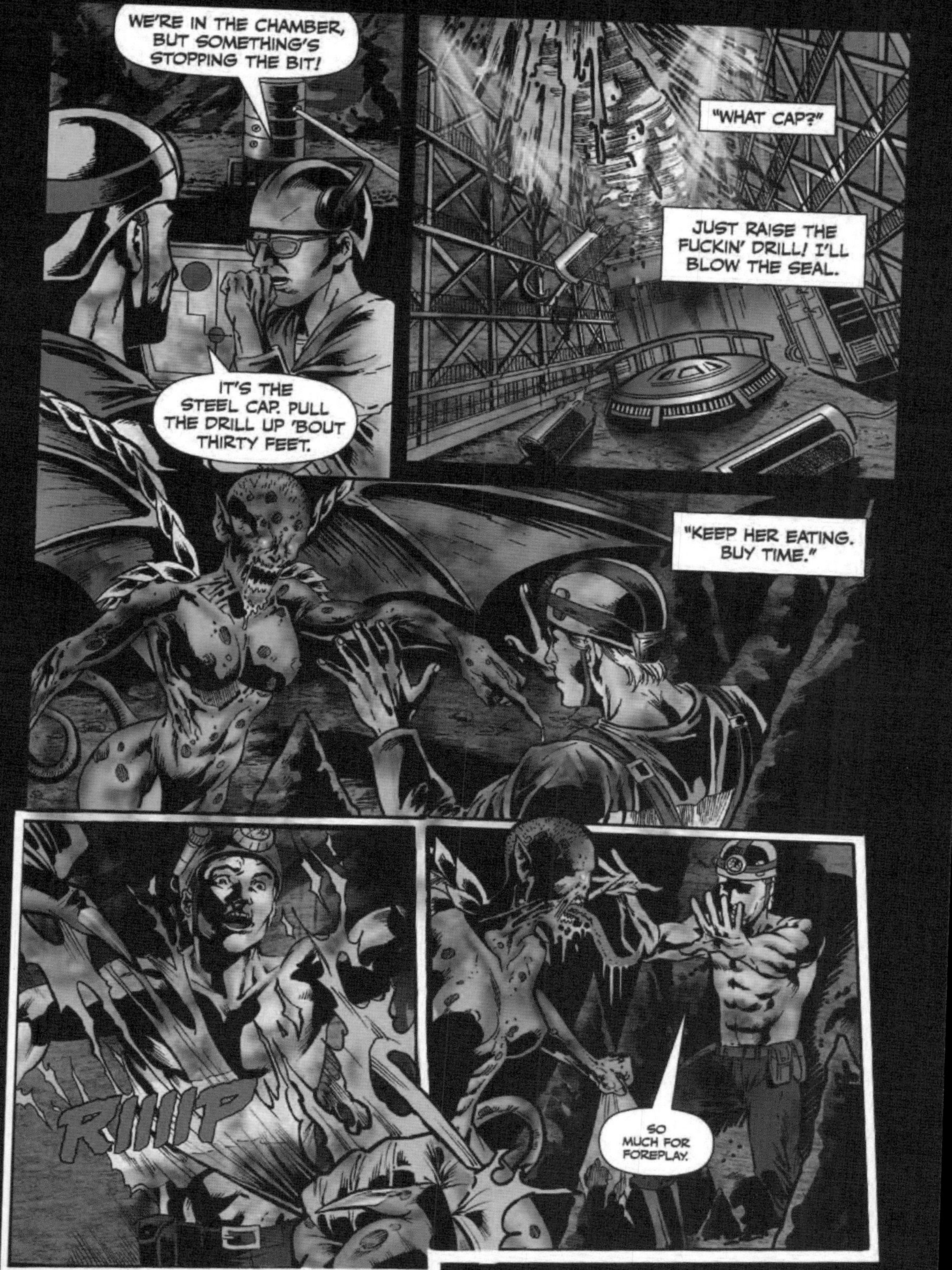
WE'RE IN THE CHAMBER, BUT SOMETHING'S STOPPING THE BIT!
IT'S THE STEEL CAP. PULL THE DRILL UP 'BOUT THIRTY FEET.
"WHAT CAP?"
JUST RAISE THE FUCKIN' DRILL! I'LL BLOW THE SEAL.
"KEEP HER EATING. BUY TIME."
RIIIIP
SO MUCH FOR FOREPLAY.

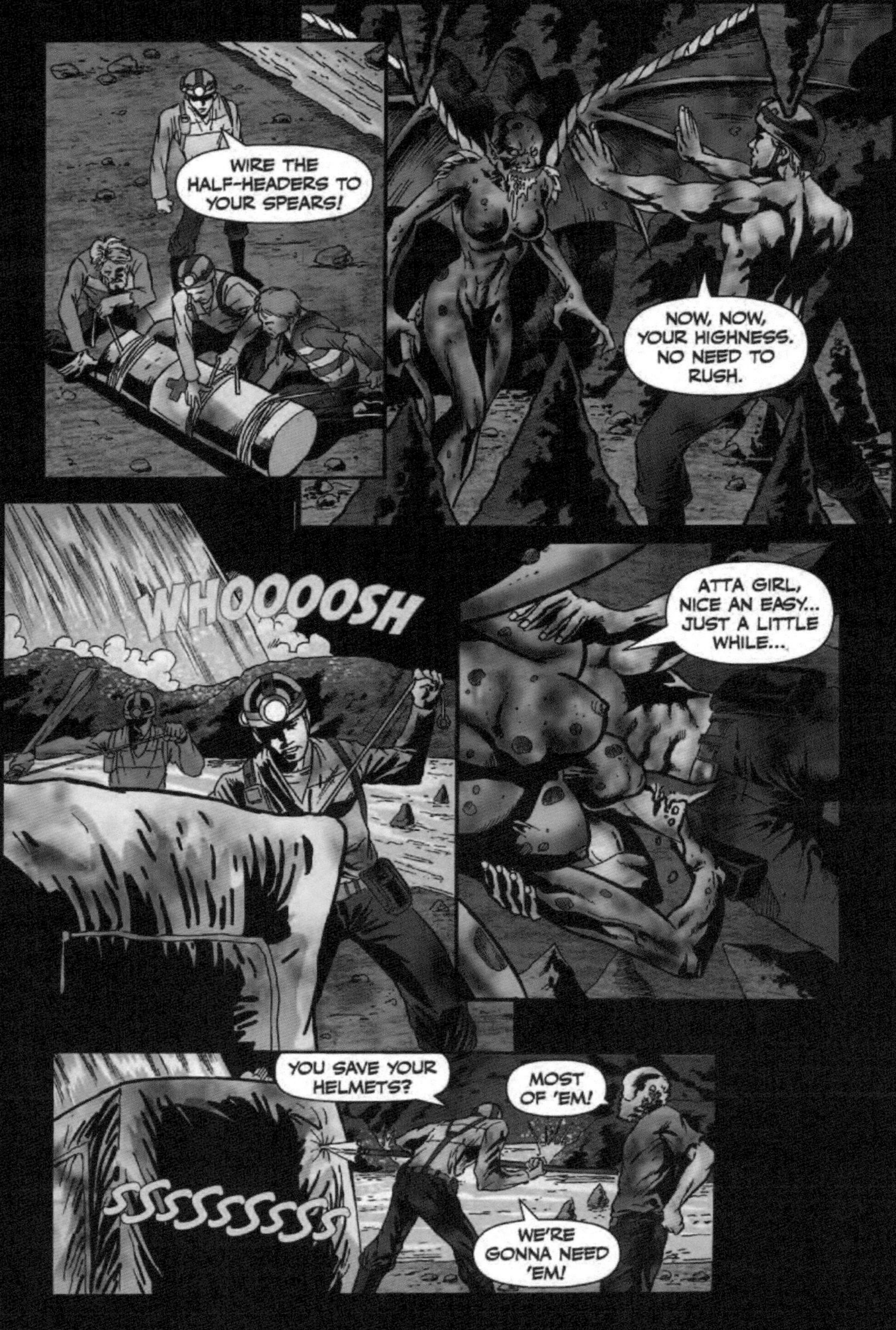
WIRE THE HALF-HEADERS TO YOUR SPEARS!
NOW, NOW, YOUR HIGHNESS. NO NEED TO RUSH.
WHOOOOSH
ATTA GIRL, NICE AN EASY... JUST A LITTLE WHILE...
YOU SAVE YOUR HELMETS?
MOST OF 'EM!
SSSSSSSSS
WE'RE GONNA NEED 'EM!

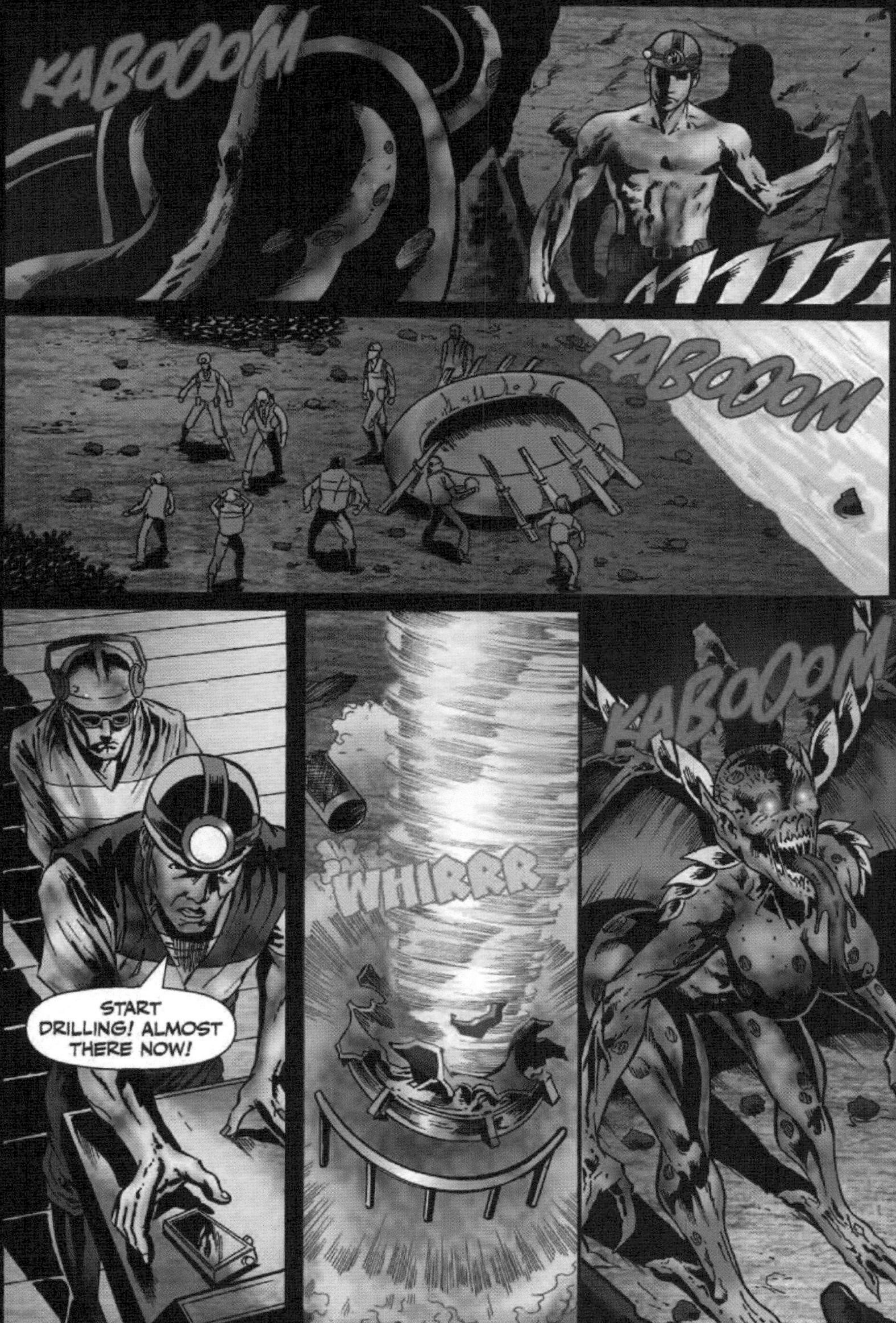
KABOOOM
KABOOOM
START DRILLING! ALMOST THERE NOW!
WHIRRR
KABOOOM

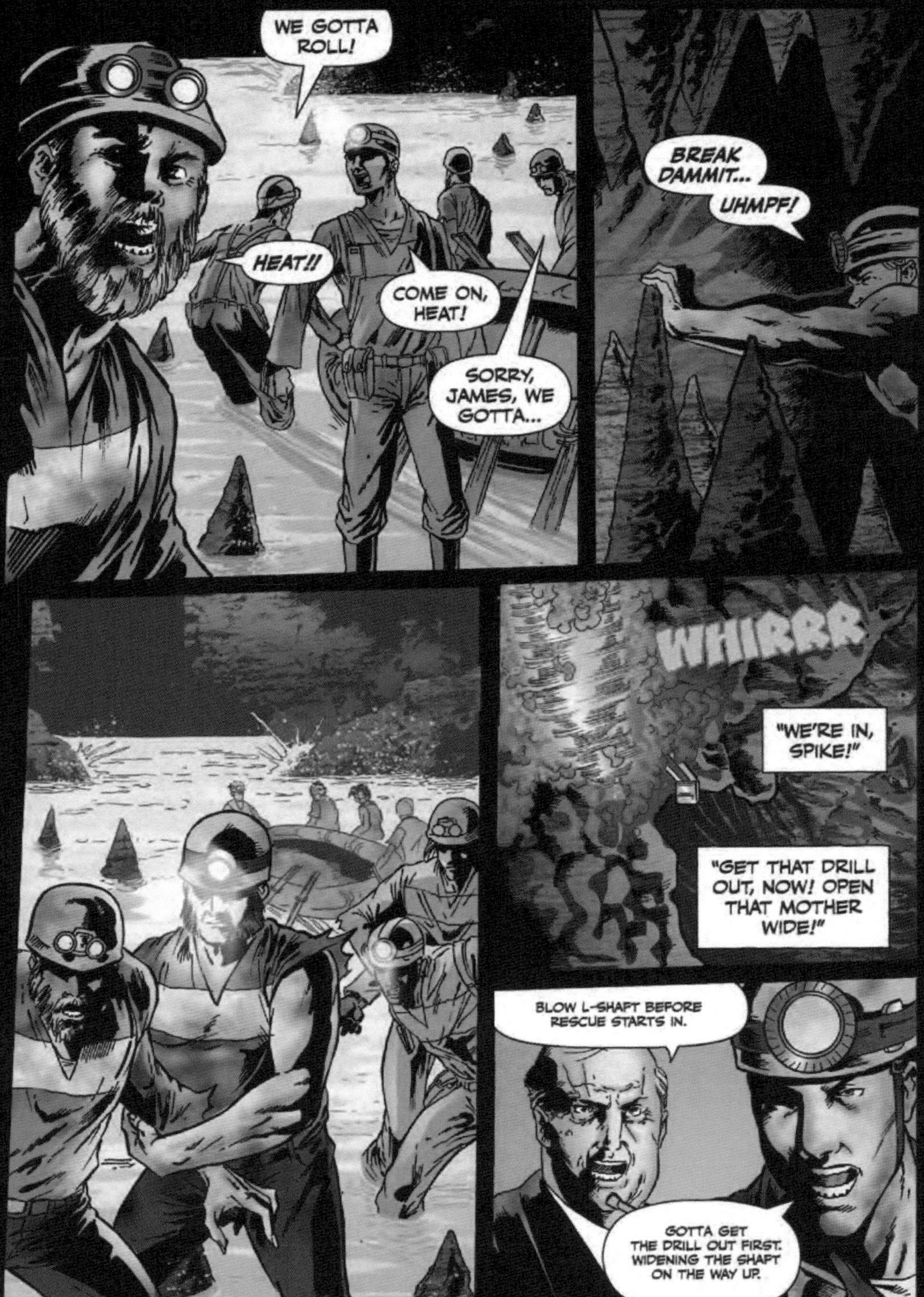

WE GOTTA ROLL!
HEAT!!
COME ON, HEAT!
SORRY, JAMES, WE GOTTA...
BREAK DAMMIT... UHMPF!
WHIRRR
"WE'RE IN, SPIKE!"
"GET THAT DRILL OUT, NOW! OPEN THAT MOTHER WIDE!"
BLOW L-SHAFT BEFORE RESCUE STARTS IN.
GOTTA GET THE DRILL OUT FIRST. WIDENING THE SHAFT ON THE WAY UP.
WE IN, SPIKE!? OVER!
ALMOST. GOTTA TEST THE AIR. STAND BY. OVER.

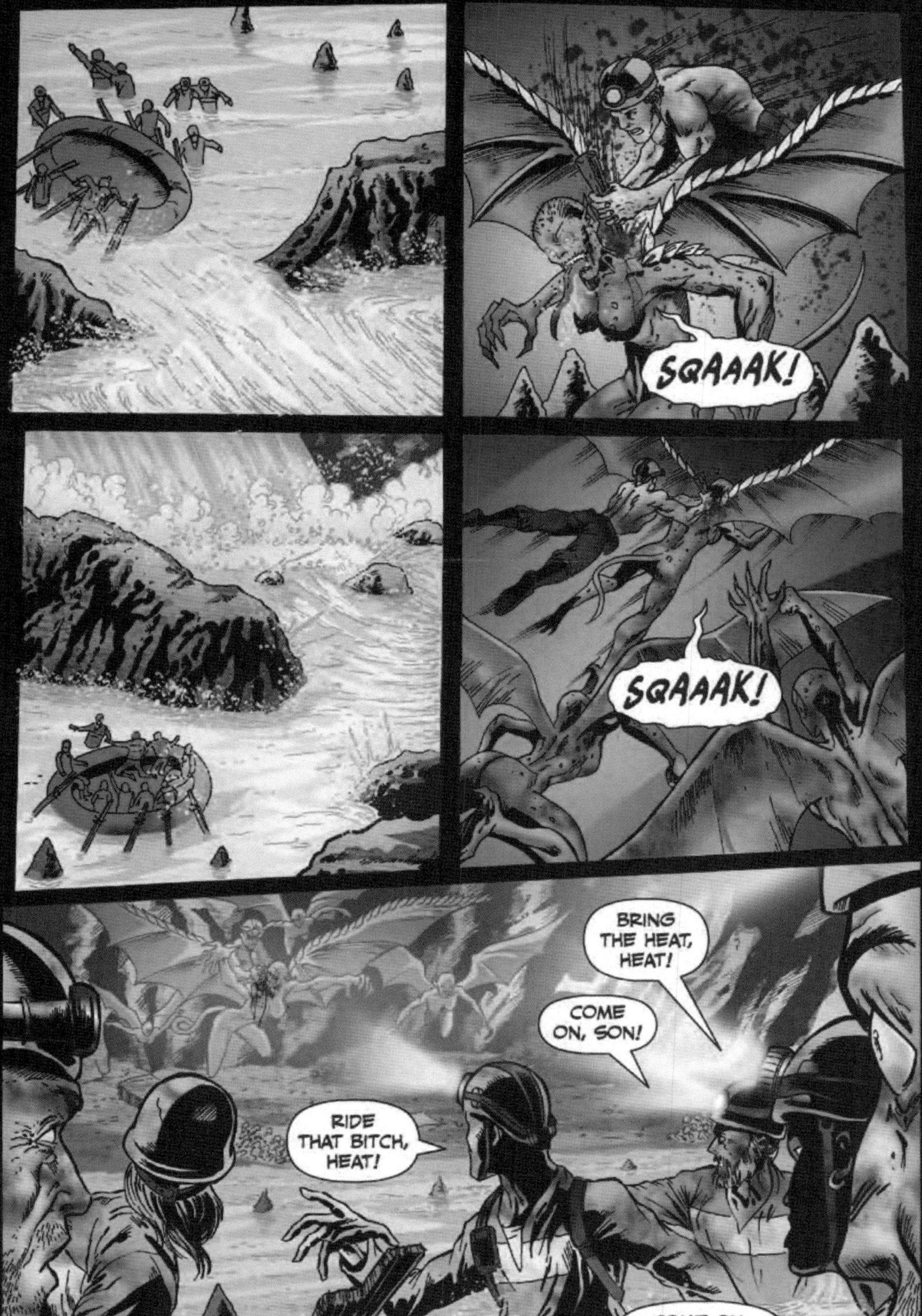
SQAAAK!
SQAAAK!
RIDE THAT BITCH, HEAT!
BRING THE HEAT, HEAT!
COME ON, SON!
COME ON, YOU CAN MAKE IT...

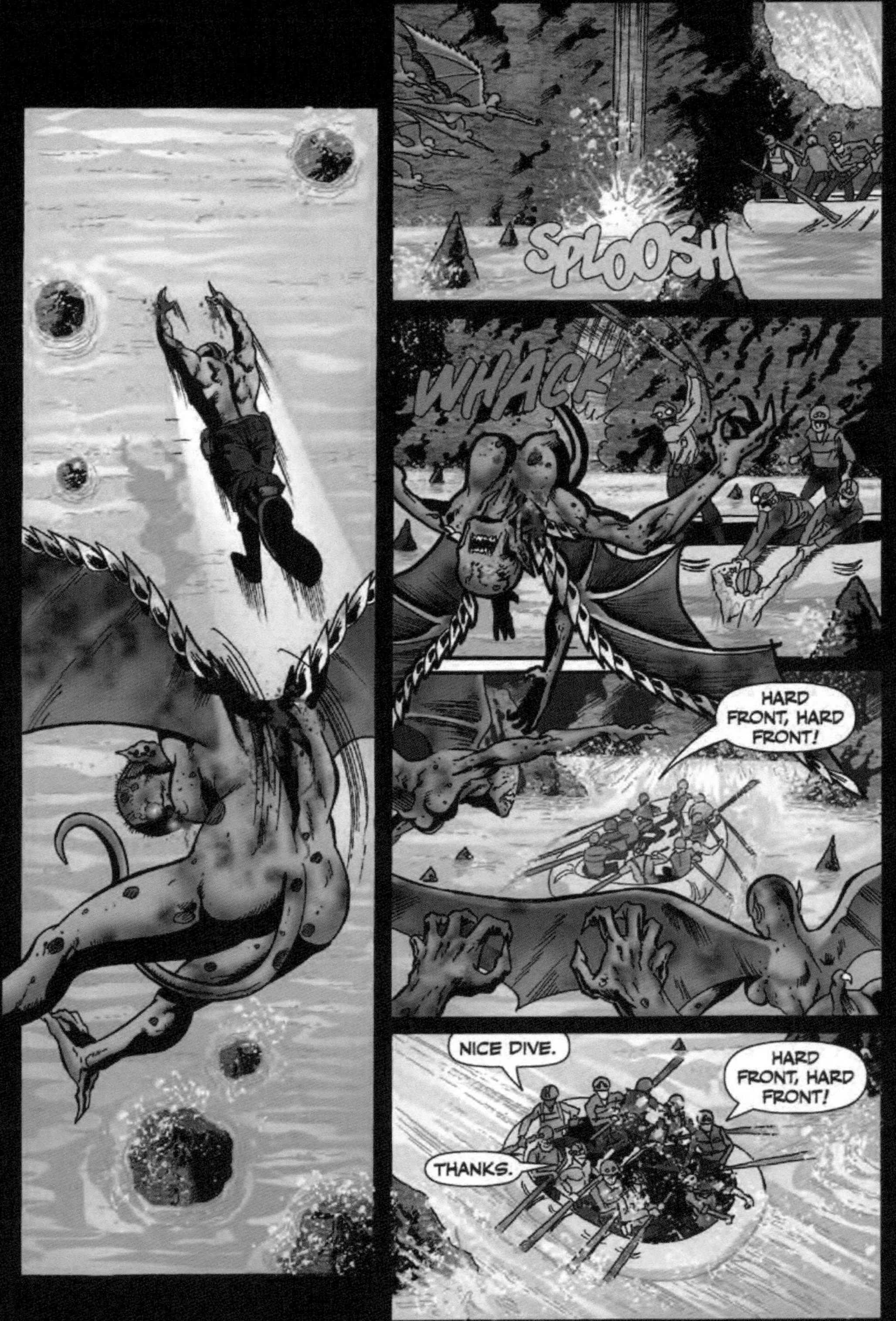
SPLOOSH
WHACK
HARD FRONT, HARD FRONT!
NICE DIVE.
HARD FRONT, HARD FRONT!
THANKS.

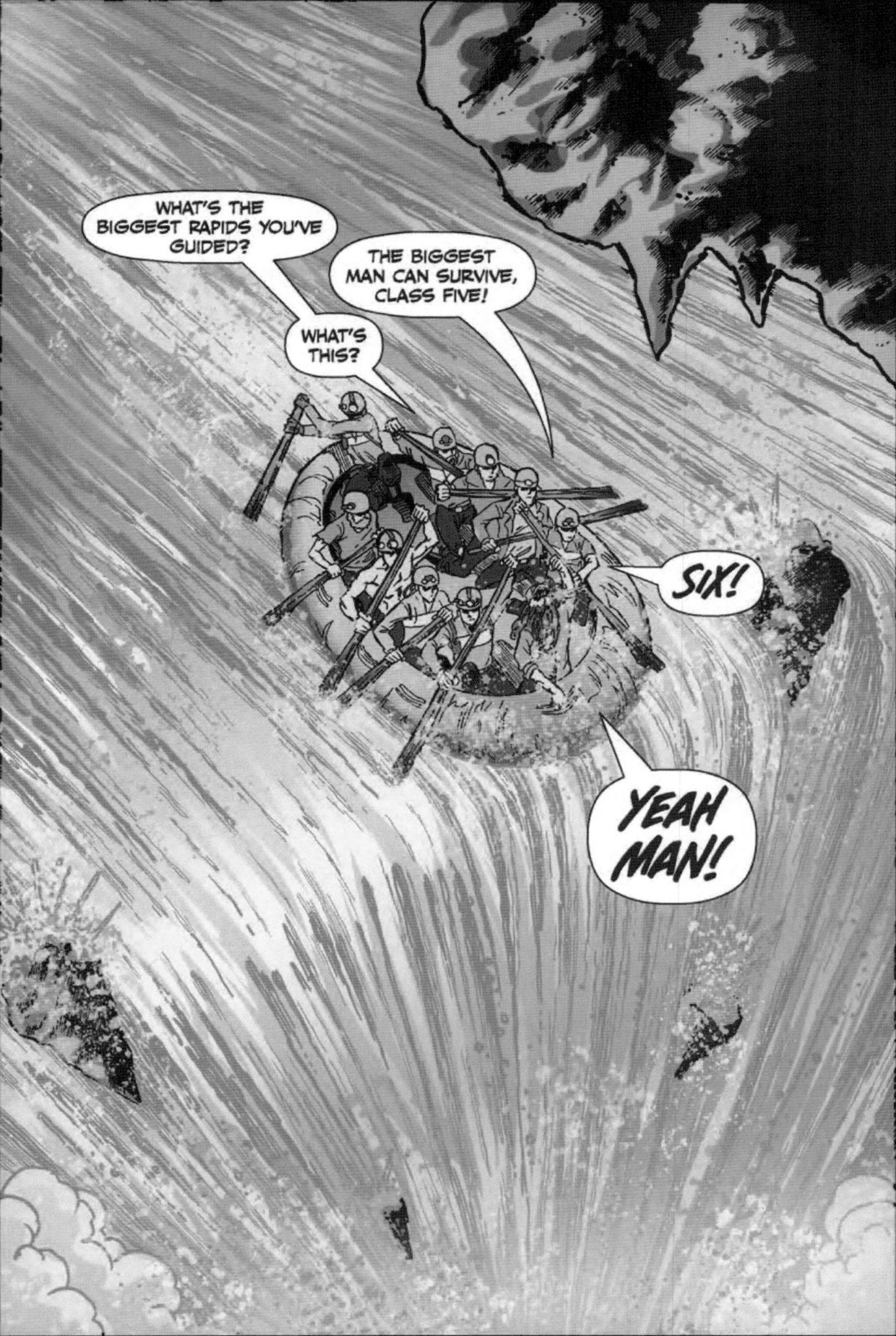
WHAT'S THE BIGGEST RAPIDS YOU'VE GUIDED?
THE BIGGEST MAN CAN SURVIVE, CLASS FIVE!
WHAT'S THIS?
SIX!
YEAH MAN!

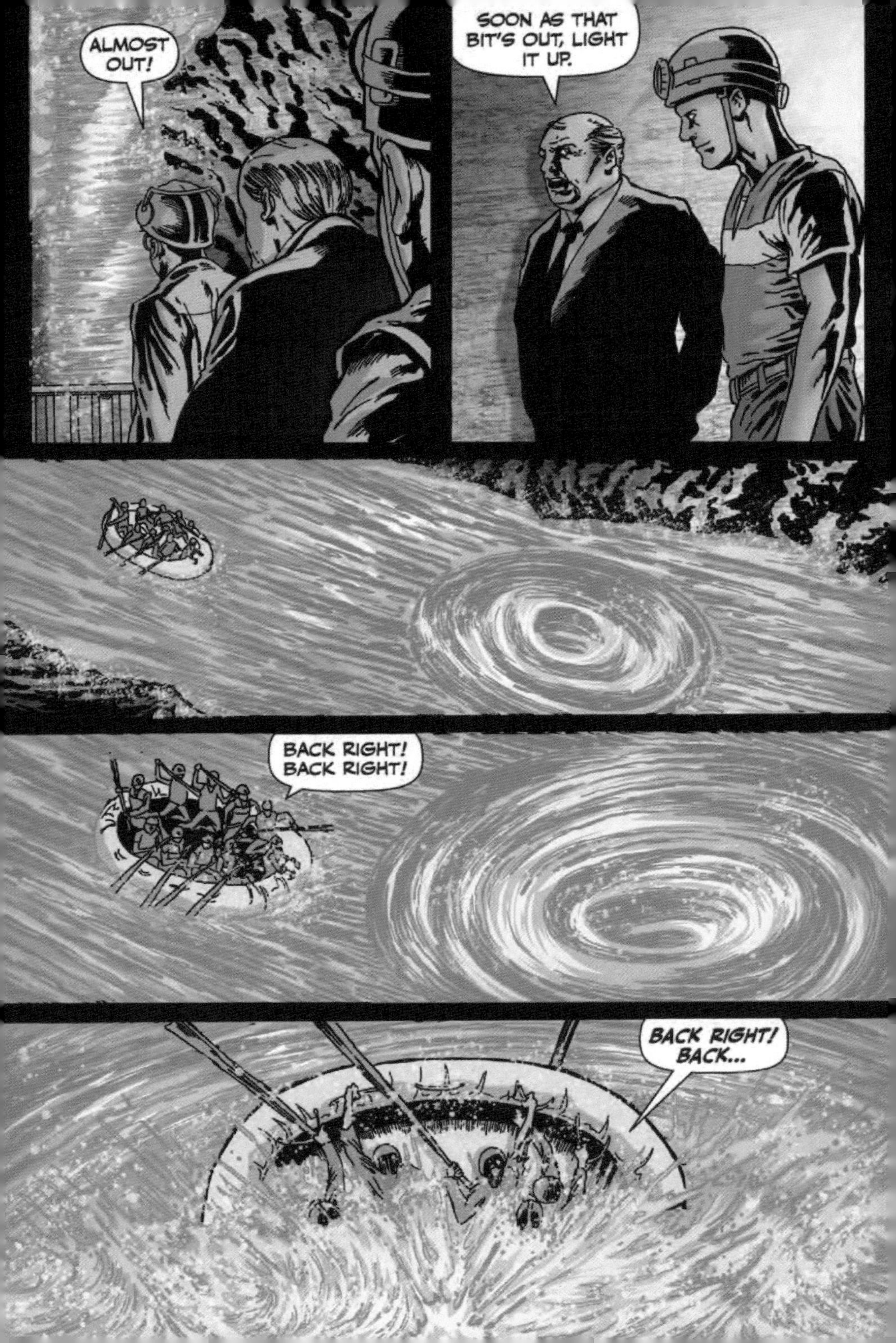
ALMOST OUT!
SOON AS THAT BIT'S OUT, LIGHT IT UP.
BACK RIGHT! BACK RIGHT!
BACK RIGHT! BACK...

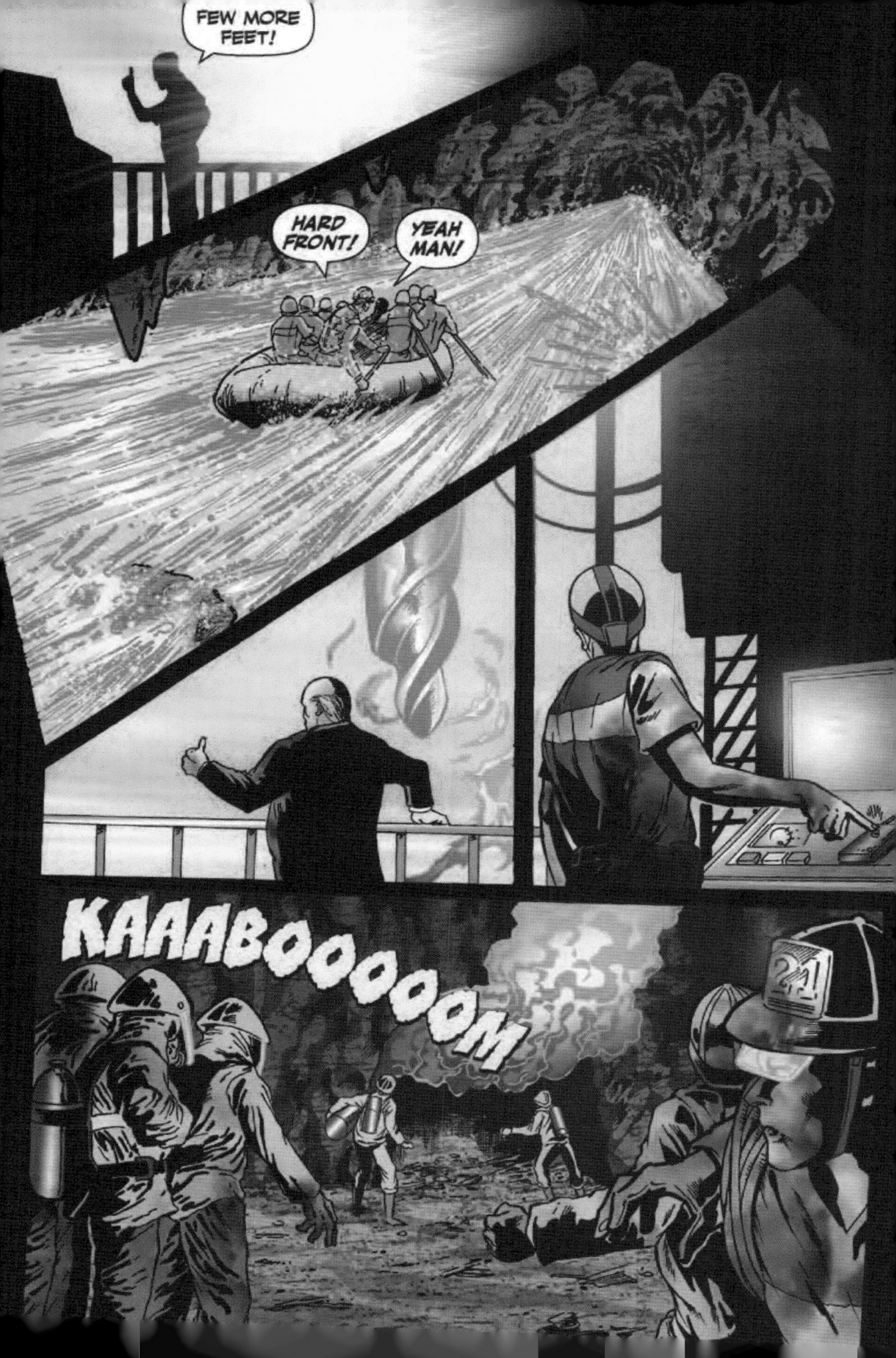
FEW MORE FEET!
HARD FRONT!
YEAH MAN!
KAAABOOOOOOM

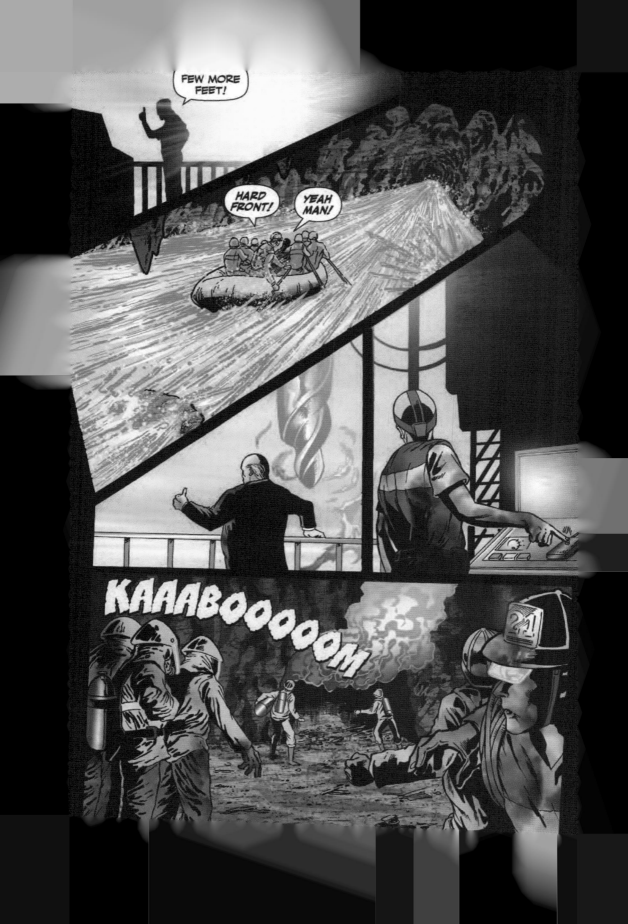

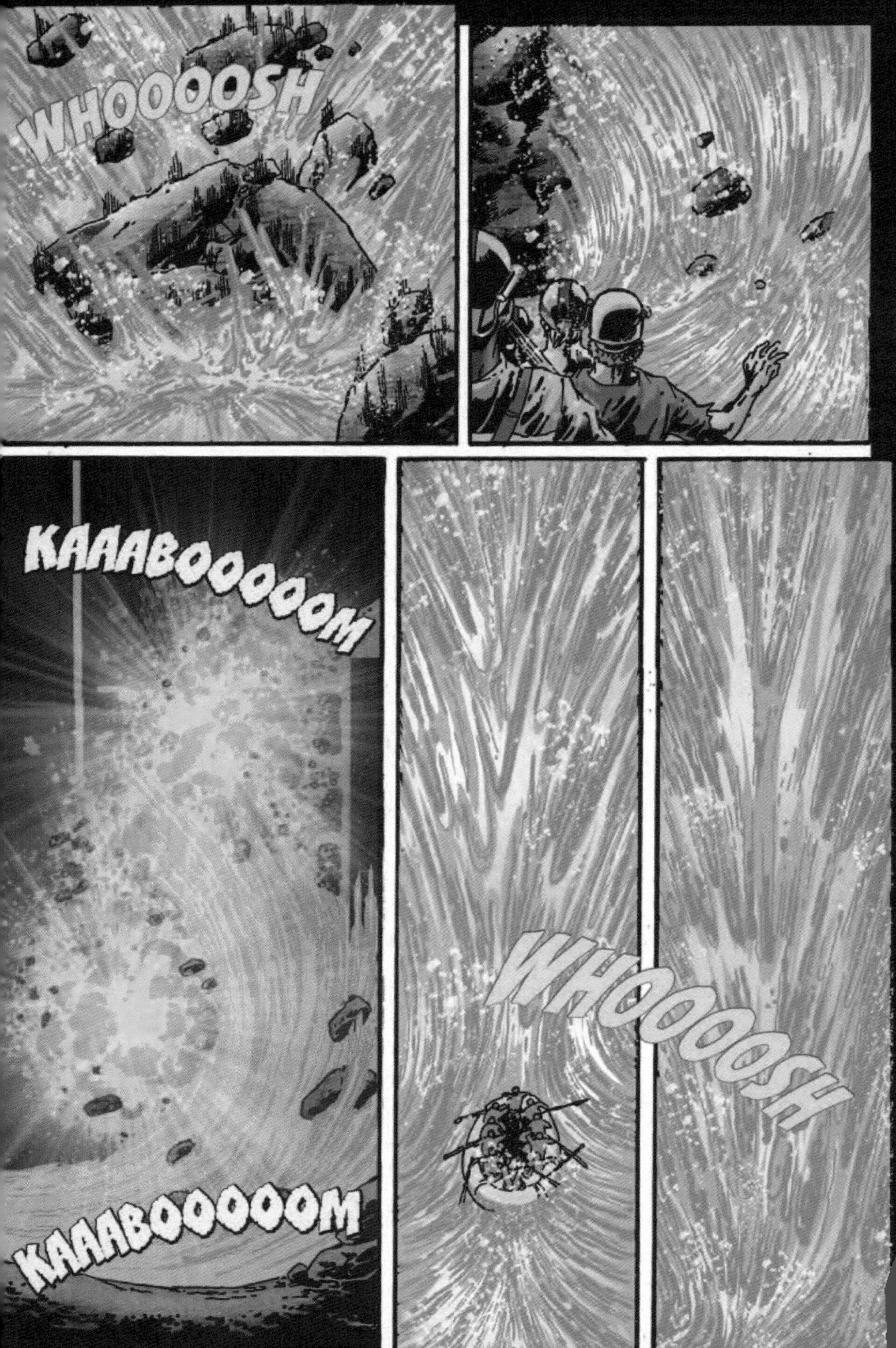
WHOOOOSH
KAAABOOOOOOM
KAAABOOOOOM
WHOOOOSH

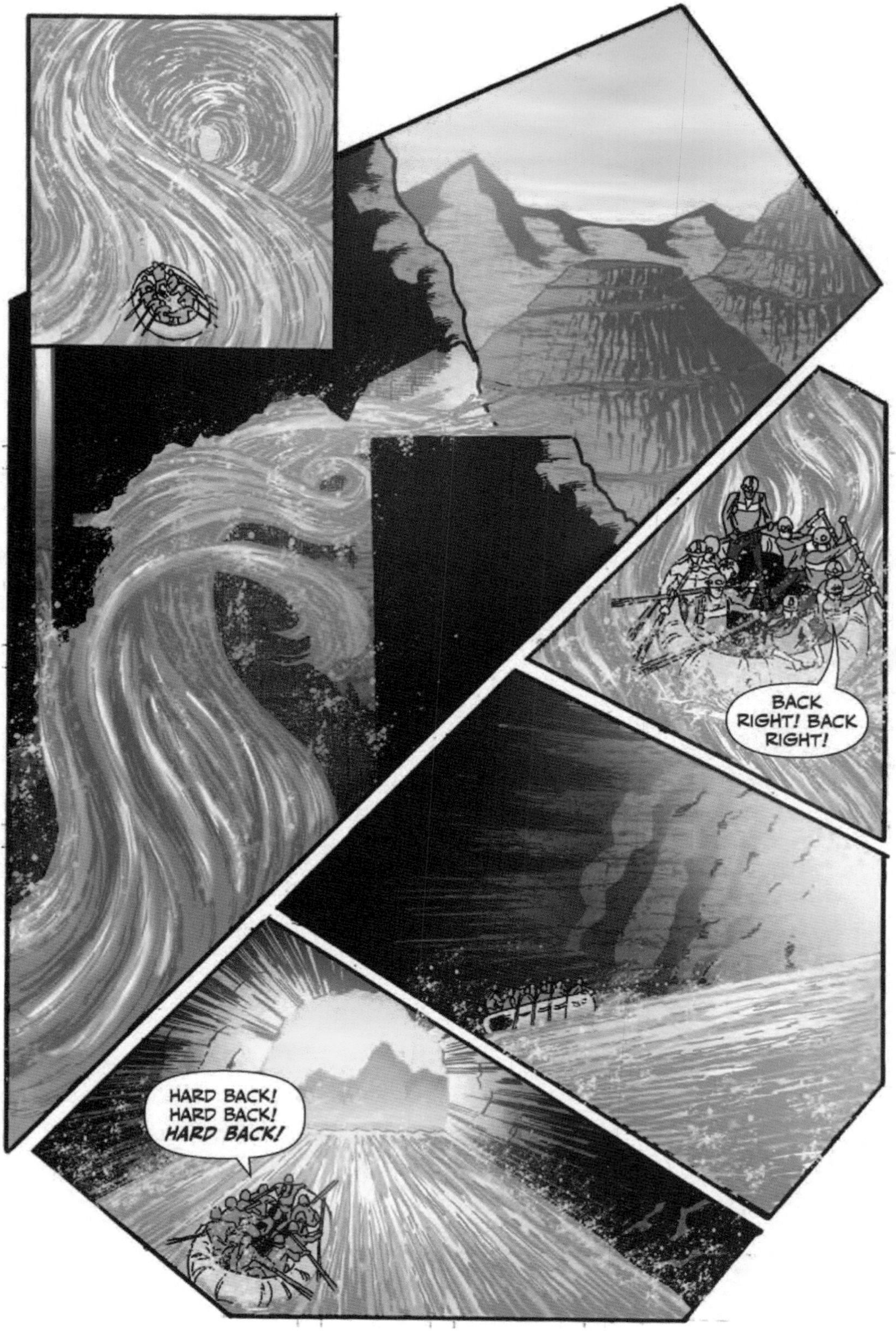
BACK RIGHT! BACK RIGHT!
HARD BACK! HARD BACK! *HARD BACK!*

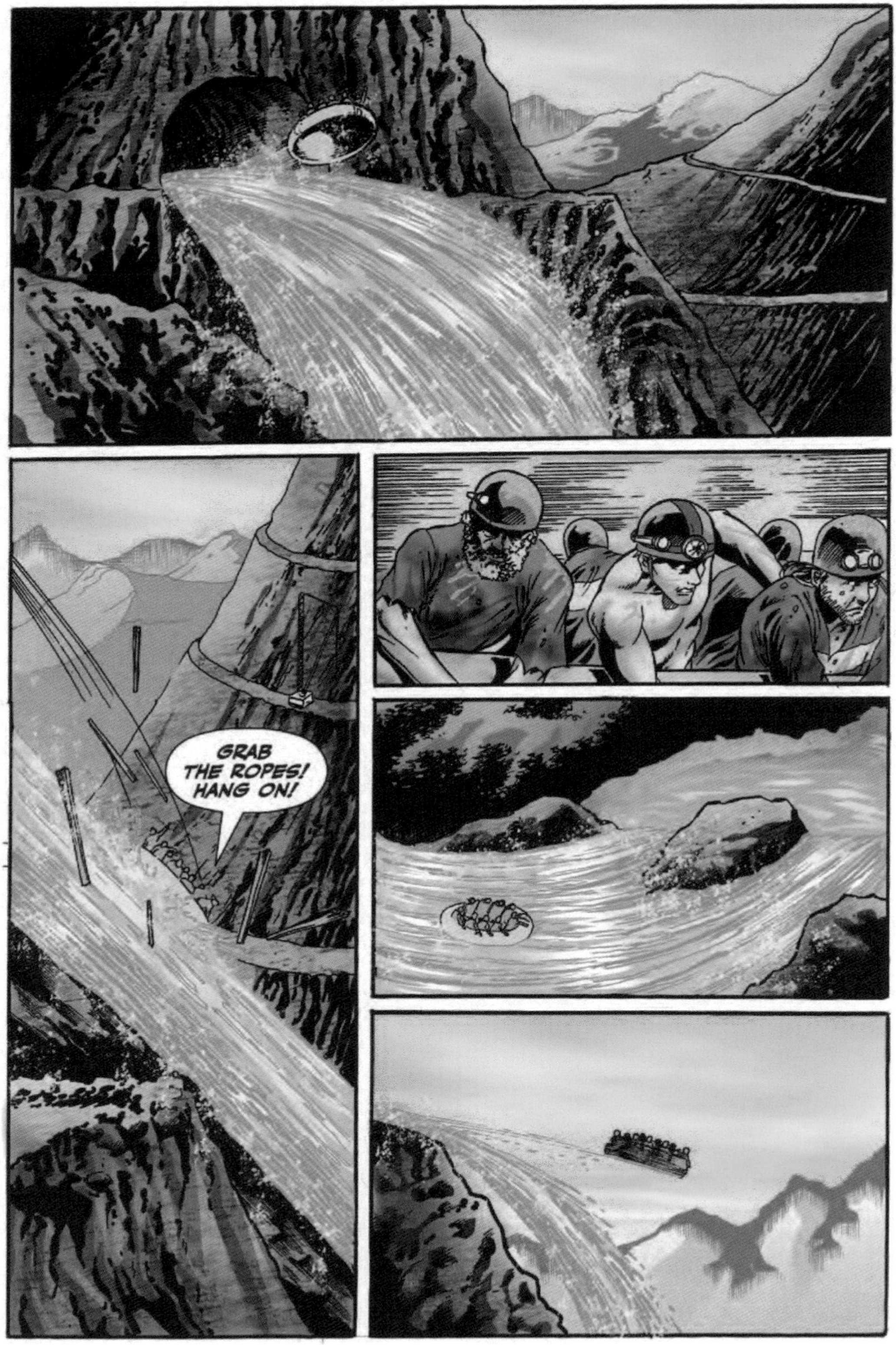
GRAB THE ROPES! HANG ON!

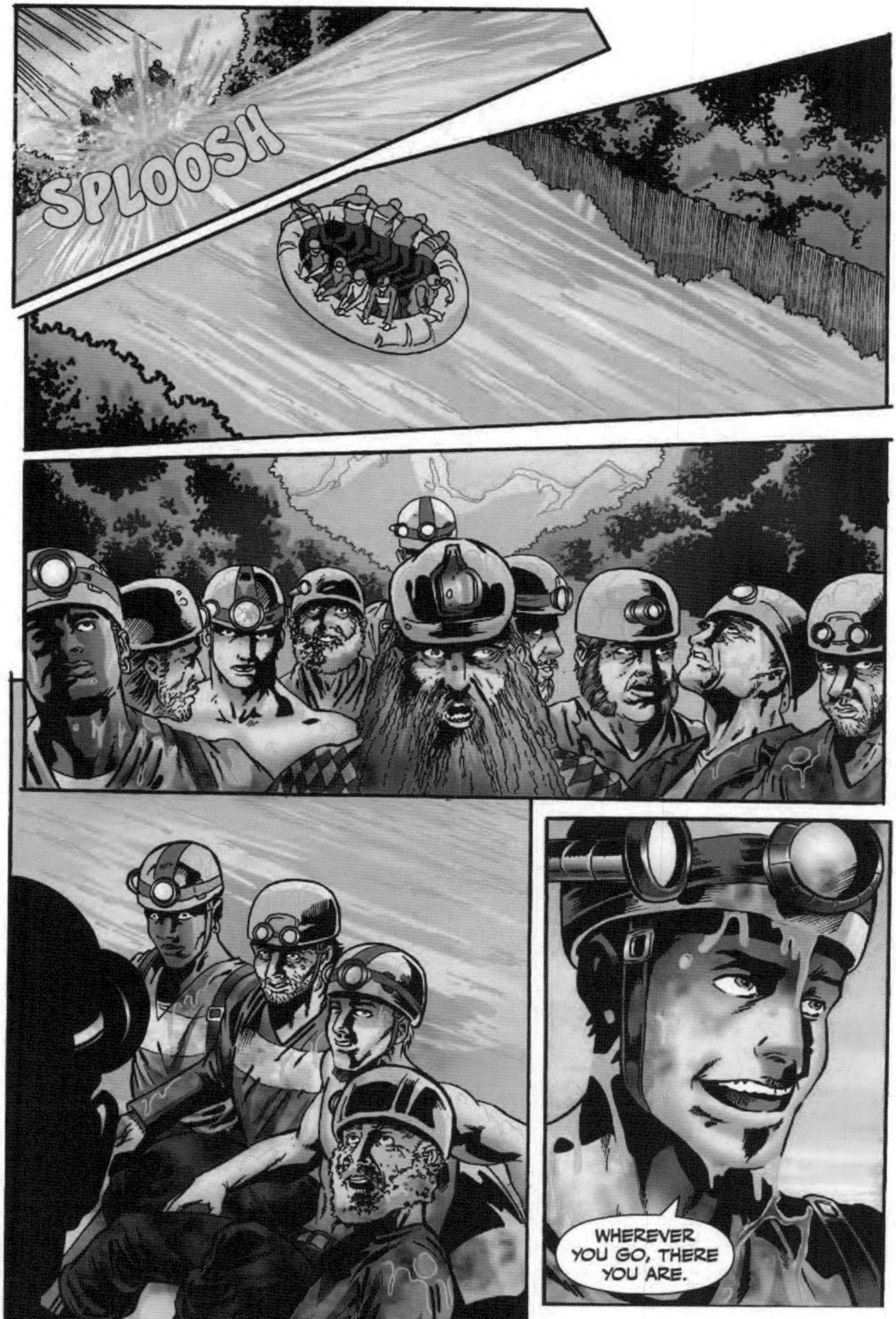
SPLOOSH
WHEREVER YOU GO, THERE YOU ARE.

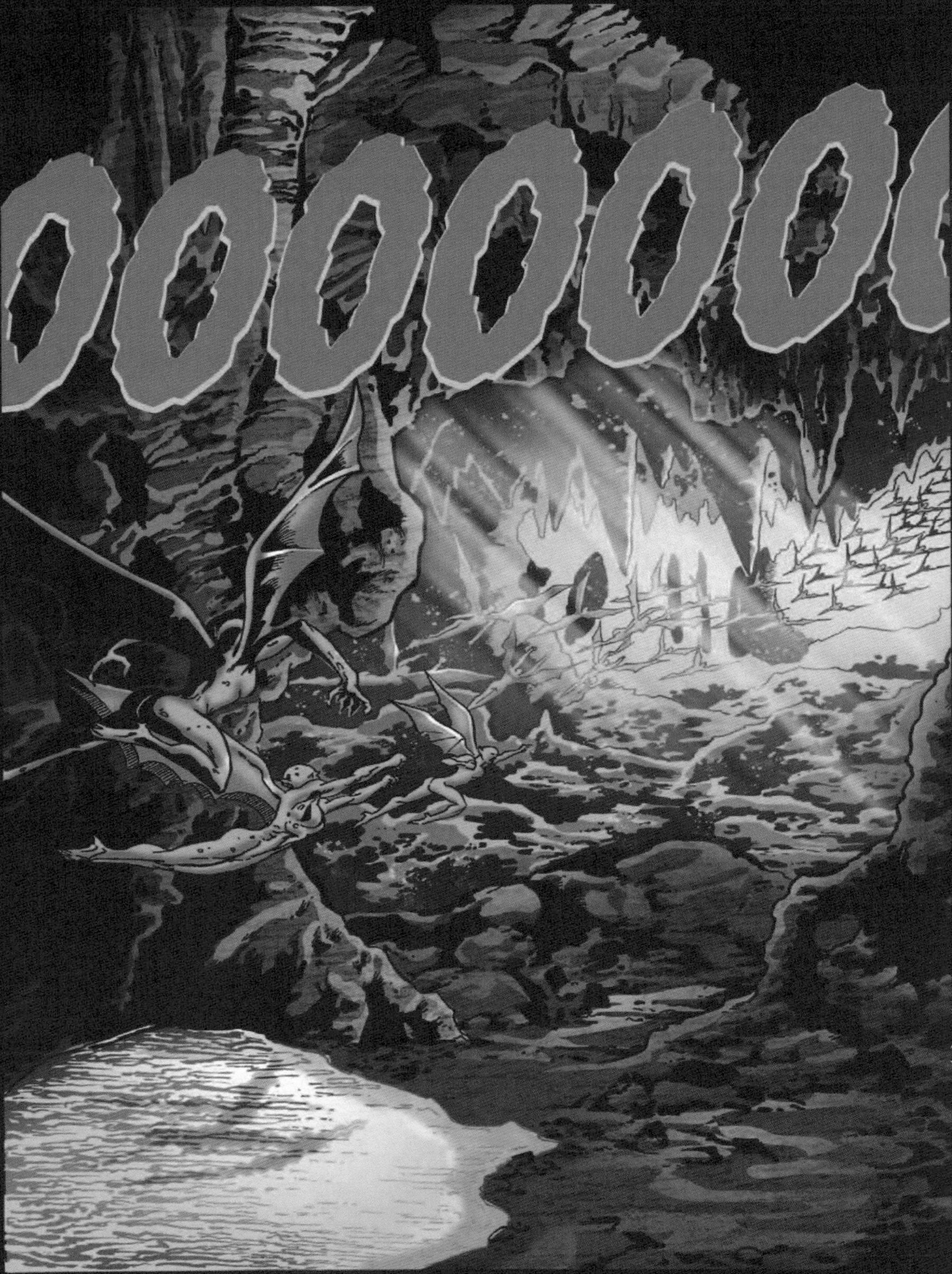
OOOOOOO

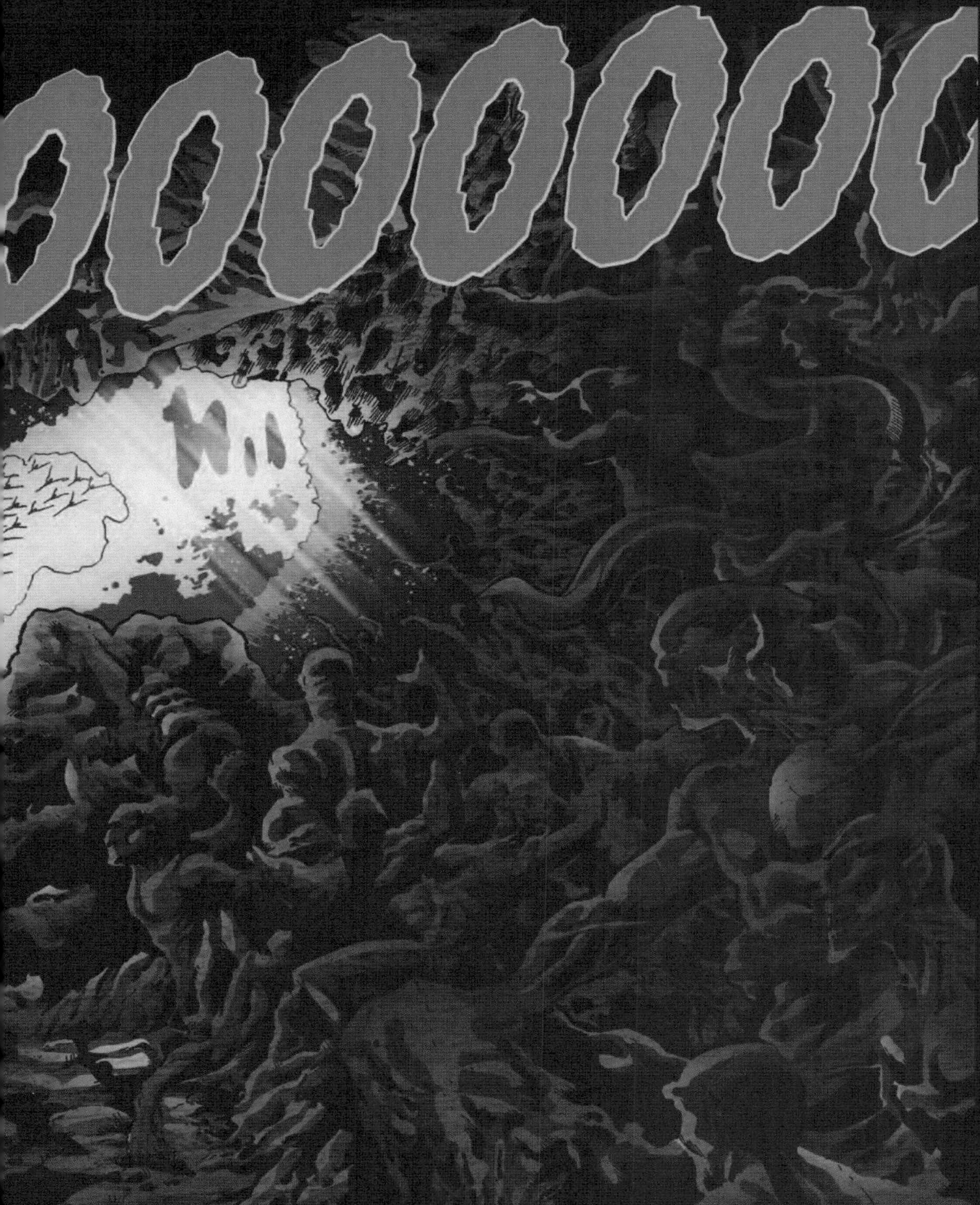
OOOOOOO

END BOOK II

BOOK IV

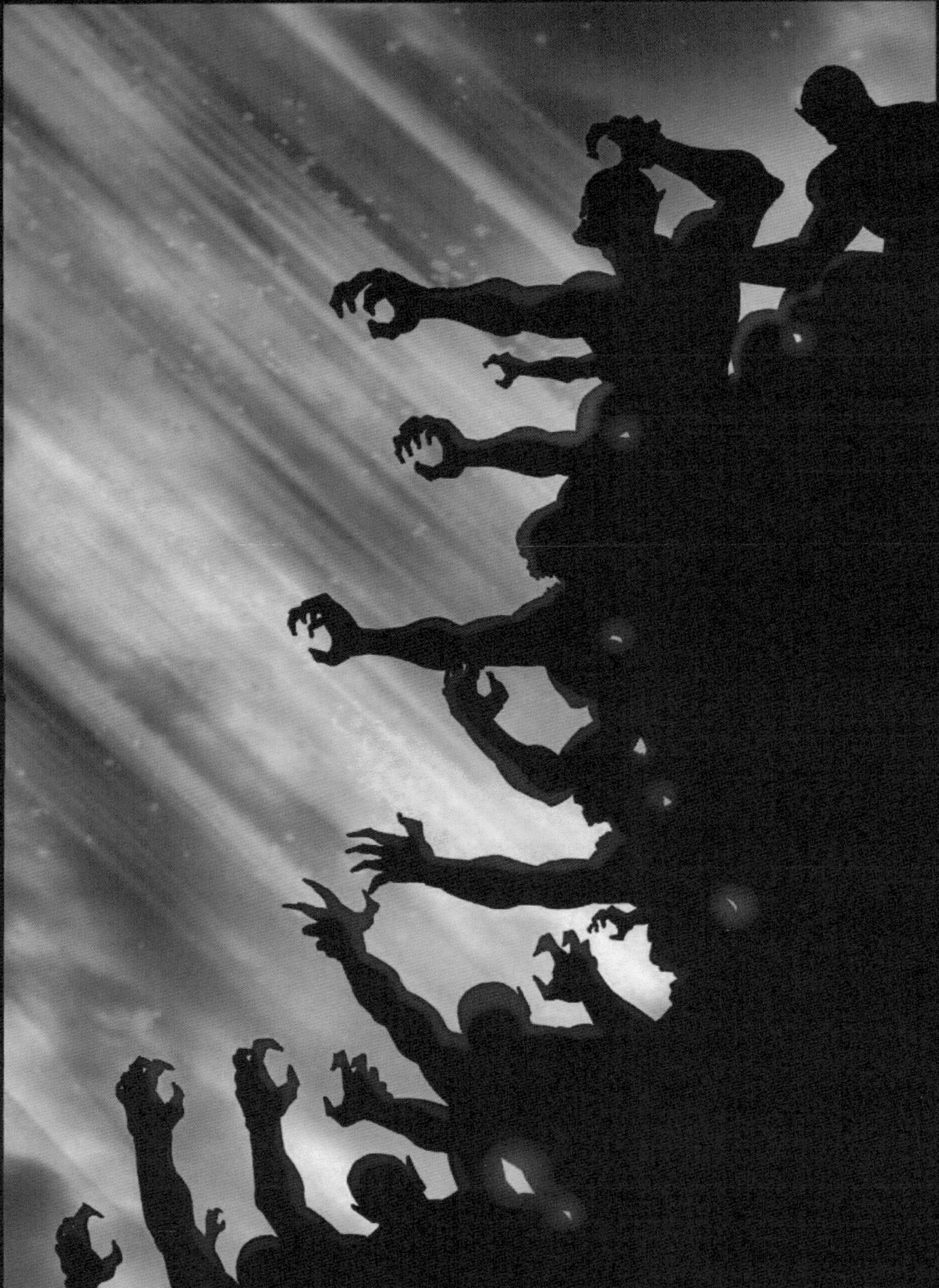

AWAKENING

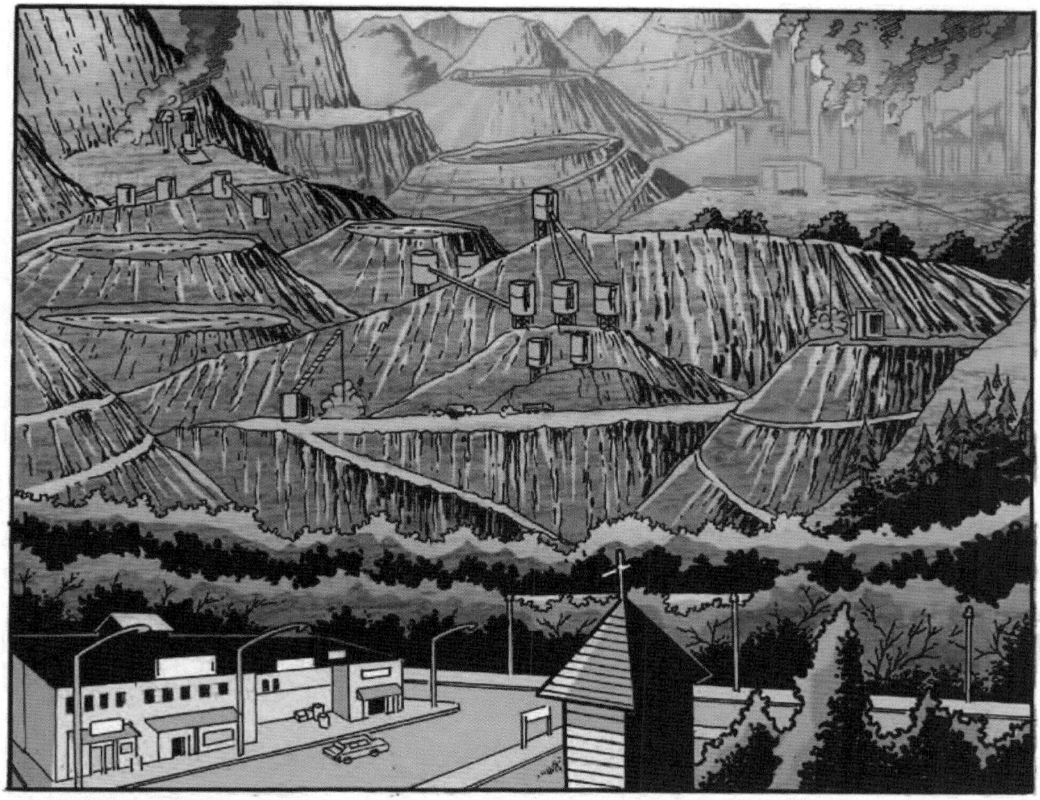

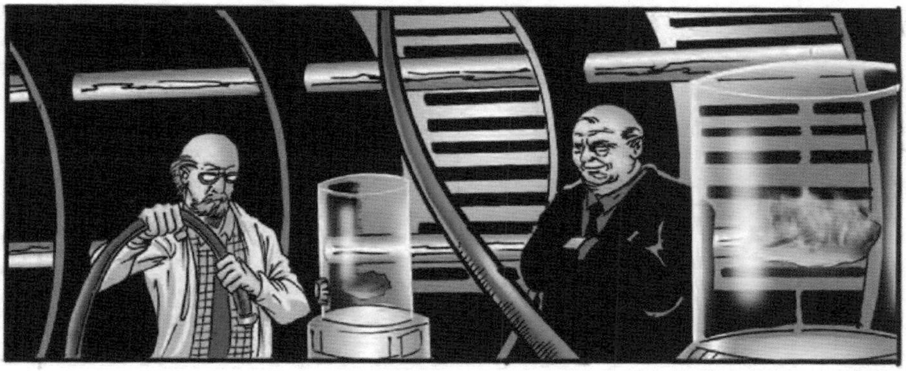

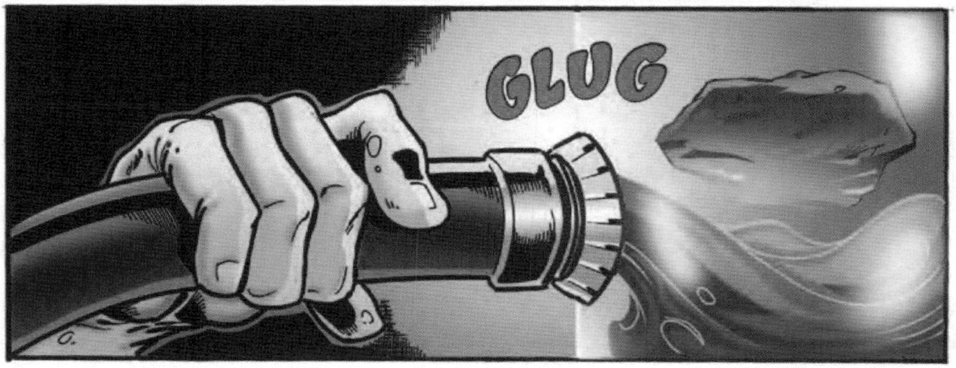
GLUG

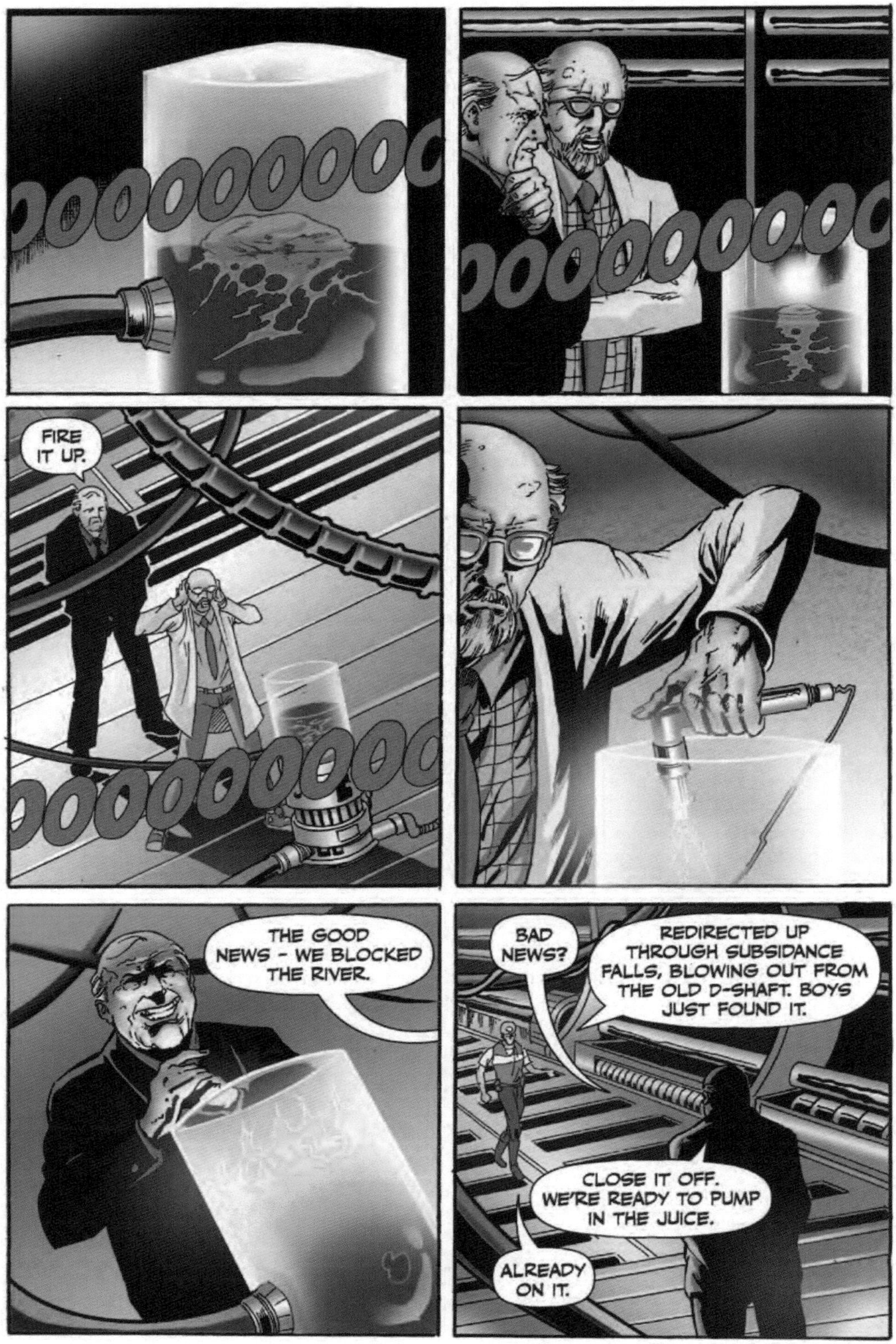
OOOOOOOOOO
OOOOOOOOOO
FIRE IT UP.
OOOOOOOOOO
THE GOOD NEWS - WE BLOCKED THE RIVER.
BAD NEWS?
REDIRECTED UP THROUGH SUBSIDANCE FALLS, BLOWING OUT FROM THE OLD D-SHAFT. BOYS JUST FOUND IT.
CLOSE IT OFF. WE'RE READY TO PUMP IN THE JUICE.
ALREADY ON IT.

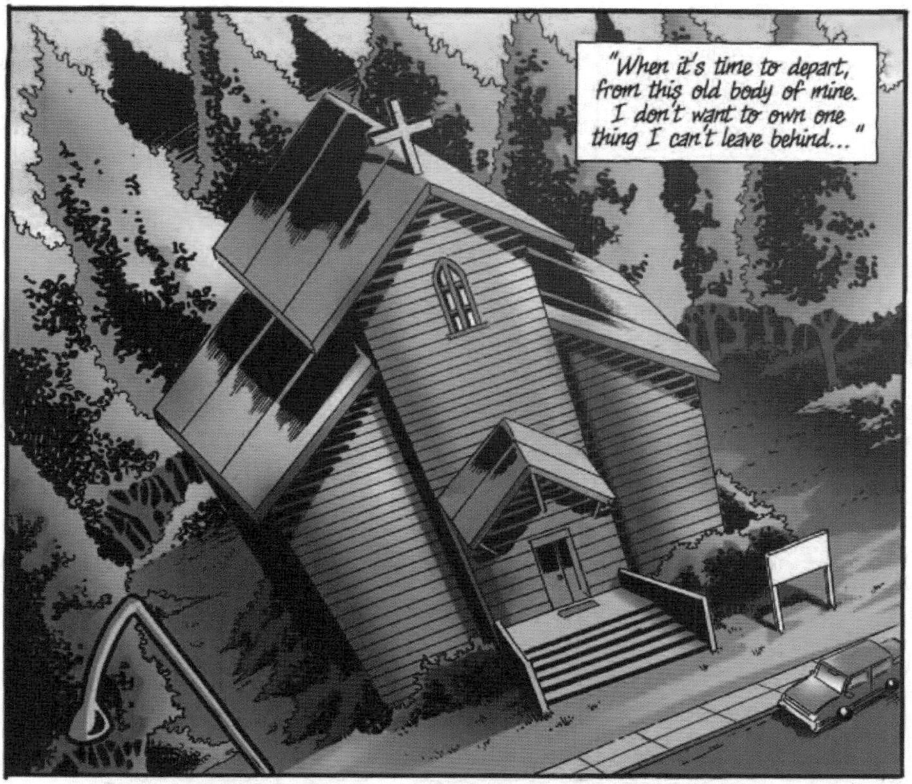
"When it's time to depart, from this old body of mine. I don't want to own one thing I can't leave behind..."

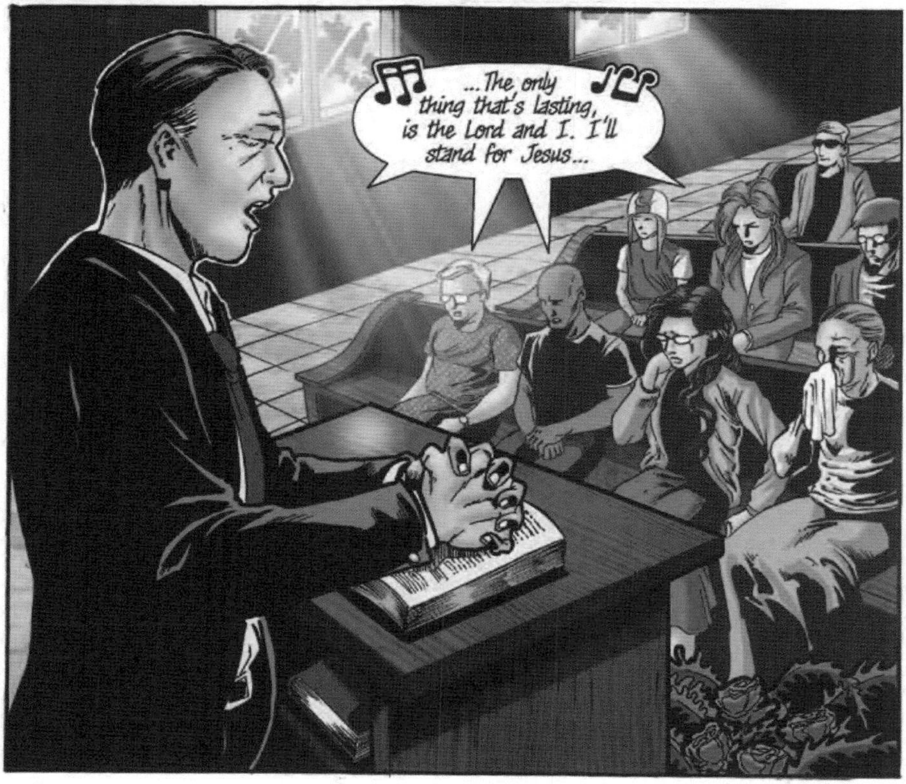
...The only thing that's lasting, is the Lord and I. I'll stand for Jesus...

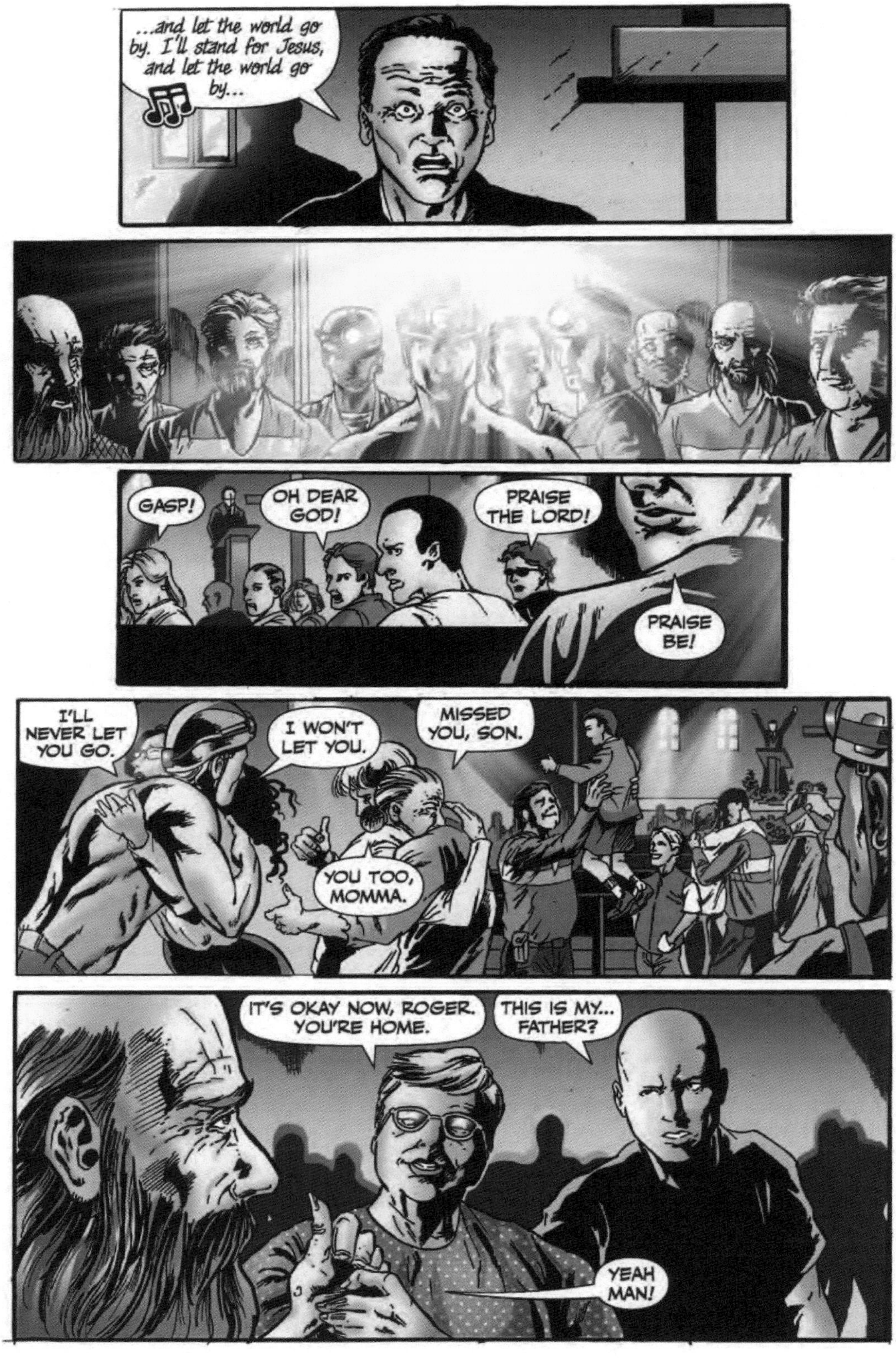
...and let the world go by. I'll stand for Jesus, and let the world go by...
GASP!
OH DEAR GOD!
PRAISE THE LORD!
PRAISE BE!
I'LL NEVER LET YOU GO.
I WON'T LET YOU.
MISSED YOU, SON.
YOU TOO, MOMMA.
IT'S OKAY NOW, ROGER. YOU'RE HOME.
THIS IS MY... FATHER?
YEAH MAN!

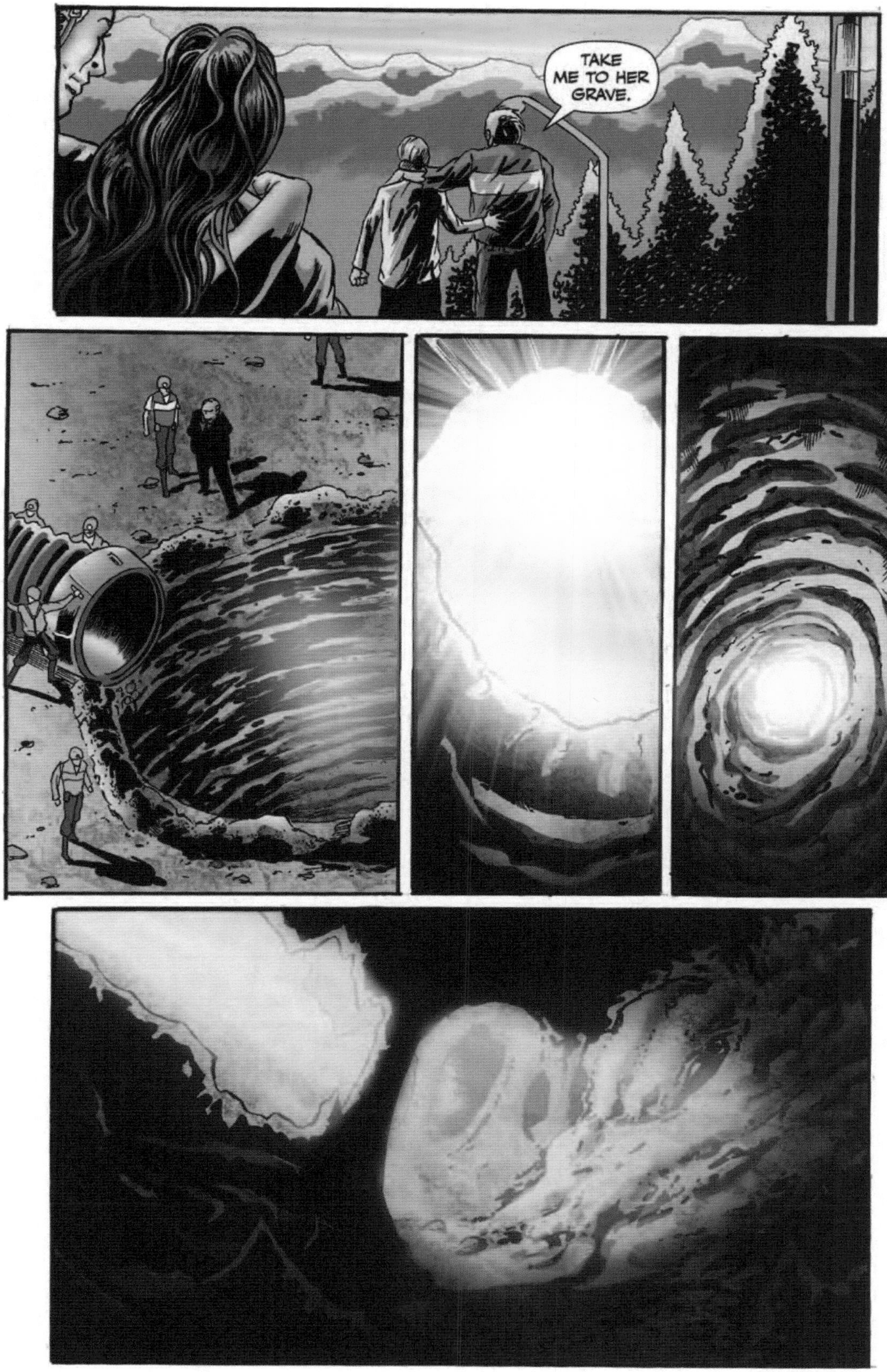
TAKE ME TO HER GRAVE.

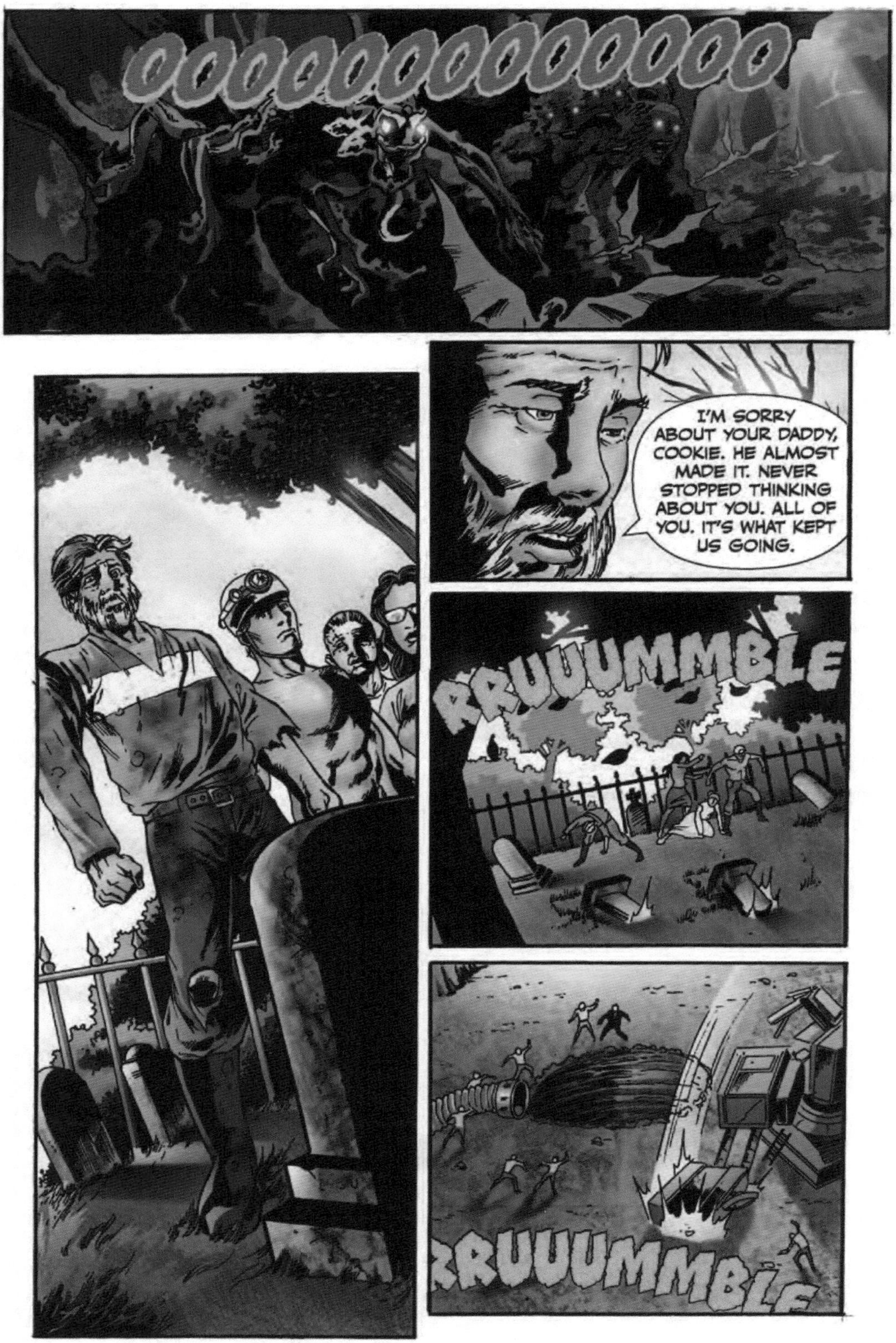
OOOOOOOOOOOOO
I'M SORRY ABOUT YOUR DADDY, COOKIE. HE ALMOST MADE IT. NEVER STOPPED THINKING ABOUT YOU. ALL OF YOU. IT'S WHAT KEPT US GOING.
RRUUUMMBLE
RRUUUMMBLE

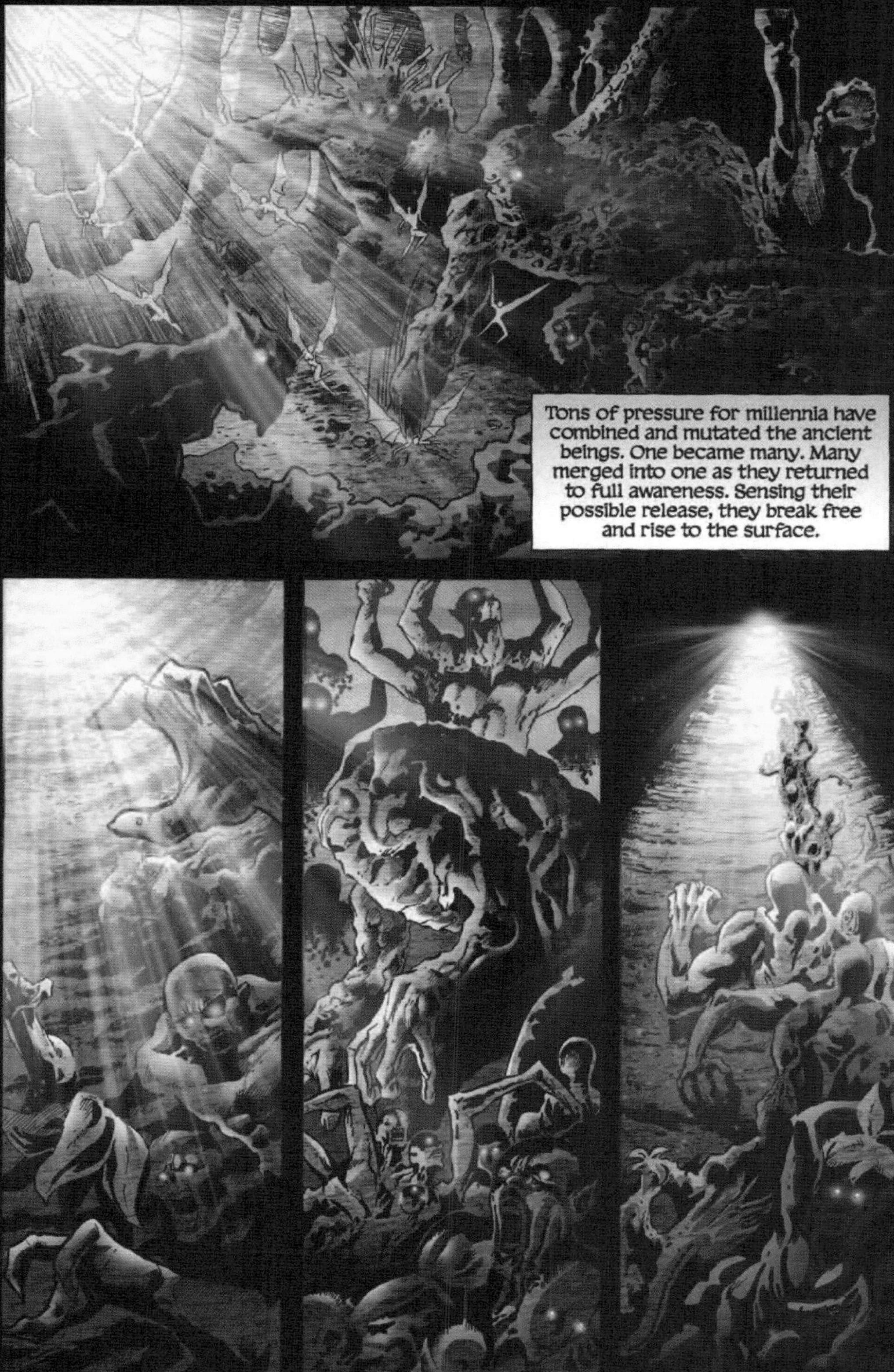
Tons of pressure for millennia have combined and mutated the ancient beings. One became many. Many merged into one as they returned to full awareness. Sensing their possible release, they break free and rise to the surface.

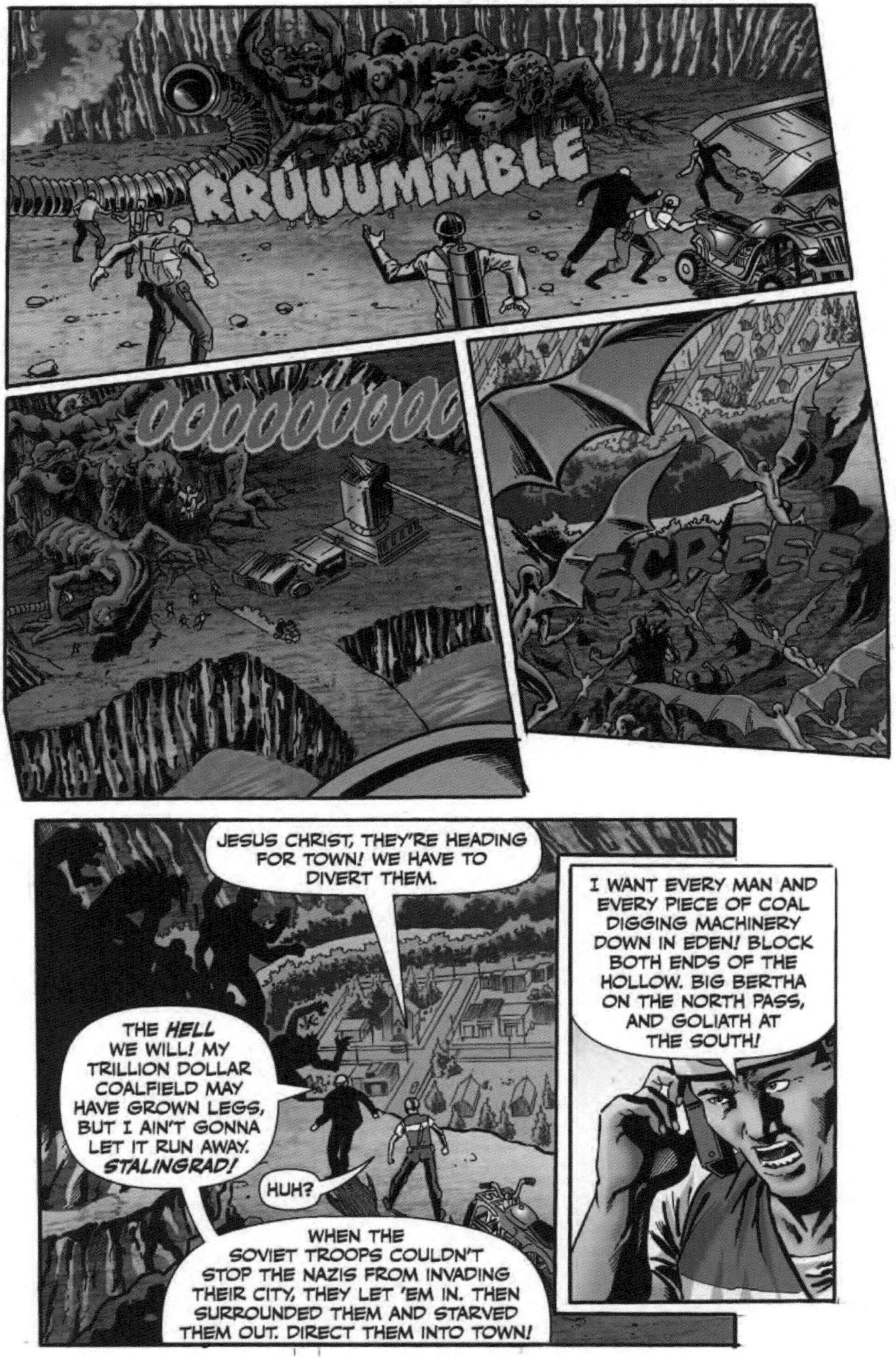
RRUUUMMBLE
OOOOOOOOO
SCREEE
JESUS CHRIST, THEY'RE HEADING FOR TOWN! WE HAVE TO DIVERT THEM.
THE *HELL* WE WILL! MY TRILLION DOLLAR COALFIELD MAY HAVE GROWN LEGS, BUT I AIN'T GONNA LET IT RUN AWAY. *STALINGRAD!*
HUH?
WHEN THE SOVIET TROOPS COULDN'T STOP THE NAZIS FROM INVADING THEIR CITY, THEY LET 'EM IN. THEN SURROUNDED THEM AND STARVED THEM OUT. DIRECT THEM INTO TOWN!
I WANT EVERY MAN AND EVERY PIECE OF COAL DIGGING MACHINERY DOWN IN EDEN! BLOCK BOTH ENDS OF THE HOLLOW. BIG BERTHA ON THE NORTH PASS, AND GOLIATH AT THE SOUTH!

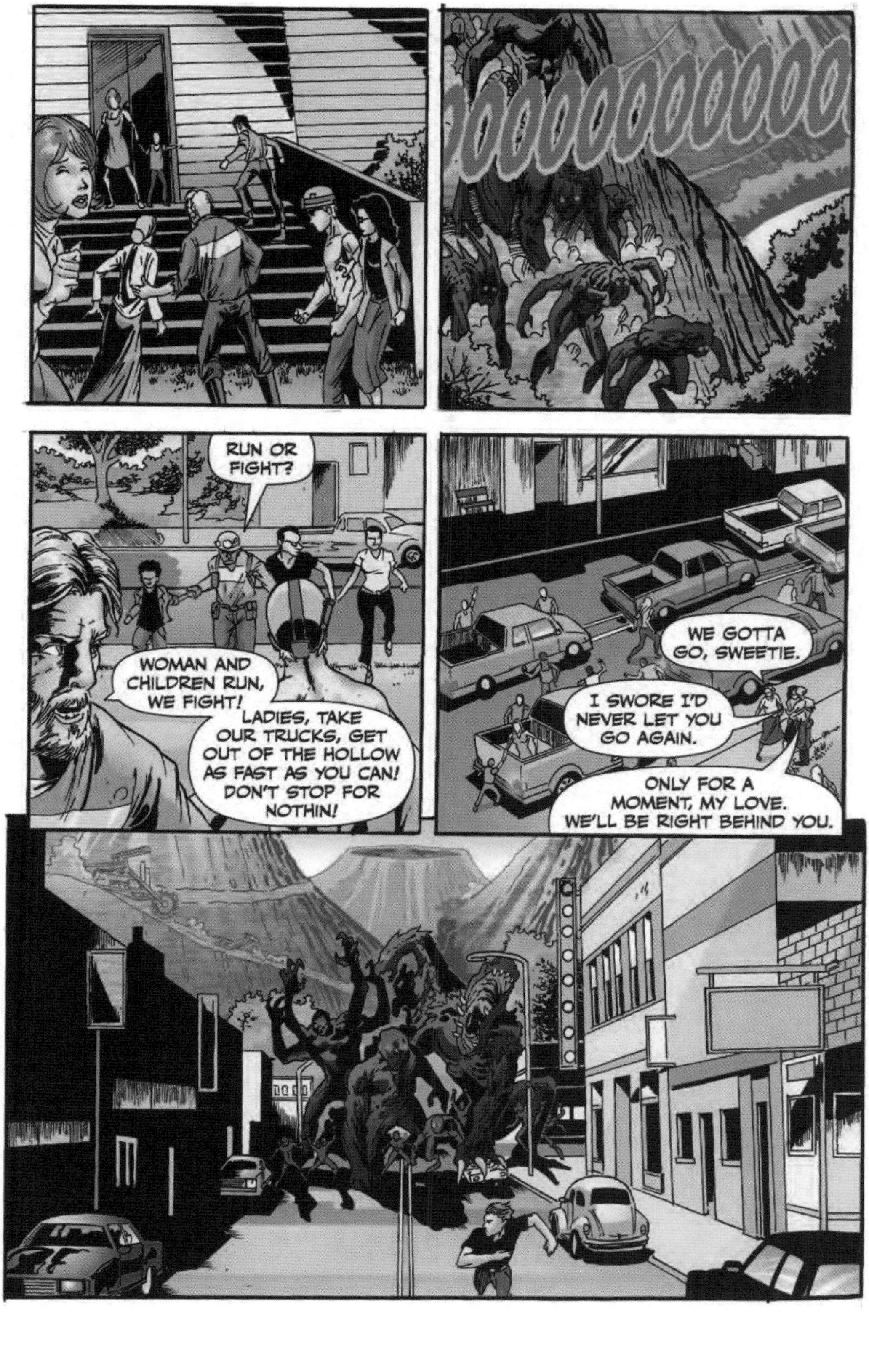
OOOOOOOOOOOO
RUN OR FIGHT?
WOMAN AND CHILDREN RUN, WE FIGHT!
LADIES, TAKE OUR TRUCKS, GET OUT OF THE HOLLOW AS FAST AS YOU CAN! DON'T STOP FOR NOTHIN!
WE GOTTA GO, SWEETIE.
I SWORE I'D NEVER LET YOU GO AGAIN.
ONLY FOR A MOMENT, MY LOVE. WE'LL BE RIGHT BEHIND YOU.

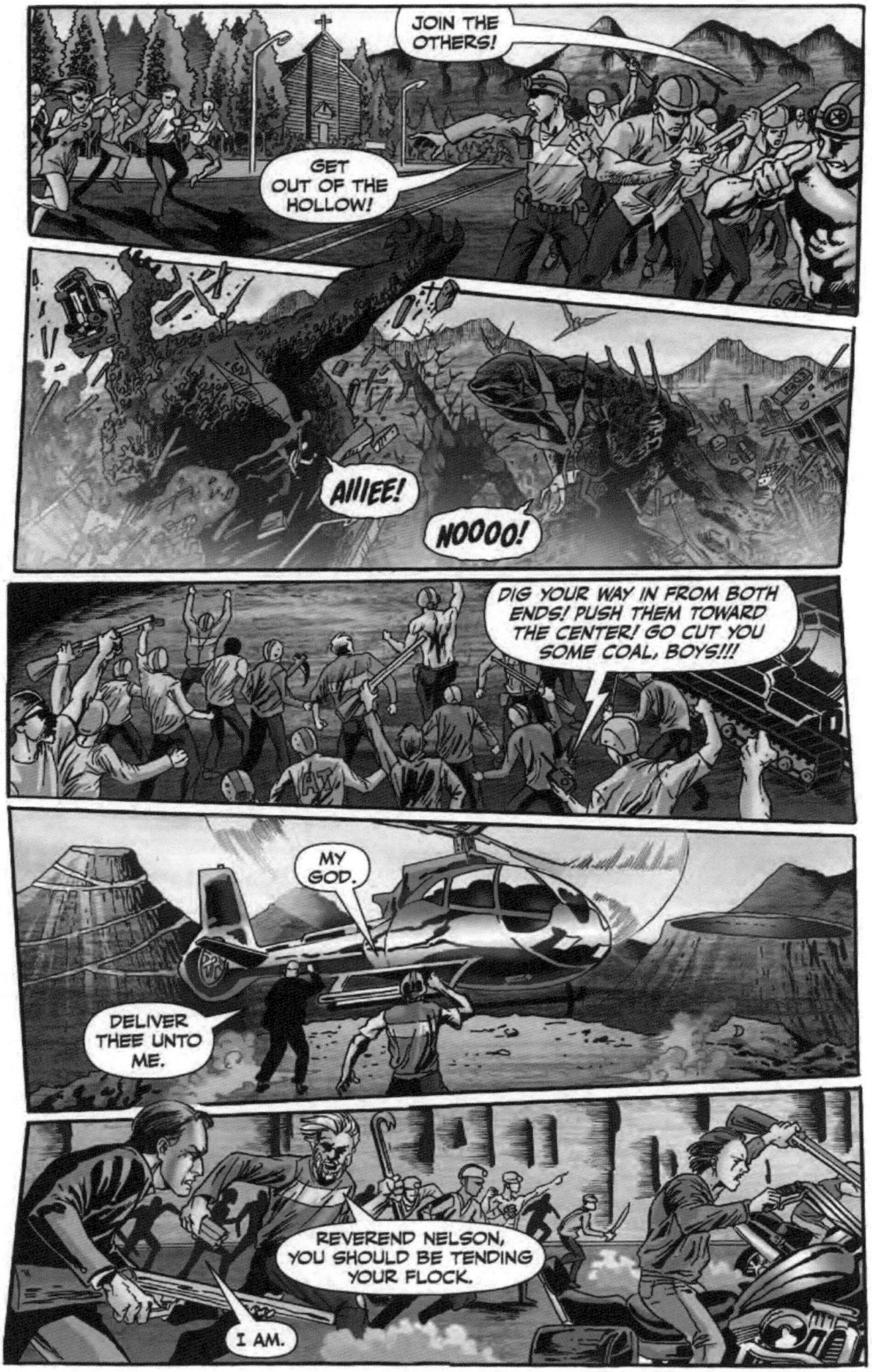
JOIN THE OTHERS!
GET OUT OF THE HOLLOW!
AIIIEE!
NOOOO!
DIG YOUR WAY IN FROM BOTH ENDS! PUSH THEM TOWARD THE CENTER! GO CUT YOU SOME COAL, BOYS!!!
MY GOD.
DELIVER THEE UNTO ME.
REVEREND NELSON, YOU SHOULD BE TENDING YOUR FLOCK.
I AM.

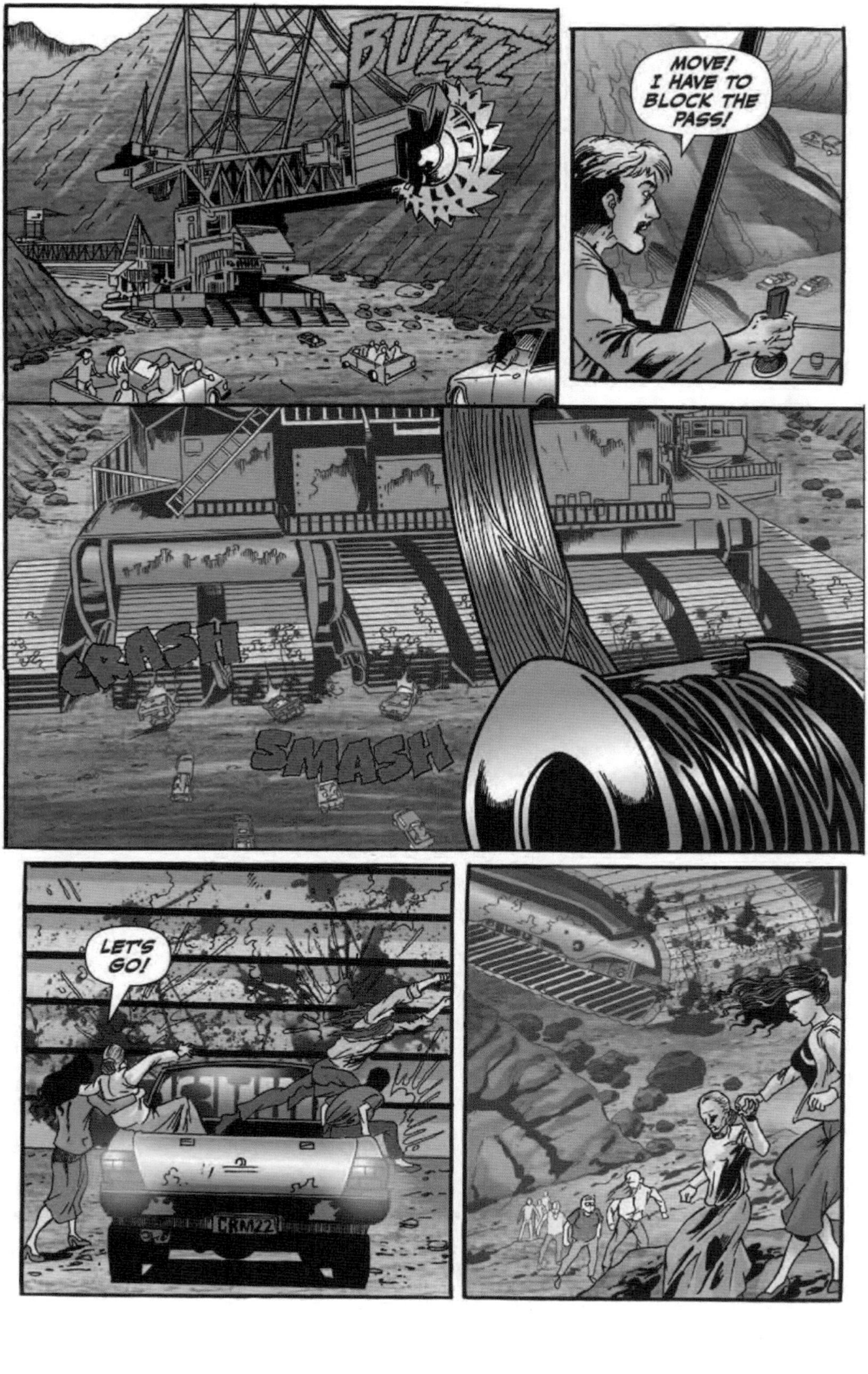
BUZZZ
MOVE! I HAVE TO BLOCK THE PASS!
CRASH
SMASH
LET'S GO!
CRM22

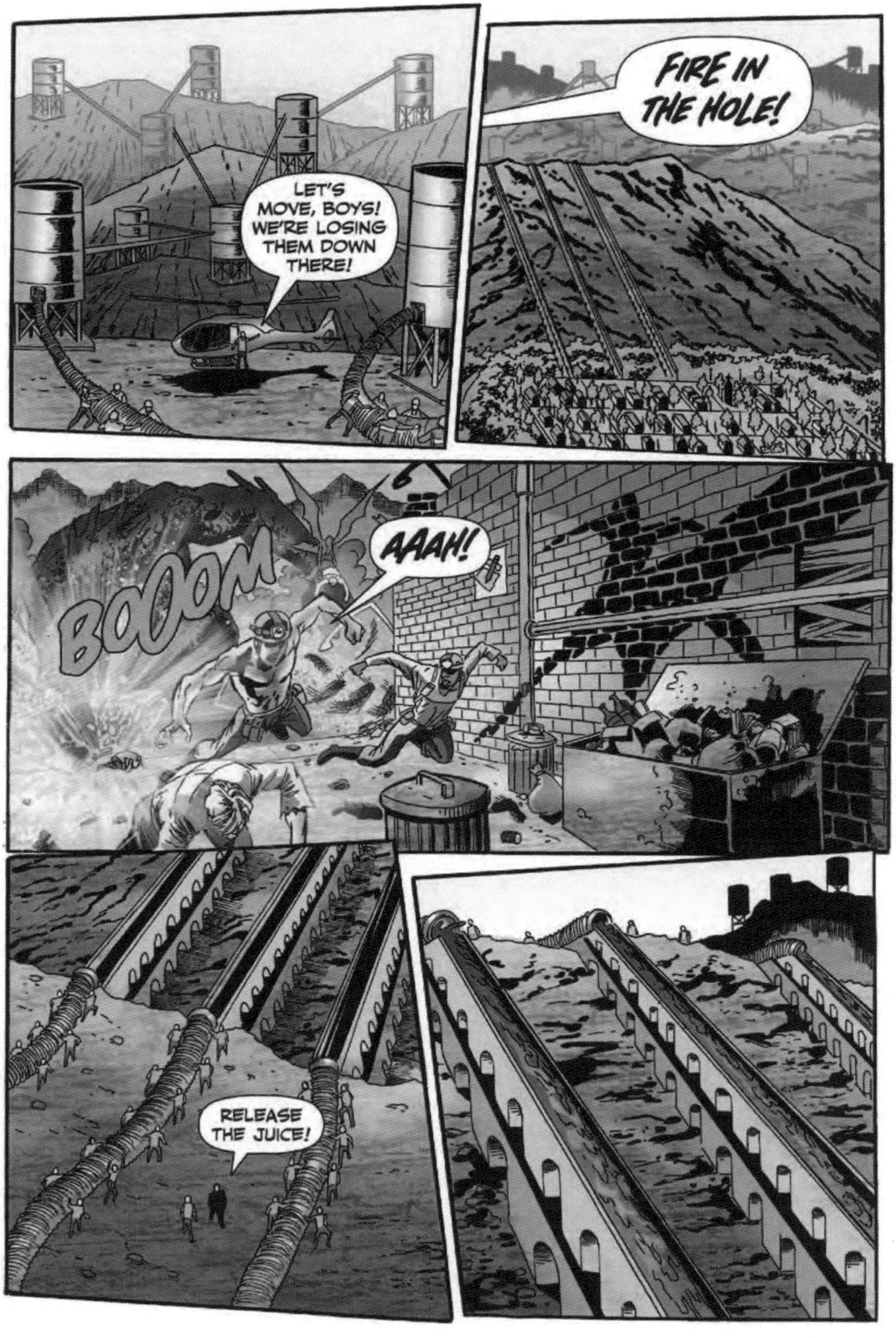
LET'S MOVE, BOYS! WE'RE LOSING THEM DOWN THERE!
FIRE IN THE HOLE!
BOOOM
AAAH!
RELEASE THE JUICE!

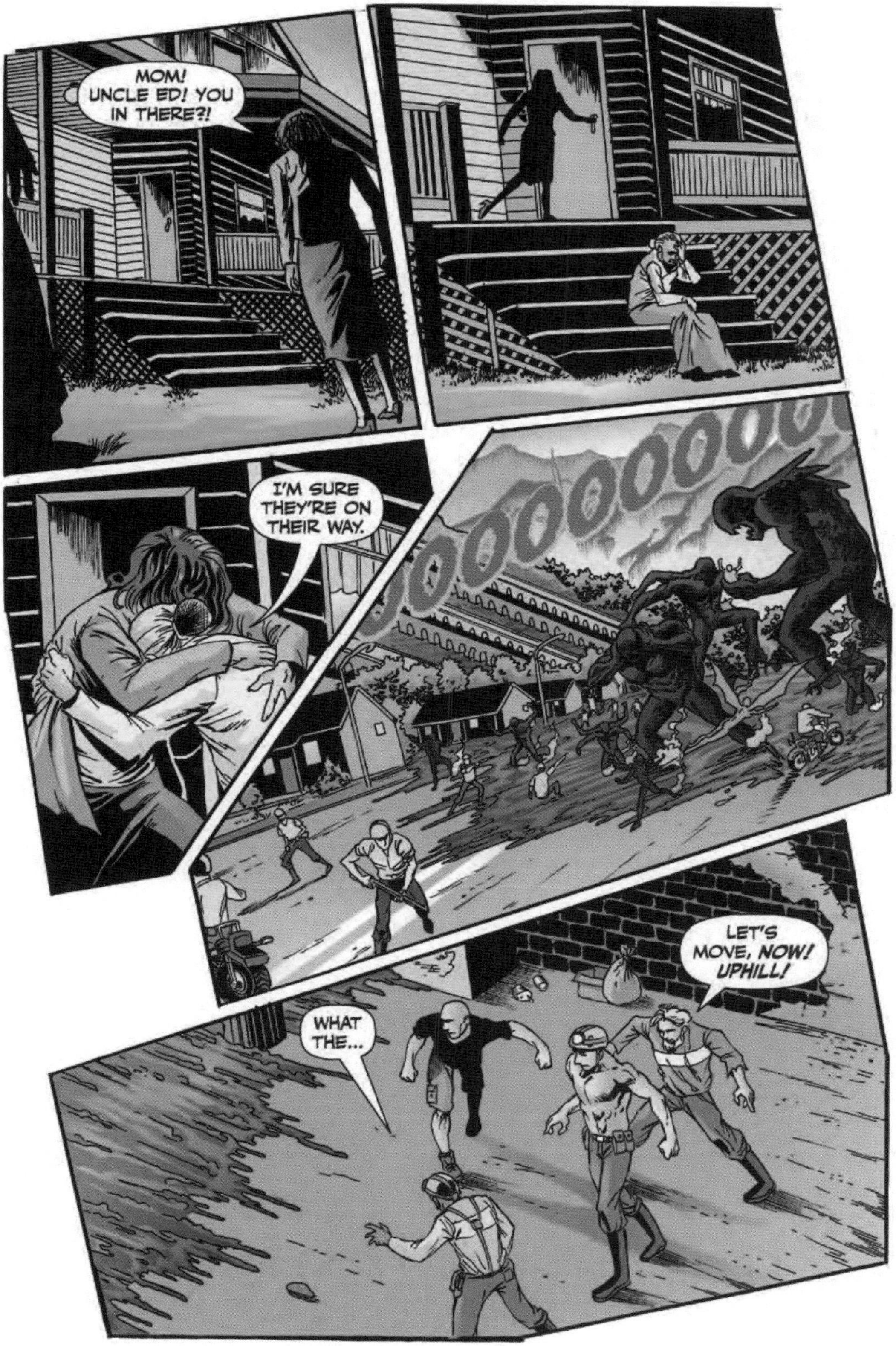
MOM! UNCLE ED! YOU IN THERE?!
I'M SURE THEY'RE ON THEIR WAY.
OOOOOOOOOO
LET'S MOVE, *NOW!* *UPHILL!*
WHAT THE...

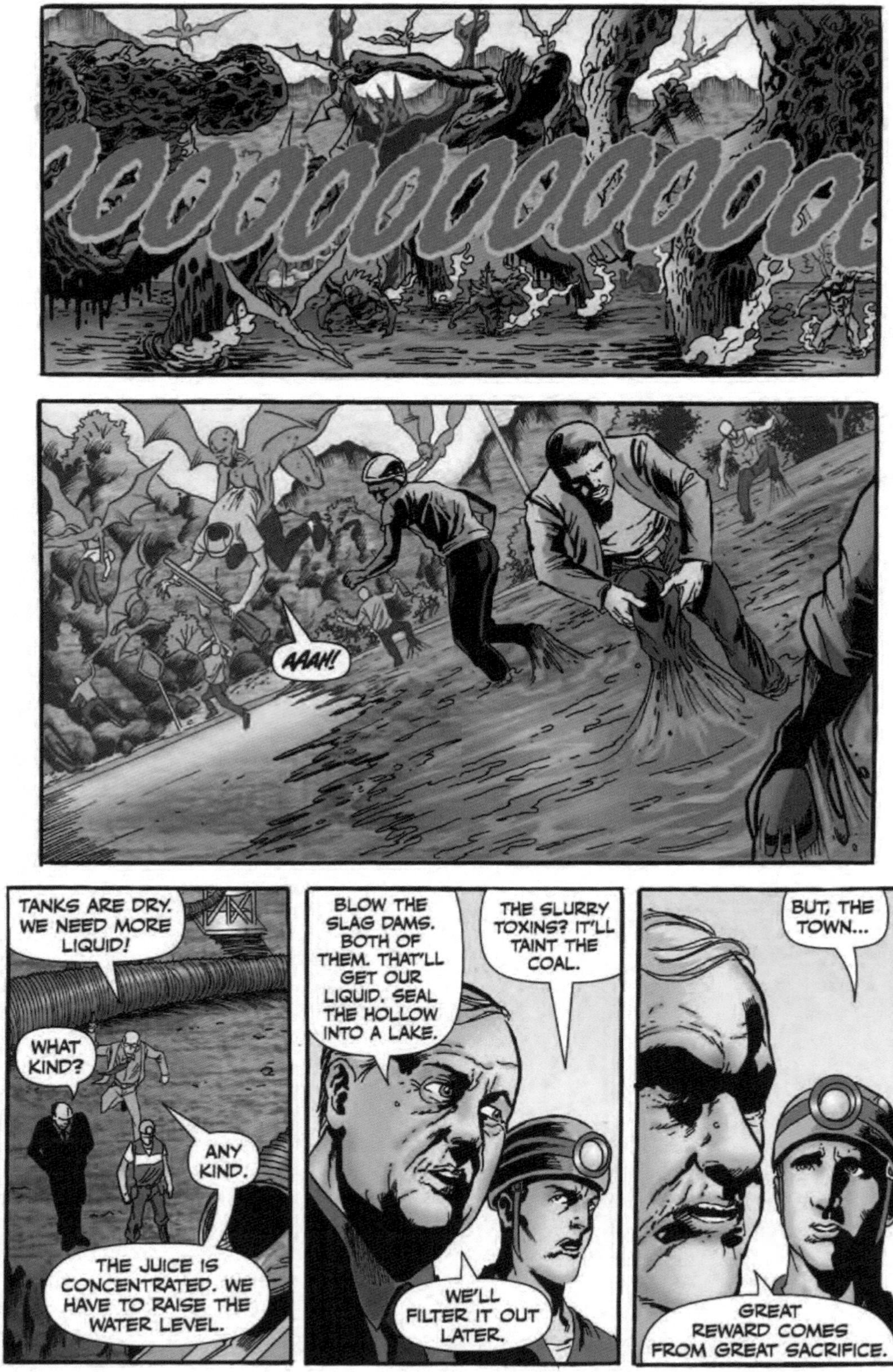
OOOOOOOOOOOOOO
AAAH!
TANKS ARE DRY. WE NEED MORE LIQUID!
WHAT KIND?
ANY KIND.
THE JUICE IS CONCENTRATED. WE HAVE TO RAISE THE WATER LEVEL.
BLOW THE SLAG DAMS. BOTH OF THEM. THAT'LL GET OUR LIQUID. SEAL THE HOLLOW INTO A LAKE.
THE SLURRY TOXINS? IT'LL TAINT THE COAL.
WE'LL FILTER IT OUT LATER.
BUT, THE TOWN...
GREAT REWARD COMES FROM GREAT SACRIFICE.

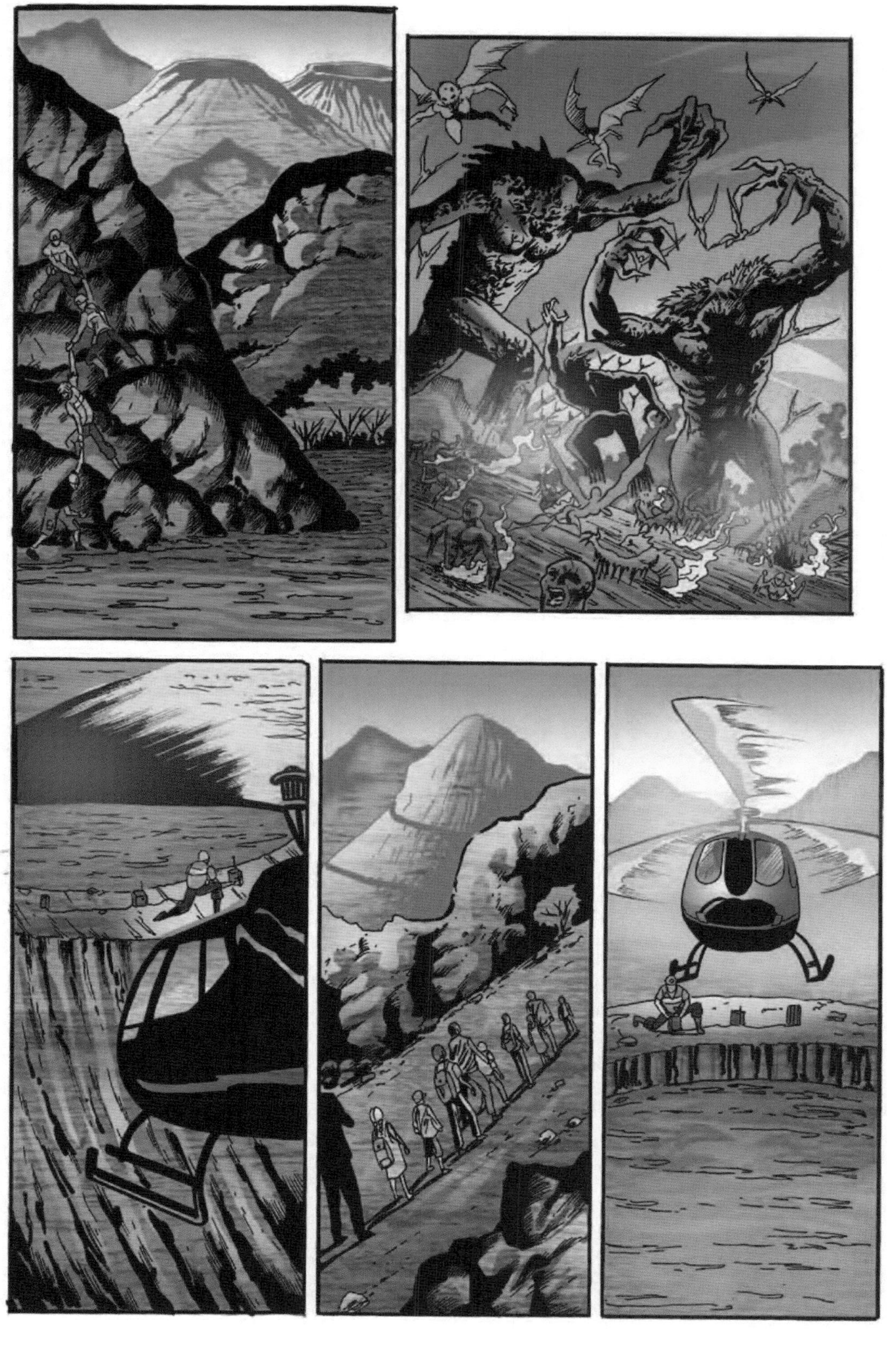

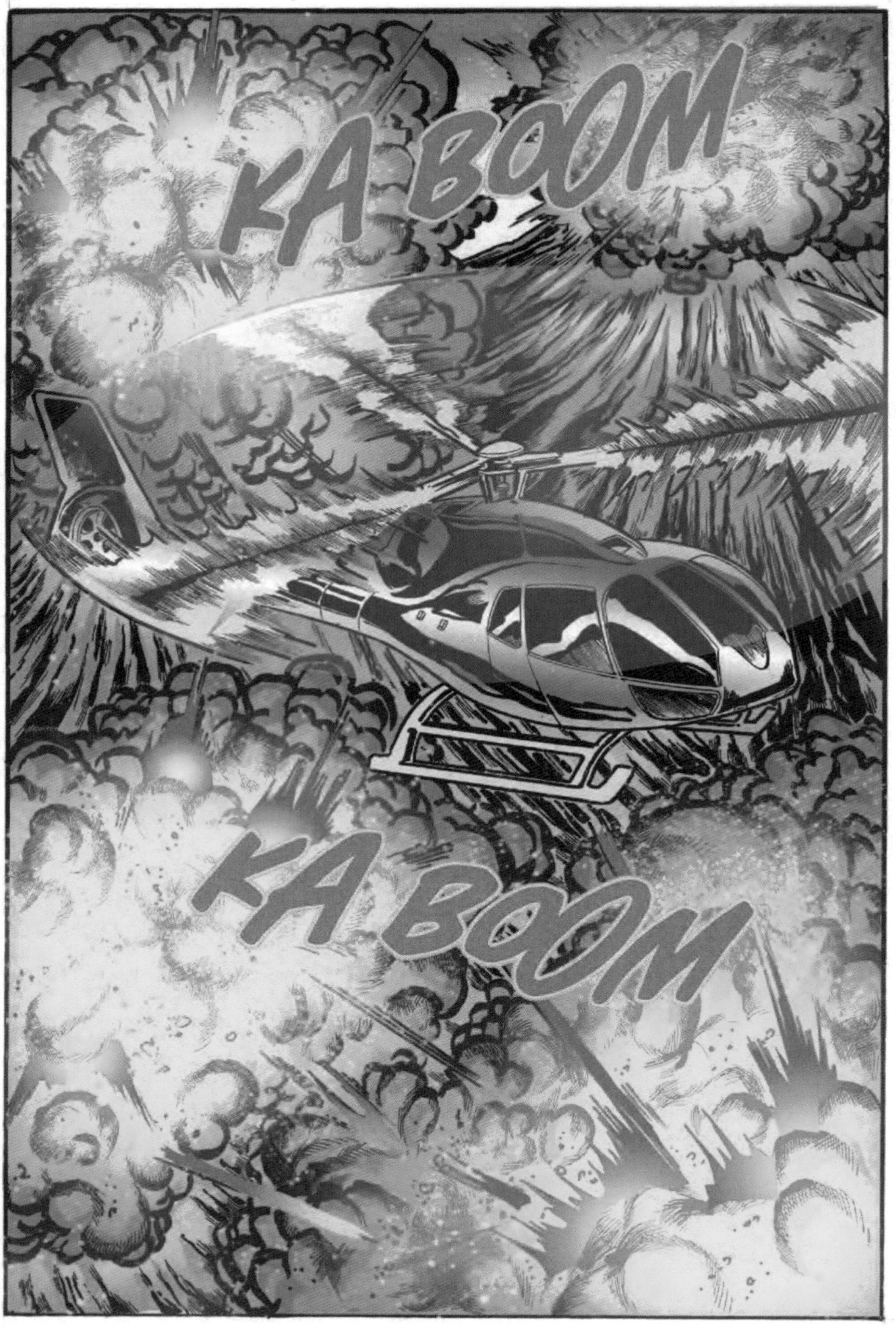
KA BOOM
KA BOOM

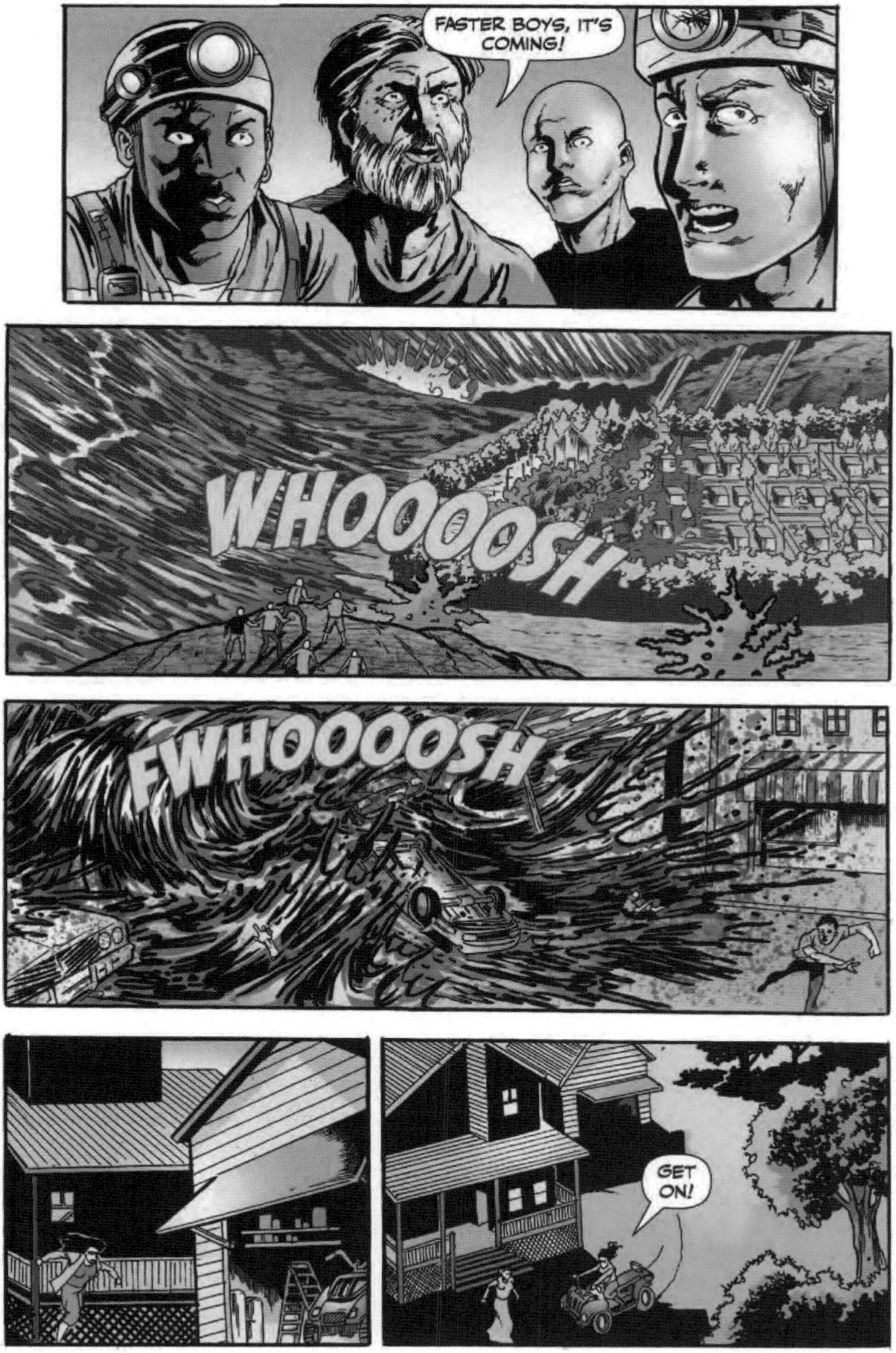
FASTER BOYS, IT'S COMING!
WHOOOOSH
FWHOOOOSH
GET ON!

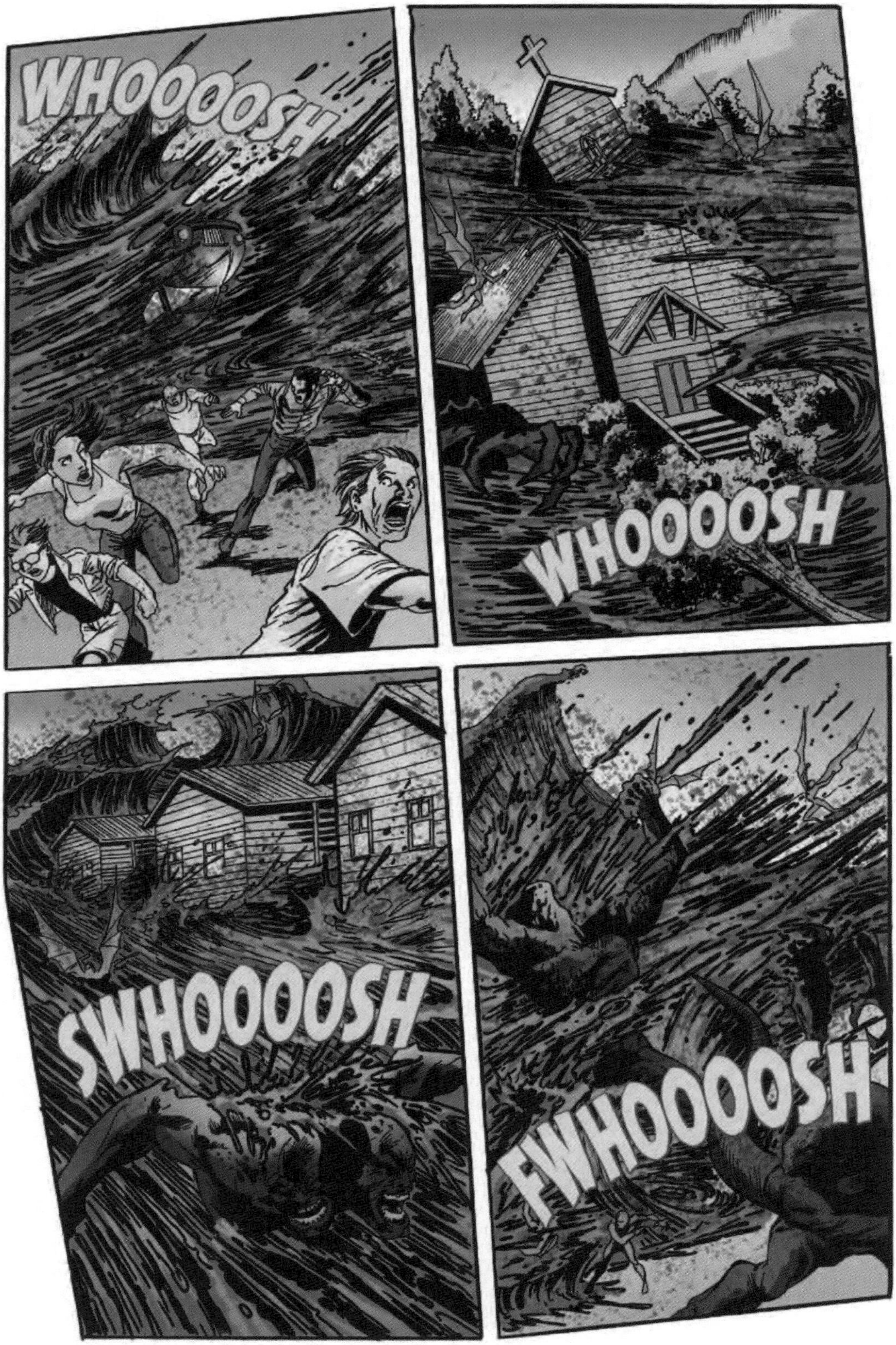
WHOOOOSH
WHOOOOSH
SWHOOOOSH
FWHOOOOSH

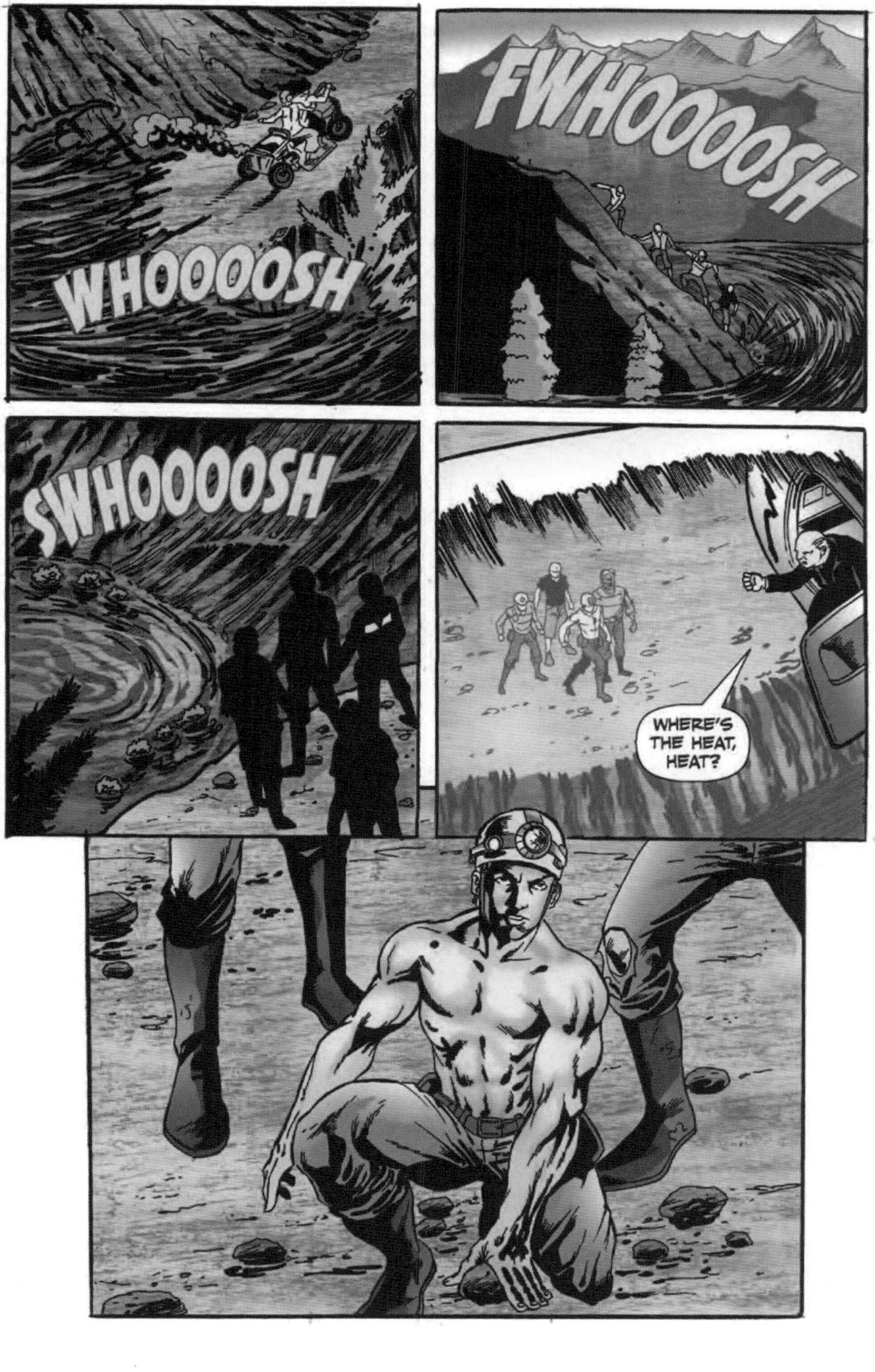
WHOOOOSH
FWHOOOOSH
SWHOOOOSH
WHERE'S THE HEAT, HEAT?

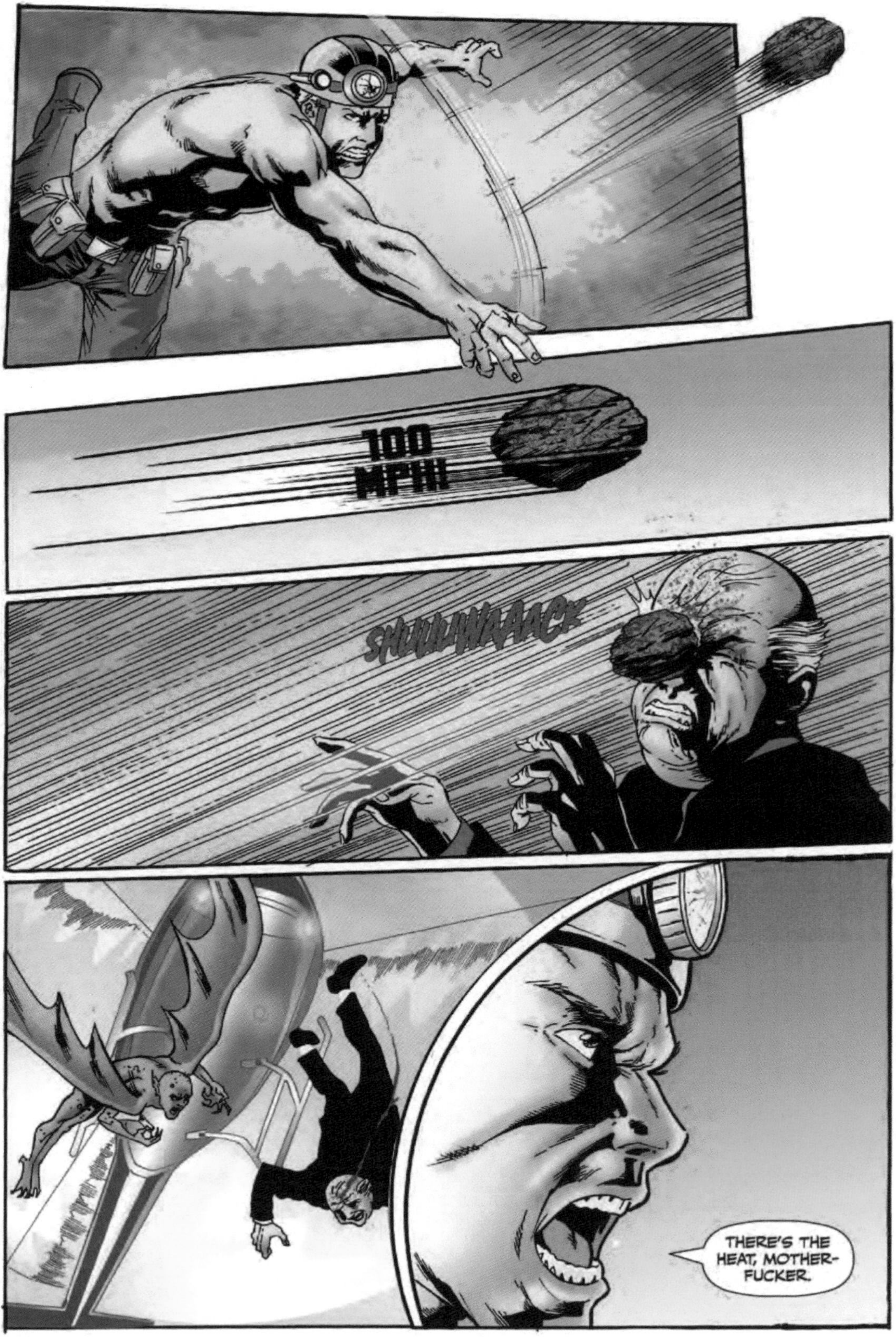
100 MPH
SHWWWAAACK
THERE'S THE HEAT, MOTHER-FUCKER.

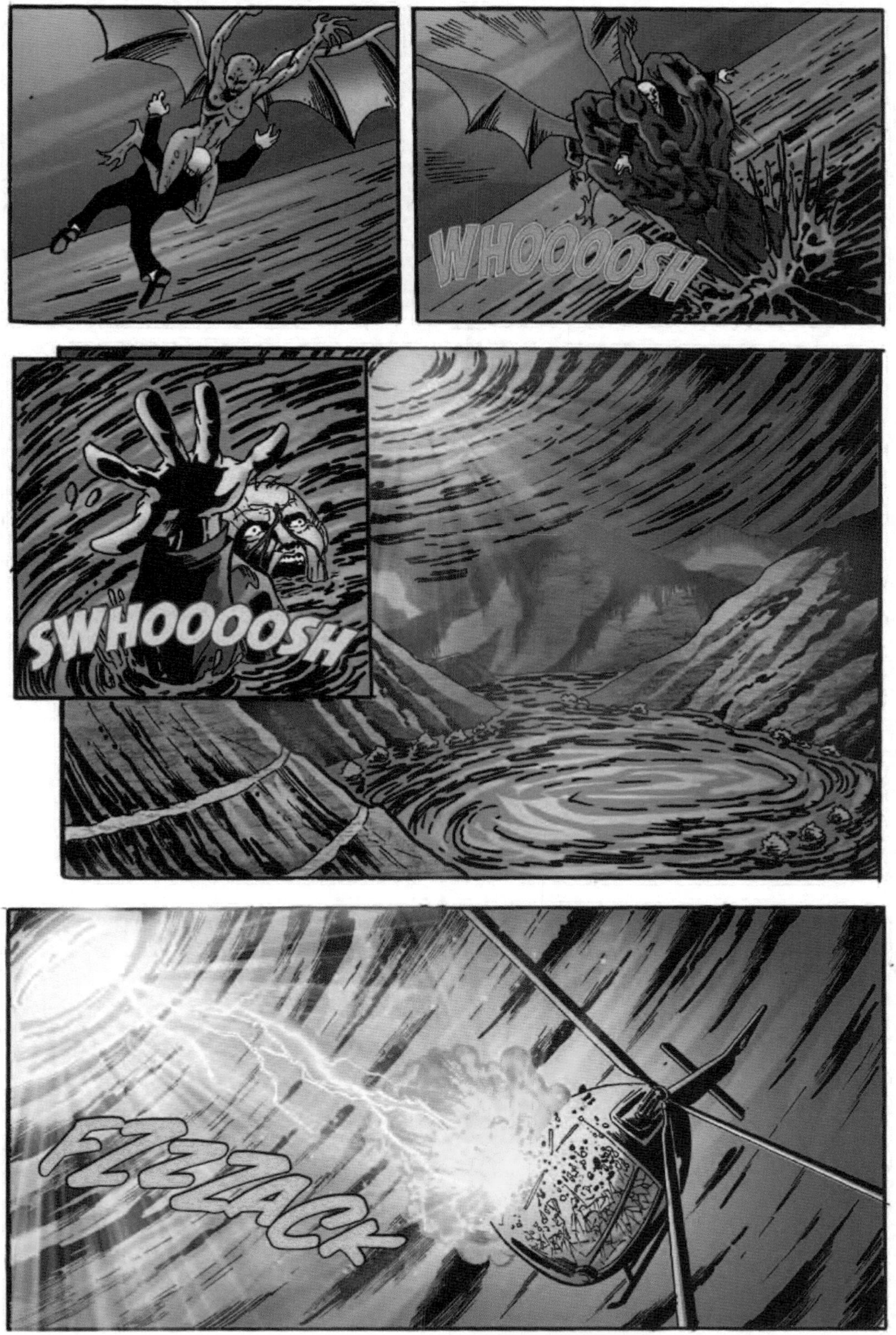
WHOOOOSH
SWHOOOOSH
FZZZACK

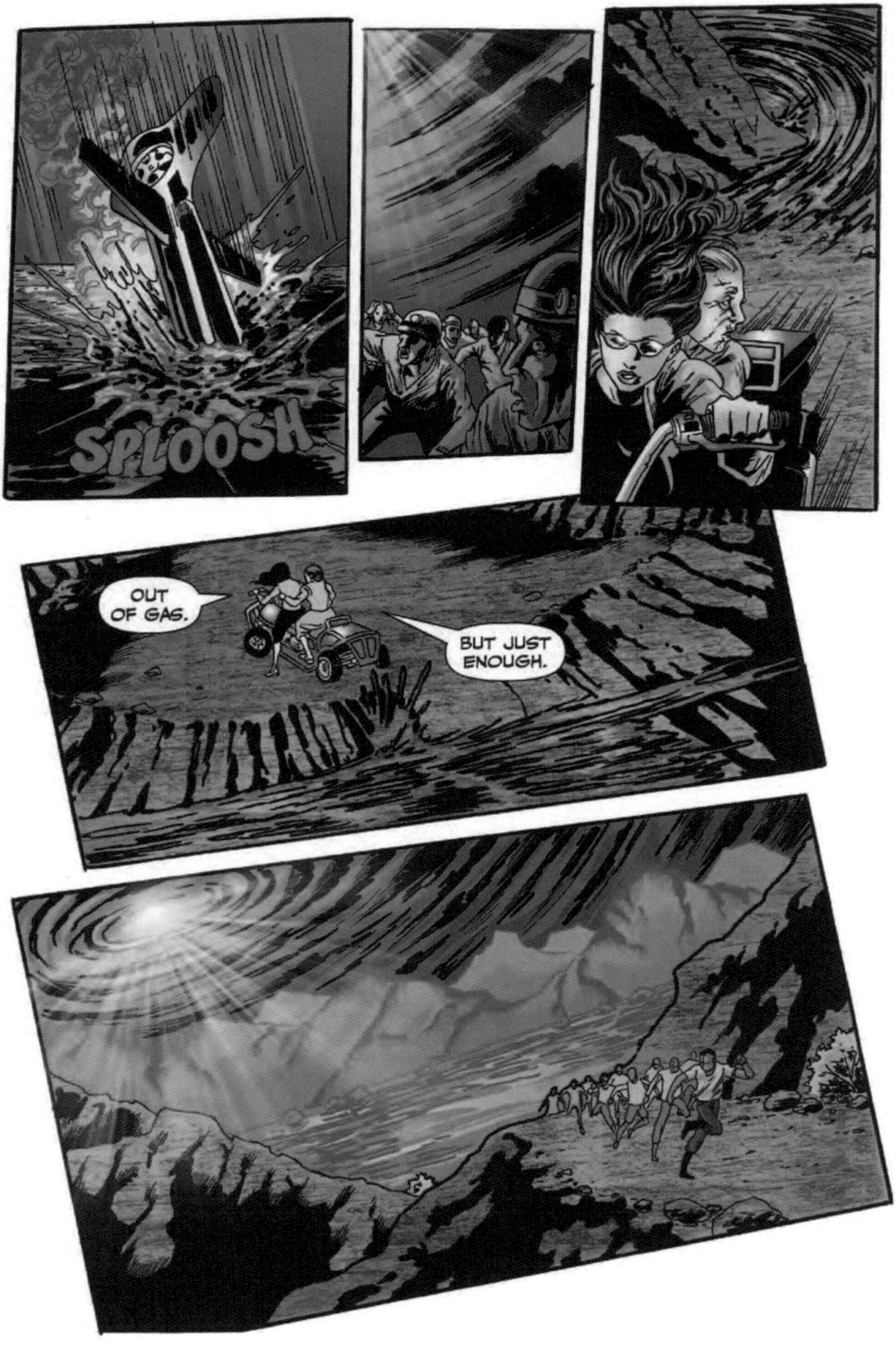
SPLOOSH
OUT OF GAS.
BUT JUST ENOUGH.

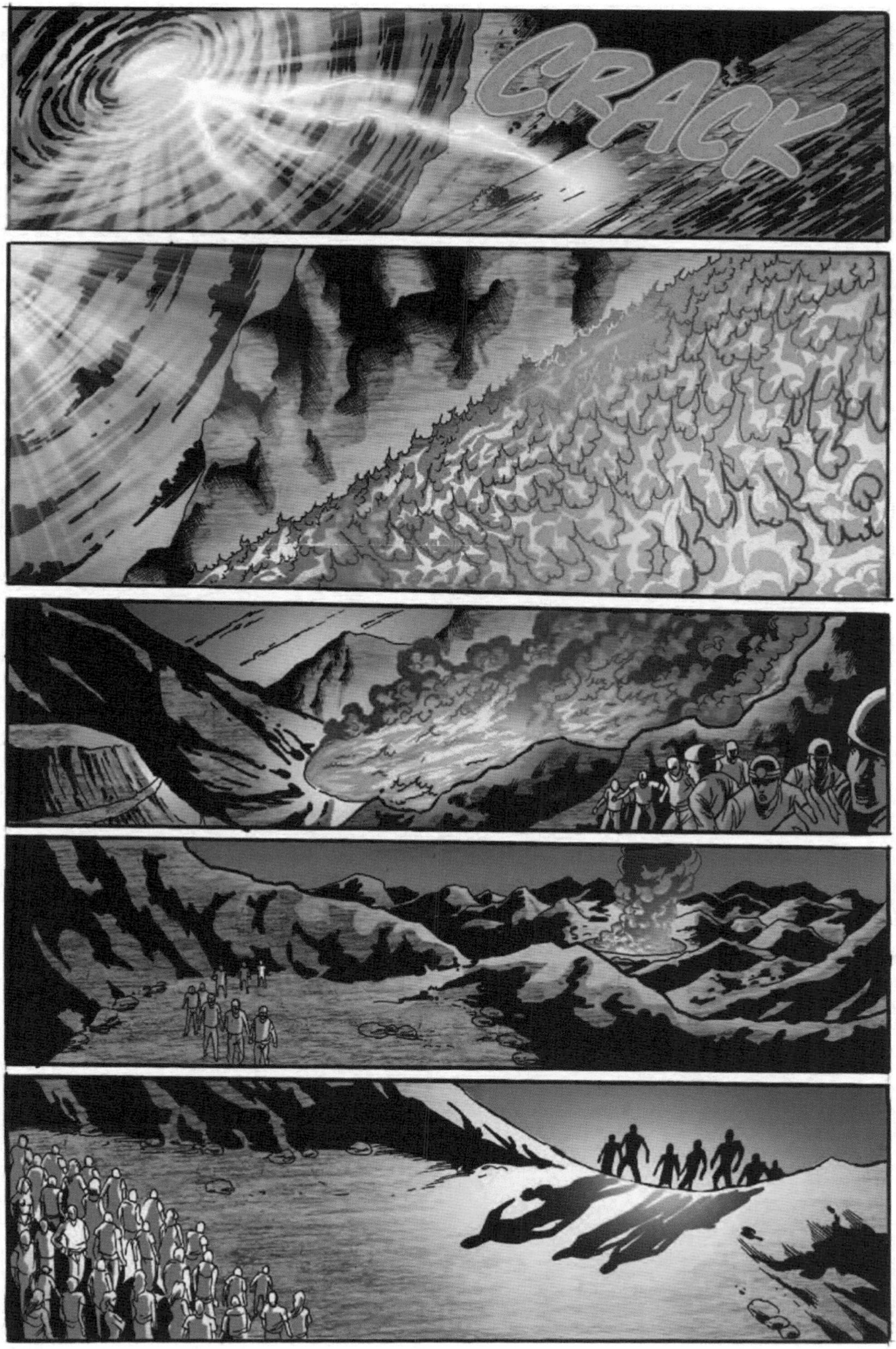
CRACK

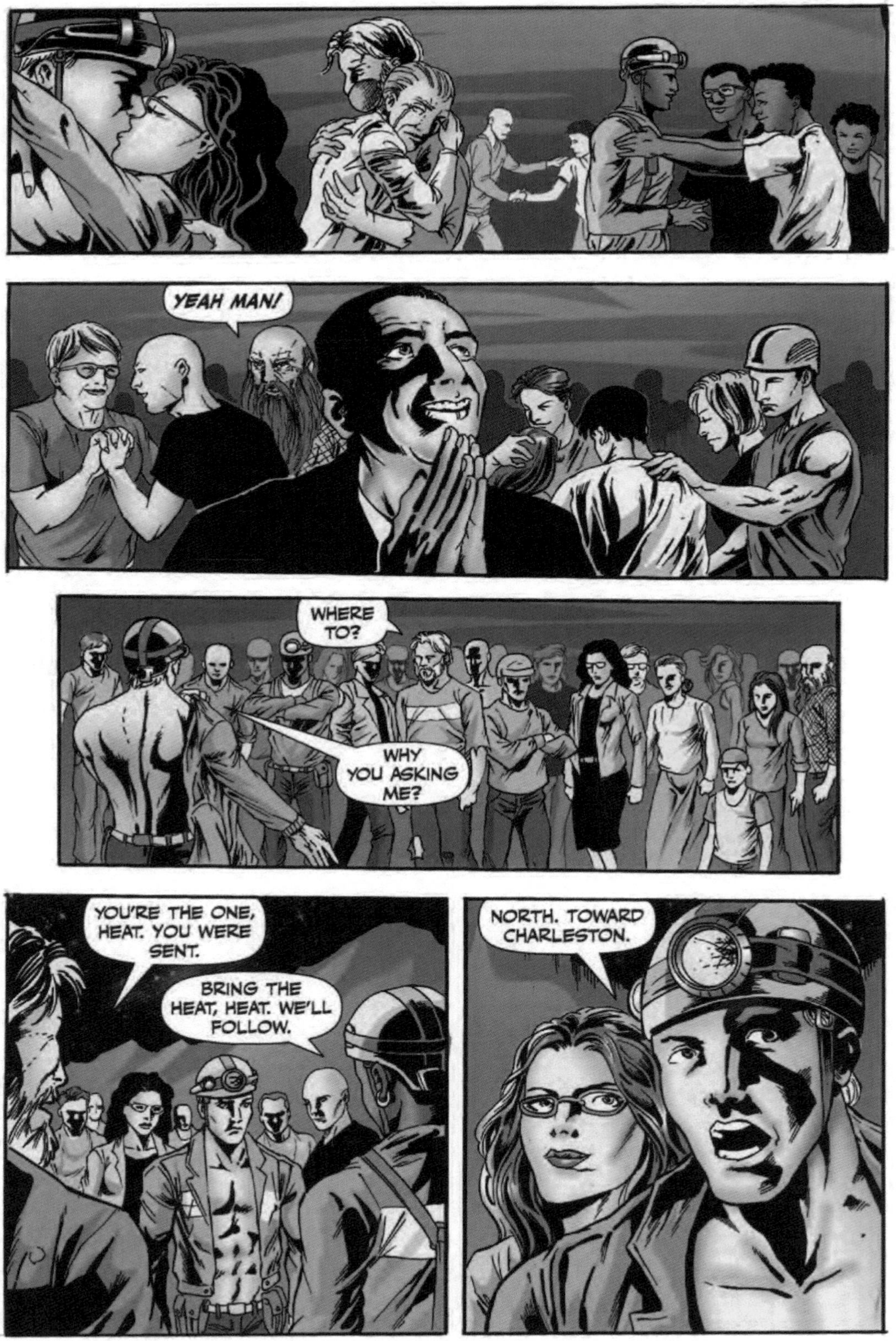
YEAH MAN!
WHERE TO?
WHY YOU ASKING ME?
YOU'RE THE ONE, HEAT. YOU WERE SENT.
BRING THE HEAT, HEAT. WE'LL FOLLOW.
NORTH. TOWARD CHARLESTON.

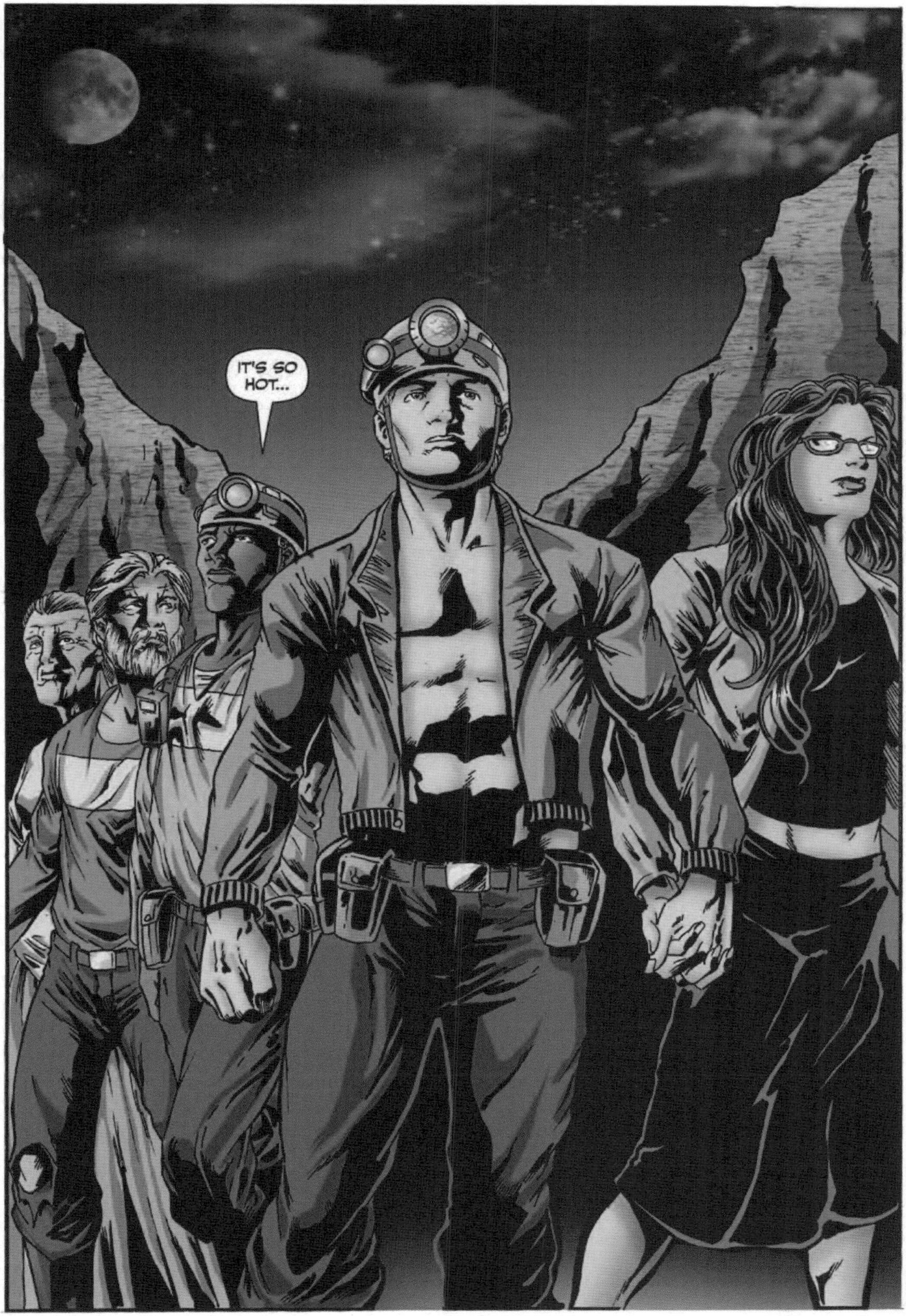
IT'S SO HOT...

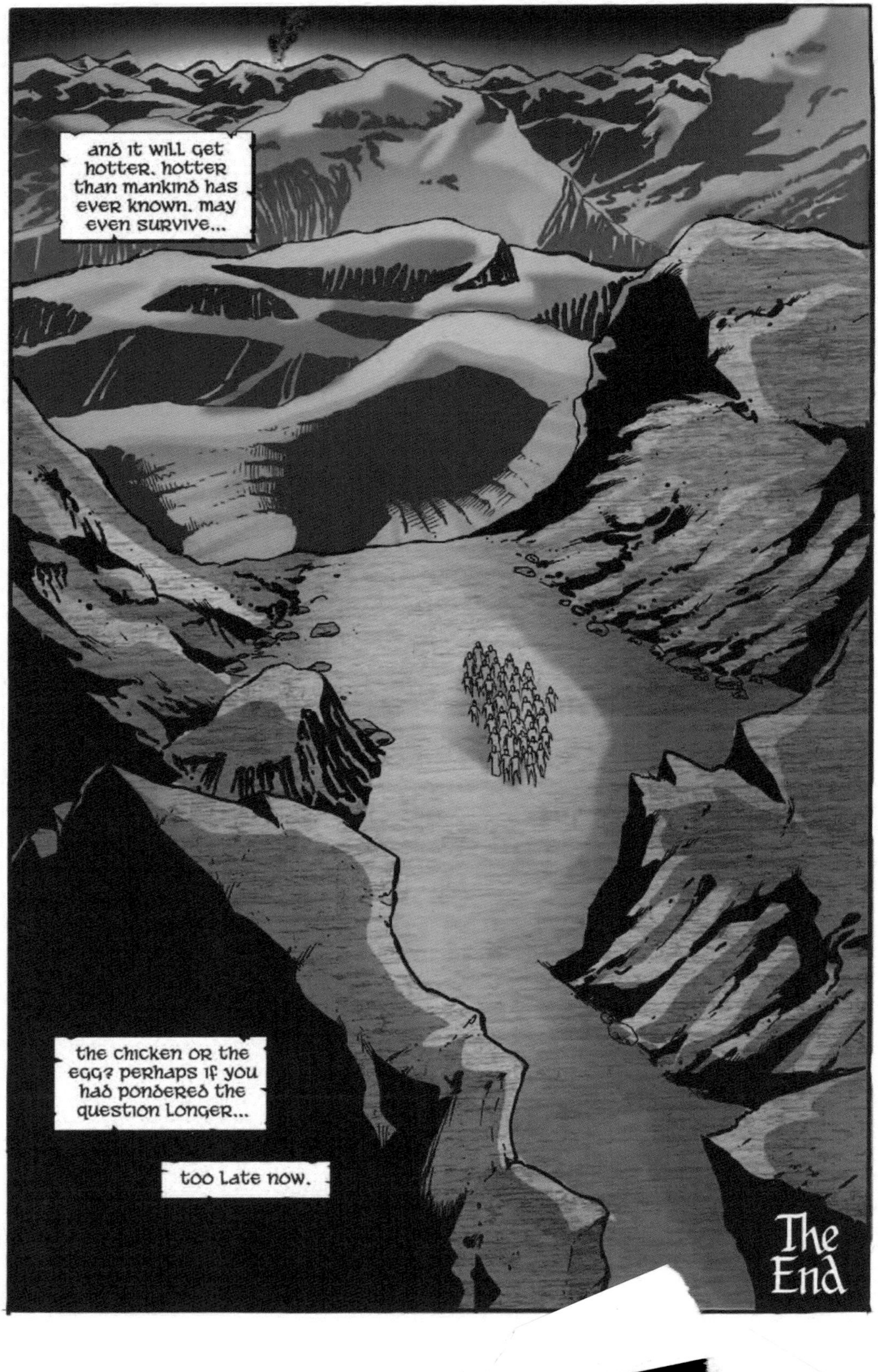
and it will get hotter. hotter than mankind has ever known. may even survive...
the chicken or the egg? perhaps if you had pondered the question longer...
too late now.
The End

AFTERWARD

Being a West Virginian, I have struggled with issues surrounding coal my entire adult life. My first professional employment was smack-dab in the billion-dollar coalfield of Mingo County. In one of the most isolated regions of the country, boy oh boy, did I get a crash course on the world of coal! Pieces of that rich part of my life have made it into nearly all of my creative works in my 30+ year career since. But I could never come up with one good, full-length creative property that would entertain while reflecting my views on this volatile subject. Then it hit me.

Coal is carbon. We are carbon. Plant and animal life is slowly transformed into a solid, burnable mineral because of the carbon that is the element of life. What if the process were reversed? It was that what if? that sparked the plot idea for this book, CARBON.

CARBON is obviously a work of fiction, a sensationalized fiction at that. The primary goal is to entertain. As I teach my media students, regardless of what we have to say—what "message" we present—we must first entertain or we have failed. Where the plot is sensationalized fiction, the canvas on which it is drawn reflects my views on several of the complicated issues related to coal: worker health and safety concerns, the destructiveness of mountaintop removal to both the land and water (and oh boy, see my "Water" update in PS!) and the communities, and the current global issue of coal's direct effect on climate change.

We West Virginians are a close-knit community, and coal is one of our primary lifelines. That makes this quite a sticky wicket for us. It is perhaps the most divisive issue for us since the Civil War, the conflict that formed our state.

The Baldwin-Felts thugs hired in the early 20th century by the coal companies to control their labor interests have been replaced by slick public relations people who use T-shirts, bumper stickers, university sports sponsorship, and Hank Jr. concerts rather than guns and clubs as their persuasion weapons. But the industry strategy remains the same: generate fear with misinformation to distract and unite a desperate population. In a masterful game of bait and switch, they have taken the heat off themselves by serving up fall guys—people of influence who suggest burning coal might not be the best way to go—as enemies in the so-called "war on coal." They have us fighting windmills rather than addressing the reality that the use of coal is winding down. We should be focusing on ways to transition and survive the change.

The smoke-and-mirrors takes the attention off their other nefarious intentions, like eliminating the earned health and retirement benefits of miners, while profiting up to the very last black rock dug from our ground. The industry knows what is coming; it has for a long time. You can bet they're not only executing their coal exit strategy, but already have another lucrative landing pad in place. If they can just keep us occupied fighting windmills, we won't notice them gone until the coal dust settles—gone like thieves in the night.

Coal is at the center of a worldwide conversation today. It has been the center of conversation in West Virginia for over a century. With mounting support from the national and international community, and now the federal government taking direct action to limit—and, in the not-too-distant future, eliminate-coal as a power-generating fuel source, West Virginia and other states that rely heavily on coal mining, are

DANIEL BOYD

between a black rock and a hard place.

Unless you think the world is flat, it is a fact that burning coal produces more greenhouse gasses than any of the other fossil fuels. Thus, it is a primary contributor to climate change, the destructive results of which become clearer with every passing season. What really sucks is that coal is commercially the most valuable natural resource in West Virginia. It has been both a blessing and a curse since its discovery and implementation as the fuel source that drove the Industrial Revolution of the late 19th and early 20th centuries.

We have had a history of other super-negatives surrounding our "black gold," starting long before the current global climate change conversation. The people didn't get rich off the ga-billions that were extracted and exported; the out-of-state industrialists did. After decades of labor struggles, our miners eventually made a fair living. Even with politicians and policy makers in the pocket of King Coal, over time adequate extraction taxes were legislated that generated enough state revenue to raise the overall standards of the state. And we became dependant on coal.

Mine worker health and safety issues have been at the forefront of controversy since the commercialization of coal mining. Under the best of conditions underground mining is one of the most dangerous occupations in the world. Significant progress was made throughout the 20th century, but the business formula remains the same: the less you spend on extraction, the greater the ultimate profit. Company greed still often trumps worker health and safety.

We relearned this brutal lesson recently when we had not one, but two cataclysmic mining disasters within four years. The Sago Mine disaster of January 2nd, 2006, killed 12 of the 13 trapped miners. The Upper Big Branch Mine disaster of April 5th, 2010, killed 29 out of the 31 miners at the site. Both were proven to be the direct result of willful neglect of state and federal safety regulations. There are scores of smaller fatal accidents every year that do not make national and international news.

No matter which side of the environmental argument they are on, most agree that the people who mine our coal are some of the most courageous human beings in the world. Like John Sayles did in his 1987 masterpiece film, "Matewan," I wanted CARBON to showcase the heroism of these usually unseen people. They are heroes. In the case of CARBON, when we find ourselves on the edge of the end of the world, these courageous miners become superheroes.

Over the years I have resisted the temptation to respond in traditional activist ways, choosing instead to integrate, where appropriate, these views into my works of fiction. I realized that at best I am just an entertainer, not an expert spokesperson or policy maker. As I learned early on from my greatest influence, Rod Serling ("The Twilight Zone"), sometimes the best way to widen the discussion of critical, highly divisive issues is to package them into more inviting and easier to digest forms of entertainment. Like Serling, my genres of choice have been those of the "fantastic." My views have trickled into many of my works over the years. Now, with CARBON, I'm finally able to tear into the topic like a continuous miner on a rich coal seam.

To create CARBON I also needed to re-shuffle the deck on our conventional spiritual beliefs. For the record, I am neither anti-coal nor anti-religion. With religion being used by both sides of the coal issue to justify their views, I decided to re-image the origin of God so we might look at things through a different lens. John Lennon's song, "Imagine," dared us to imagine there was no heaven so we could focus more on the world that we live in while we're living in it. For CARBON, I did not eliminate a heaven but gave humankind more direct ownership and responsibility in God and His original mandate.

Yeah, I know, it's just a comic book set in an isolated part of the country. But if coal is at the center of of climate change, West Virginia is at the center of coal. The state has always been the center of my universe, so I thought it quite fitting that it be the center of the universe for Book 1 of a planned trilogy (with SALT and GOLD to follow). Here at the crossroads of the local-global debate, perhaps CARBON can bring a new and different audience to the conversation, packaged as entertainment rather than the typical venomous misinformation generated by bought pundits and propagandists.

I'm just a comic book writer.

Here's hoping!
Daniel Boyd

WHOA.. HOLD THE PRESSES!!!

As I was waiting for a publication date for CARBON on January 9th, I came home to a sickly-sweet smell in the air so strong that I walked around my house checking for fire. The odor has since been described as a licorice smell. Well maybe if it came from a giant butt-crack candy factory. For sure, those of us who experienced, and continue to experience the effects of the toxic chemical - MCHM, gushing into our water supply, will never forget the smell. And not just a few of us. Some 300,000 customers of our for-profit water company were, and continue to be, directly affected.

We were initially commanded not to drink, bathe, or... hell, do anything with the water except flush toilets or put out our fires if we must. Even though we were given the official "all clear" to drink five days later, most of us still didn't. As I write this, nearly two months later, many of us still won't.

Unlike CARBON, this incident is not sensationalized fiction set in an isolated area, far from public view like our coal fields. This is real, and began right in the middle of our state capitol before quickly spreading to eight surrounding counties on that public water system. Kinda hard to hide or cover that one up.

During the initial emergency-live press conference, our Governor felt the need to clarify to the world, twice that I remember, "This was not a coal-company incident. This was a chemical-company incident." Really? MCHM is a toxic chemical used to treat coal, to clean coal. And as it turns out, the violating company, "Freedom Industries" is a part of network of shell corporations that tie directly to coal mining. The only thing the Governor clarified to me is who buys his drinks.

Officials continue to step on their weenies in attempts to reassure us that they are in control and that all is well. Again, Really? The new F-word around here has become the S-word: Safe. No one will say that the water is "safe." They use words like "adequate." The truth is they don't know. The stuff was never tested on humans. It took a lot of it to kill a few lab rats, but who knows about the long-term effects on humans. The short-term is pretty unpleasant, that's for sure. And we should now feel reassured hearing from the same officials that allowed an outlaw toxic chemical company to exist unregulated a mile upstream from the intake of the largest water supplier in state?

And if you think MCHM is bad, put dozens more toxic nasties in a stew and you have coal slurry - the solid/liquid byproduct of the coal mining preparation process. To add insult to our recent injury, 33 days later, February 11th, over 100,000 gallons of that crap spilled into Fields Creek that feeds directly into the Kanawha River – the same major waterway the Elk River drained the MCHM into.

None of this is a surprise to the people who have lived, and continue to try and live in our coal fields. Their water has been being poisoned for decades. I invite you to flip back through the pages of this book and see how central water is to the whole issue of coal and the plot of CARBON. The water of coal mining brings destruction at two speeds: A slow death through gradual contamination and human consumption of polluted water supplies. And sometimes, a fast death as was depicted in the climax of CARBON. That event was inspired by the real-life event of the Buffalo Creek, West Virginia, disaster of 1972 when a coal impoundment dam broke and approximately 132,000,000 gallons of toxic slurry flooded the valley, killing 125, injuring 1,121 and leaving over 4,000 homeless.

I had coal as the star and water the co-star in CARBON. I've known all along that if I am able to continue the trilogy, that in the next book, water is the headliner. I had hoped not to show that hand just yet. But our recent water crisis changed things. So in the next book, SALT, oh boy howdy are we going there! When you boil all of these issues down, It's All About the WATER!

At the end of CARBON, I lit the fuse that will speed up the possible death of the Earth for humans. It is sensationalized fiction to show "what if" the whole climate change thing was greatly accelerated. I thought the more realistic worst-case scenario of the Man versus Nature commercial exploitation magilla was the eventual cumulative effects of climate change/global warming, where the point of no return was still a few clicks away. Maybe even not too late to change this genocidal direction. But when I see things like mega nuclear facilities built on coastlines near major geologic fault lines (Fukushima, Japan), and unregulated toxic chemical companies operating a mile upstream from the intake of the largest water company in a state, I become worried about the present. I have always been a "glass half full" kind of person. But right now it not only seems a "glass half empty," but what's actually in the glass can kill us. We may be just one click away.

My survivor-heroes are heading to Charleston, West Virginia at the end of CARBON. I did not rewrite this to coincide with our recent disaster. I wrote the book nearly five years ago, and the end remains exactly the same.

My fictional heroes may, or may not make it, but there are many more real-world ones who will. So, big-business mass-Earth assassins, and you elected and appointed officials who protect them, instead of us - Beware!

DB

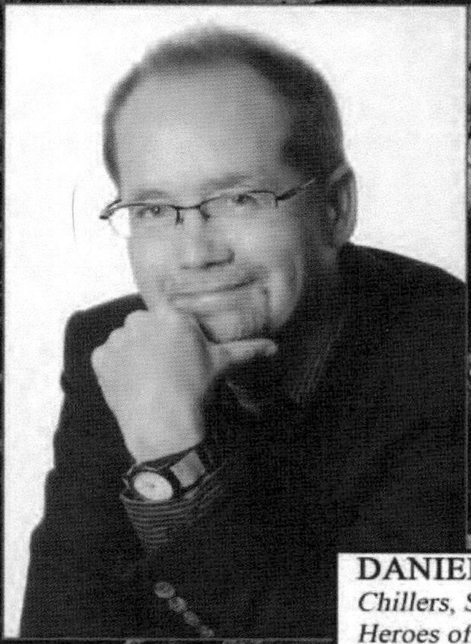

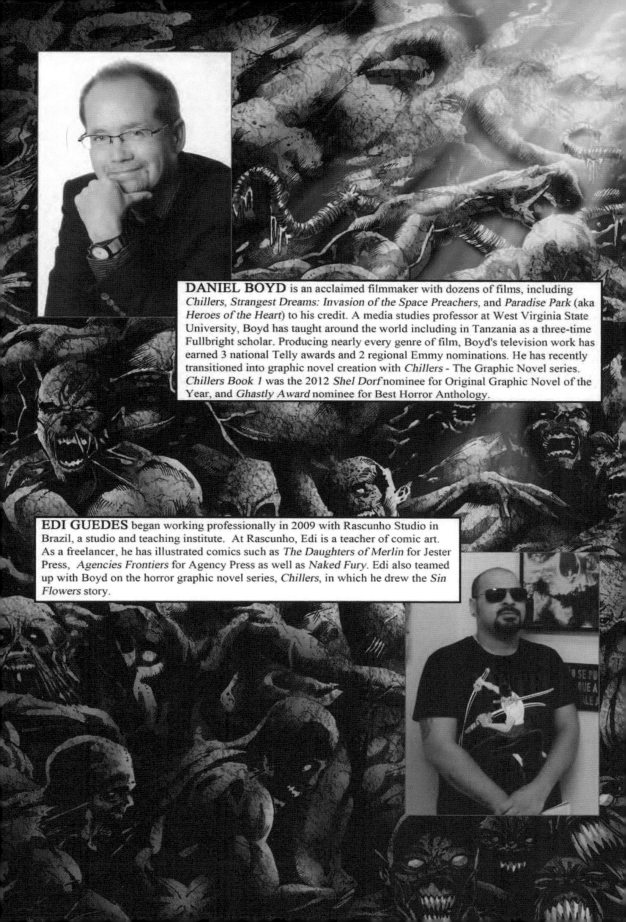

DANIEL BOYD is an acclaimed filmmaker with dozens of films, including *Chillers*, *Strangest Dreams: Invasion of the Space Preachers*, and *Paradise Park* (aka *Heroes of the Heart*) to his credit. A media studies professor at West Virginia State University, Boyd has taught around the world including in Tanzania as a three-time Fullbright scholar. Producing nearly every genre of film, Boyd's television work has earned 3 national Telly awards and 2 regional Emmy nominations. He has recently transitioned into graphic novel creation with *Chillers* - The Graphic Novel series. *Chillers Book 1* was the 2012 *Shel Dorf* nominee for Original Graphic Novel of the Year, and *Ghastly Award* nominee for Best Horror Anthology.

EDI GUEDES began working professionally in 2009 with Rascunho Studio in Brazil, a studio and teaching institute. At Rascunho, Edi is a teacher of comic art. As a freelancer, he has illustrated comics such as *The Daughters of Merlin* for Jester Press, *Agencies Frontiers* for Agency Press as well as *Naked Fury*. Edi also teamed up with Boyd on the horror graphic novel series, *Chillers*, in which he drew the *Sin Flowers* story.

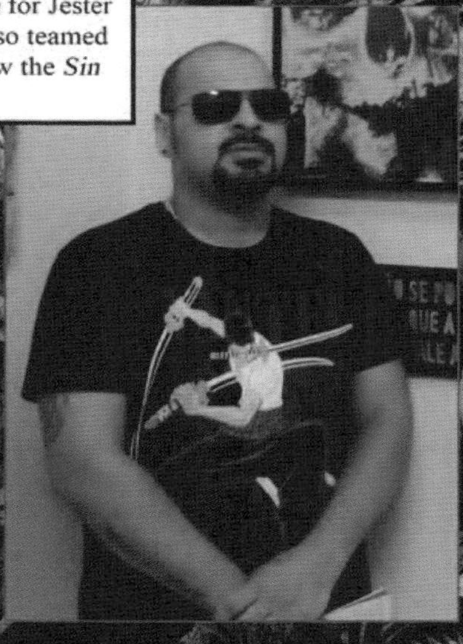

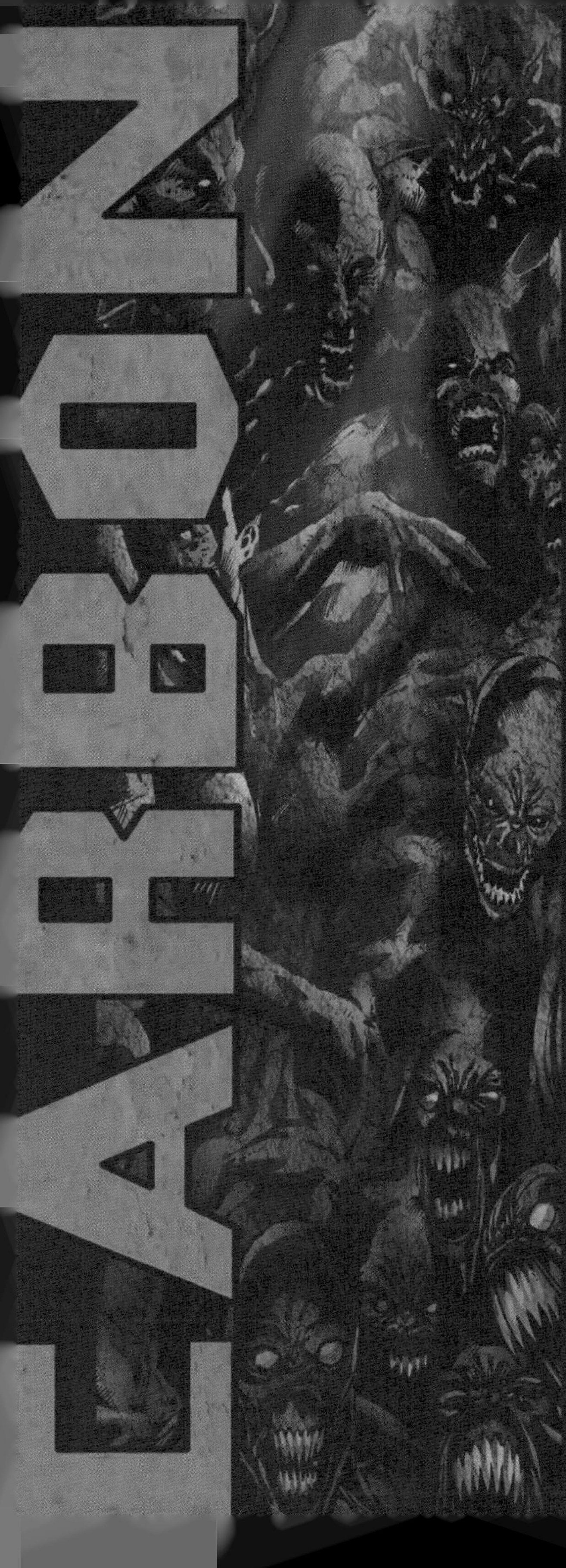
CARBON

VERY SPECIAL THANKS TO

Susan & Bob Maslowski
Guy Nelson & Gary Fish
Brendan Deininger
Randy Smith
Curtis Baskerville
Jeff & Joyce Berryman
Lorre & Steve Wilson
Adam Castleman
Chris Rodrigues
Bill Richardson

AND

Kelly Baker, Mark Martin, JV Poore, Rick Kelly, John McIntyre, Jim Van Metre, Barbara Leonard, Marina Hendricks, Sherry Skidmore

35043518R10066

Made in the USA
Lexington, KY
29 August 2014